RENAISSANCE CULTURE
A New Sense of Order

The Cultures of Mankind

Renaissance
Culture

A New Sense of Order

Edited by Julian Mates
and Eugene Cantelupe

George Braziller · New York

For information, address the publisher,
George Braziller, Inc.
One Park Avenue, New York 16
Library of Congress Catalog Card Number: 66-15759

First Printing

Printed in the United States of America

DESIGN BY JULIUS PERLMUTTER

ACKNOWLEDGMENTS

The editors and publisher have made every effort to determine and credit the holders of copyrights of the selections in this book. Any errors or omissions may be rectified in future editions. The editors and publisher wish to thank the following for permission to reprint the material included in this anthology:

Brander Matthews Dramatic Museum of Columbia University—for "The New Art of Writing Plays" by Lope de Vega, translated by William T. Brewster. Appeared in *Papers on Playmaking*, edited by Brander Matthews, published by arrangement with Hill and Wang, Inc., 1957. Reprinted by permission of the Brander Matthews Dramatic Museum of Columbia University. All rights reserved.

Columbia University Press—for selections from *Defensor Pacis* by Marsilius of Padua, translated by Alan Gewirth, 2 vols., 1956.

Doubleday & Co., Inc.—for selections from *Discoveries and Opinions of Galileo*, translated by Stillman Drake. Copyright © 1957 by Stillman Drake. Reprinted by permission of the publisher.

Farrar, Straus & Giroux, Inc.—for selections from *The Complete Poems of Michelangelo*, translated by Joseph Tusiani. Copyright © 1960 by Joseph **Tusiani**. Reprinted by permission of the publisher.

ACKNOWLEDGMENTS

Sears Jayne—for selections from his translation of "Marsilius Ficino's Commentary on Plato's *Symposium*," originally published by the *University of Missouri Studies*, XIX:I, 1944.

Liveright Publishing Corp. and Leonard Opdycke—for a selection from *The Book of the Courtier* by Baldesar Castiglione, translated by Leonard Eckstein Opdycke. Copyright, 1901, 1903 by Leonard Eckstein Opdycke, copyright 1929 by Leonard Opdycke. Black and Gold Library, 1929.

David McKay Co., Inc.—for selections from *The Sonnets of Petrarch*, translated by Joseph Auslander, copyright 1931, 1959 by Joseph Auslander. Reprinted by permission of the publisher.

Estate of Curtis Hidden Page—for "Ere Love from Barren Chaos . . ." and "When You Are Very Old . . ." from *Songs and Sonnets of Pierre de Ronsard*, translated by Curtis Hidden Page.

Philosophical Library, Publishers and Lutterworth Press—for selections from *Reform Writings of Martin Luther*, translated by Bertram Lee Woolf, 1953. Reprinted by permission of the publisher.

G. P. Putnam's Sons—for "The Boatwoman" by Marguerite de Navarre from *The Palace of Pleasure* by Harry Levtow and Maurice Valency, Capricorn edition. Copyright 1960, Capricorn Books. Reprinted by permission of the publisher.

Gisela M. A. Richter—for selections from *The Literary Works of Leonardo da Vinci*, edited by J. P. and I. A. Richter, 2 vols., London, Oxford University Press, 1939.

Russell & Russell, Inc. Publishers—for a summary of the scenario of "The Three Cuckolds" [*Li Tre Becchi*] from *Italian Population Comedy* by Kathleen M. Lea, 1962.

Stanford University Press—for selections from *The Complete Works of Montaigne*, translated by Donald M. Frame. © Copyright 1948, 1957, 1958 by the Board of Trustees of the Leland Stanford Junior University. Reprinted by permission of the publisher.

University of California Press—for a selection from *Andreas Vesalius of Brussels*, edited by C. D. O'Malley, 1964.

The University of Chicago Press—for selections by Pompanazzi and Pico from *The Renaissance Philosophy of Man* by Cassirer, Kristeller and Randall. Copyright © 1948 by The University of Chicago. Reprinted by permission of the publisher.

The Viking Press, Inc. and Cassell and Co., Ltd. Publishers—for a selection from "Don Quixote" from *The Portable Cervantes*, translated and edited by Samuel Putnam. Copyright 1949 by The Viking Press, Inc. Reprinted by permission of the publisher.

to Elaine and Jean

PREFACE

We have tried to do, in the following pages, what is, after all, impossible. How does one describe the Renaissance in a few pages, see the ocean in a drop of dew? Maybe not at all, but we were determined our failure should be if not glorious at least interesting. Therefore we used the Introduction to set out the story of the Renaissance as a new ordering of life, and the anthology which follows illustrates aspects of this ordering. But the selections are so much more—they are to catch the spirit, if we're lucky, of the Renaissance. And they are to be delightful reading in their own right. We have taken long pieces entire when we liked them and short pieces entire for the same reason; we have often retitled pieces; we have kept original spelling and punctuation when possible, finding the Renaissance attitude toward these sacred cows both refreshing and pleasurable to read; we have omitted irrelevant or dull passages (always indicated by ellipses or three centered dots); sometimes we spilled blood by including only a little of a work in order to give the reader a sense of what it is like. Always we have tried with as great delicacy as possible to maintain a tension between the significant and the delightful—and we were always aided by the Renaissance itself, a period when the difference between the two was likely to be thoroughly obscured.

Helpful, kind criticism was proffered by many of our colleagues and friends, especially Arnold Berleant, Stan Brodsky, Donald Frank, Elaine Mates, Raoul Pleskow, and Michael Pressman. We also are grateful to C. W. Post College for a grant enabling us to reproduce much of the material.

Brookville, 1966

7

Contents

PART I

The Unraveled Tapestry:

New Ordering of Political Science and History

PART II

The Greeks and Nature:
New Ordering of the Visual Arts, Music, and Literature

PART III

The Here and Now:
New Ordering of the Sciences

PART IV

A Trinity of Ideas:
New Ordering of Philosophy and Religion

List of Illustrations

13

1. *David*, Michelangelo.

INTRODUCTION

THE NEW SENSE OF ORDER

Byron claimed that he woke one morning and found himself famous; but Medieval man did not wake one morning and find himself in the Renaissance. So many elements in the Renaissance were directly continuous with the Middle Ages that it would have been impossible for him to decide at any one point that a new day had dawned. Yet there was a Renaissance, and the idea of a new birth of culture was not merely the brain child of nineteenth-century historians and scholars.

Jacob Burckhardt's *Civilization of the Renaissance in Italy* (1860), is generally credited with popularizing the idea of a Renaissance, a period of intense individualism originating in Italy in the fourteenth century and reaching its climax at the beginning of the sixteenth century. But a reaction set in to Burckhardt, as reactions have a habit of doing in scholarly circles, and in the extensive literature that has since been written on the problem of periodization, the dates of the Renaissance slide from century to century, as the place of origin gravitates from country to country. Moreover, one generation of scholars and historians casts doubt on whether a Renaissance had actually come into being, suggesting rather that the Middle Ages extended into the period Burckhardt had so neatly roped off. Another generation looked upon the Renaissance as a transitional age between the Middle Ages and the Modern Era that began in the seventeenth century. Today, the notion of a Renaissance is again in the ascendant. And tomorrow?

But one idea threads through the literature, that of a new birth of the arts, of philosophy, of discovery; and one intriguing aspect of the academic discussion is the fact that a moment in history did occur

2. *The Triumph of Venus,* North Italian birth salver.

when man was aware of a great change in his view of himself, of his God, of the world around him—when he gulped life in huge draughts. He lacked the historical perspective to see his debt to Medieval art, Medieval philosophy, Medieval learning—indeed he was not psychologically disposed toward such a view—but he was aware that something new had happened. Italian humanists and writers of the fourteenth century, particularly Petrarch, inveighed against a period of darkness (Medieval World) that separated them from a period of light (Classical World); and they saw the dawn of a new era in the attempt to emulate and reconstruct a golden age.

There is no question that life was changing. Modern ways of understanding the universe date, not from the Medieval point of view, but from the Renaissance. And more than anything else the Renaissance meant a new sense of order, not order as opposed to disorder or chaos, but as a method of experiencing the universe in a manner different from that of Medieval man. Believing himself capable not merely of experiencing but of doing, he felt confident of his ability to make **his own** world ("Knowledge is power," said Francis Bacon), to control his environment. Man still viewed himself as located in the center of the universe, but it was now a universe he was capable of understanding and fashioning for his own purposes. Nature was viewed not as symbol but as reality; life was no longer a vestibule to eternity but a place of wonder and joy and fulfillment which God wanted man to experience before he attained Heaven (St. Francis of Assisi, for example, felt one reached God by enjoying Nature); the leader on earth was not the priest but the prince; and man achieved a new identity in the great chain of being—he was no longer an insignificant speck in the universe but a unique creation, lower than angels but higher than animals, endowed with the divine faculty of reason. "What a piece of work is a man," says Hamlet, reflecting the Renaissance view. "How noble in reason! how infinite in faculty!" This new sense of order can be seen in all aspects of the Renaissance—in politics and the sense of history, in philosophy and religion, in art, in science—and it helps make clear why the Renaissance is the threshold to today's world.

The Unraveled Tapestry:

New Ordering of Political Science and History

The fourteenth through the seventeenth centuries saw tremendous changes in European man's conception of the state. Economic and technological developments such as the expansion of trade with the East and the introduction of gunpowder resulted in more and more power falling into temporal hands, thus sharpening the conflict between Pope and Prince. The search for a way to divorce theology from politics was a full-time occupation for educated men. If organized society existed to aid men achieve grace, then the priest was crucial and the Pope superior to all. The Renaissance, concerned with the fact that the Church's hierarchy of values seemed unbreakable, yet needing reasons to defend a new approach to power, opted to ignore ultimate questions of purpose and to concern itself with more immediate problems. For example, Marsilius of Padua (c. 1277-1342), who borrowed heavily from a secularism based on natural law (or Aristotle as interpreted by Averroës) approached political questions via means rather than ends. Typically, he assumed the necessity of the state for a "sufficient life," and he discussed the functioning of authority rather than its justification. Theorists became interested in power rather than in justice; the concern was what people want, rather than what people ought to have. Machiavelli is perhaps the best example of a man ignoring ultimate questions, and in *The Prince* (written in 1513) he attempted to make clear the role of command in a secular world.

Authority divorced from God led to the major political problem in the Renaissance: state sovereignty, its means and methods, limits and legal basis. Bodin, in his *Republic* (1576), attempted to define sovereignty for the era. Politics was no longer in the Church's hands, and lawyers could take over—canon law was replaced by Roman law, piety was replaced by patriotism, and the modern world could be seen over the horizon.

The new Renaissance order was apparent in the writing of history as well. Whereas Medieval historians often wrote theological history, in which historical events were determined by supernatural causes, Renaissance historians wrote literary narrations of political and military events (the models were such classical authors as Herodotus and Livy). Renaissance historians also began, for the first time, to discern periods of history as separate secular entities rather than to view all events as a Biblical continuum from Genesis to their own day. The new dynamic, secular view of history reached its peak in the works of Machiavelli and Francesco Guicciardini (1483-1540). Machiavelli's assorted works of history are concerned with local events objectively viewed. But Guicciardini was a better historian, indeed the best the Renaissance had to offer. He developed a critical history (see his *History of Florence*) as he slighted the old chronologically-oriented historiography in favor of a more comprehensive, a more psychological interpretation of history. Portraiture became as important in the writing of history as it became in Renaissance art and biography. Guicciardini's *History of Italy* (1536) in twenty books frequently massacred style in favor of verbiage, but it stressed analysis of events rather than the mere recording of them.

In England, too, history came to be interpreted in a secular fashion. The works of Halle and Holinshed perpetuated the Tudor myth, that is, the idea that the Battle of Bosworth Field in 1485 had brought together the warring houses of York and Lancaster and led to a united England under Henry VII. Their lucid writing, their attention to detail, their devotion to style, formed excellent sources for the chronicle-history plays to come, particularly those of Shakespeare.

Perhaps the outstanding quality of Renaissance historians was their ability to view the past without interference from moral passions, preconceived judgments, or philosophical dogmas. Historical writing, as Erwin Panofsky has pointed out, offered, even as did art, "focussed perspective."

The Greeks and Nature:

New Ordering of the Visual Arts, Music, and Literature

"Out of the thick Gothic night our eyes are opened to the glorious torch of the sun," exclaimed Rabelais, reflecting on the separation Renaissance man felt between his Medieval heritage of religious and social dogma that held earthly life insignificant, and his own humanistic age that found in a revival of the antique an emphasis upon the here and now. Even though a study of the past had been an aspect of Medieval thought, still the Renaissance stress derived ultimately from the Greek notion of man as the measure of all things. No better illustration of this humanistic theme can be found than in the visual arts, particularly in Italy, where there appeared a parade of such artistic geniuses as the Western World has not seen again.

In painting, the new realistic style was launched by Giotto (1266-1336). Breaking with the traditional Italo-Byzantine style, best represented by such artists as Simone Martini (1284-1344), he worked in fresco rather than tempera and oil; he replaced a gold background that symbolized eternity with a deep blue that signified earth; and he peopled his compositions not with the stylized, bodiless types found in Byzantine mosaics, but with flesh and blood individuals plastically rendered. Still utilizing Biblical subject matter and employing an economy of means seldom equalled, Giotto created a psychological and visual realism that gave direction to Western painting for over five hundred years.

For almost a century, most artists found Giotto's new realism difficult to understand and to imitate—except Masaccio (1400-1427). He was the true inheritor of the Giotto manner and his frescoes in the Brancacci Chapel in Florence not only continued Giotto's style but also prepared for the High Renaissance style—monumentality of the human figure, focal perspective, and psychological drama—as developed by Leonardo da Vinci (1452-1519), Raphael (1482-1520), and Michelangelo (1475-1564). This stylistic phase ended in Venice, in a blaze of color and decorative splendor favored by Titian (1477-1576), Tintoretto (1518-1594), and Veronese (1528-1588); but not before it had radiated throughout Northern Europe, particularly to Germany. In his portraits of the Tudors, Hans Holbein the Younger (1497-1543) revealed a Renaissance mastery over pictorial elements to delineate character; and in his voluminous output, Albrecht Dürer (1472-1528), as curious about the environment as Leonardo, showed the influence of his Italian journey in his geometric designs and the solidity of his figures.

Brief reference must be made to the movement known as Mannerism, a reaction to the style of the High Renaissance, which appeared throughout Europe between 1520 and 1620. A style of deliberate distortions and disharmonies, yet replete with devices of fancy, surprise and invention, its Italian representatives include Jacopa da Pontormo (1494-1557), Angelo Bronzino (1502-1572), and Michelangelo himself in such late works as the *Last Judgment* in the Sistine Chapel; as well as Lucas Cranach the Elder (1472-1553) and François Clouet (1516-1572). Subjective and often tormented, neo-Gothic in spirit and anti-classical in method, Mannerism no doubt reflected the disenchantment and dislocation that the Reformation and Counter-Reformation introduced into Renaissance Europe.

Renaissance sculpture follows a path similar to that of Renaissance painting, except that the new style antedates Giotto's by at least twenty-five years—perhaps because sculptors, unlike the painters, had before them Graeco-Roman statues and carvings. Where Medieval sculpture, used to decorate cathedrals, had been mainly columnar and distorted, so as to accentuate the verticality of the building to which it was attached, Renaissance sculpture was realistic, free-standing, and three dimensional. Subject matter remained largely Biblical but Renaissance sculptors, like the painters, emphasized the nude human body, which became the supreme vehicle for the expression of man's beauty, intellect, and ambition. For example, Donatello (1386-1466) carved a bronze rustic *David*—the first free-standing nude since the fall of Rome —and Michelangelo, preferring the same Old Testament subject, made David a marble God from Olympus.

The break with the Medieval tradition may best be seen in the pulpit panels in the cathedrals at Pisa and Pistoia. Executed by the Pisani—Nicola (*c*. 1206-1278), Giovanni (1250-1330), and Andrea (1270-1348)—these panels combine Gothic mannerisms of crowding and diminution of the human figure with the classical ones of naturalistic movement and plasticity of form, elements that betray their prototypes in classical marbles. The new style created by the Pisani was continued by Donatello, who not only studied classical models—as revealed in his *Singing Gallery* in the cathedral at Florence—but also carefully observed nature—as evidenced in his *St. George* on Or Sanmichele in Florence. Like a way station between him and Michelangelo is Andrea Verrocchio (1435-1488), whose equestrian statue of Colleoni revived a classical mode that the Medieval centuries had neglected. Finally in Michelangelo, the tradition culminates. In his *Bound Slaves* and the allegorical figures on the Medici Tombs, Michelangelo so monumental-ized man that he thunders the earth like Jove. (And again, Shakespeare couches in poetry the Renaissance theme—Caesar could bestride the world like a colossus with petty men peeping between his legs, and Antony is a "triple pillar of the world.")

More than painting and sculpture, Renaissance architecture marks a definite break with the Medieval past. Reflecting man's divine aspira-tions, Medieval buildings were almost entirely ecclesiastical, their but-tresses, windows and stone decorations dependent upon linear, vertical design to create a mystic effect. The Gothic cathedral, the most char-acteristic building of the age, was indeed what the English poet Stephen Spender termed "an immense arrow shooting heavenward." During the Renaissance, palaces, villas, and public halls were as common as churches, their horizontal design anchoring man to earth, and their classical moldings and friezes revealing the architects' intense study of Graeco-Roman ruins. Filippo Brunelleschi's (1379-1446) Pazzi Chapel in Florence, with its subtle use of classical motifs and rounded arch; Michelozzo's (1396-1472) Medici-Riccardi Palace, an immense pile of geometric stone topped with a deep cornice; and St. Peter's Basilica with its Michelangelo dome that embodies both temporal and spiritual power, are only three examples of the changes that the Renaissance brought to architecture.

Similar effects were achieved in the music of the Renaissance. Various Medieval genres began to break up as composers found they could involve a "secular" song in a Mass setting or toss out the fixed refrains of the *chanson*. The *chanson* (in its new guise, the madrigal) and the motet reached their greatest heights. The Renaissance composer achieved a new, integrated, homogeneous polyphony where one voice imitated another, where the parts were smoothly integrated, complementary, uni-fied, instead of the note-against-note idea of the Middle Ages. Secular texts were used, and as religious and civil ceremonies came to be com-bined, music moved outside the Church.

Music, which for the Medieval *cantor* or practicing musician was meant to make heavenly harmony audible to men, became, in the Renaissance, a vehicle for the expression of human emotions. Effort was made to wed music to words. Stimulated by the newly rediscovered Greek tragedies and their use of music, the Florentine Camerata (fl. 1600) expanded upon the traditional use of music in Miracle, Mystery, and Morality plays, and added music to texts with classical themes, producing a new art form—opera. Interest in the ancients and their concern with the relationship between music and numbers also furthered musical experimentation. In England, France, and Italy musical life in the Renaissance flourished and reached new heights of achievement in secular forms that reflected the period's absorbing interest in earthly man.

Renaissance literature also reflects the unique qualities of the period. Many Medieval forms of literature remained popular in the Renaissance, but many more were added until the proliferation of literary forms became itself a mark of Renaissance literature. And in this proliferation of forms came opportunity for a new ordering of experience.

The appeal of the Medieval novella, aside from that of a good story well told, had been in its realism, its satire, its convoluted love affairs, and its morality. These reasons, congruent with the Renaissance's ideas of literature, made the novella popular in both periods of history. Such works as Boccaccio's *Decameron* (published 1471), Queen Marguerite of Navarre's *Heptameron* (1553) and Cinthio's *Hecatommithi* (1566) all testify to the enduring delight of the form. It is not unnatural that the novella grew into somewhat larger works. These were frequently satirical, lusty, full-bodied, realistic, and sometimes romantic and helped pave the way for the novel. These prose narratives crossed national boundaries, and one finds them in England (Lyly's *Euphues* [1578], for example), in Spain (Cervantes' *Don Quixote* [1605]), and in France (Rabelais' *Gargantua* [1537-1564]).

Longer narratives, in verse, became popular in the Renaissance. They evinced the characteristics of the classical epic: large in effect, leisurely in presentation, supernatural in mechanics, and remote in time. Ariosto's *Orlando Furioso* (1516) handled a Medieval subject, the story of Roland, yet rendered it in the Renaissance manner—sensuous pictorial detail, richness of plot—but most of all the epic narrative reflected the Renaissance attempt to reconcile the man of action with the contemplative man. One sees the theme again in Spenser's *Faerie Queene* (1590), where moral excellence, embodied in the Medieval contemplative man (the monk) and the Medieval man of action (the knight) emerges as Sir Guyon and the Red Cross Knight.

The essay began largely with Montaigne (his *essais* [1580] were to be tentative, incomplete attempts at expressing intimate ideas—again, the Renaissance believed that what an individual thought and felt might have importance) and was practiced by such an outstanding author as Francis Bacon. Closely related to the essay was the courtesy book, a Renaissance invention which prescribed rules of conduct for the courtly gentleman and lady as well as rules for the education of the future prince and courtier. Castiglione's *Book of the Courtier* (1528) is perhaps the most outstanding example of the genre, though the English were also fond of indulging in practical advice (for example, Henry Peacham's *Compleat Gentleman,* 1622).

Biography in literature assumed great importance. The literary shift from Saints' lives to those of less holy men can be found in such works as Vasari's *Lives of the Artists* (1550) and Lydgate's *The Fall of Princes* (1431-1438). Another illustration is the multi-authored *A Mirror for Magistrates* (1599), a series of didactic tragedies of English kings who fall from high to low estate because of failure in their responsibility to God. The form satisfied the Renaissance desire to be both instructed and entertained—a desire which found its satisfaction in the drama, as well.

The major forms of Renaissance drama were partly derived from the Middle Ages and partly from the classics. If the Medieval Mystery play concerned itself with Biblical stories, the Renaissance continued these stories into more recent history, and the chronicle-history plays resulted. Tragedy, too, grew from such Medieval forms as the Morality play, but again the influence of the classics, in this case Seneca, helped a unique form to emerge. The Medieval Interlude, injected with the witty prose of John Lyly, emerged as comedy, a unique comedy, a comedy unfettered by rules when handled by Shakespeare and adapted to Aristotelian principles when created by Jonson. The *commedia dell' arte* in Italy (which was to exercise so strong an influence on the drama of France and England) grew from the improvised Italian skits but, again, it was classical comic figures which gave it its characters and its new life. Lope de Vega (1562-1635) in Spain combined Medieval chivalry with a Renaissance realistic awareness of practical life.

Of the many Renaissance poetic forms, either imitative of the antique—such as the eclogue and the epigram—or continued from the Middle Ages—such as the love allegory—none is more representative of the period than the sonnet. In a short, constricted form the poet found a means of expressing both personal emotion and attitude and suggesting a resolution—a fresh way of ordering the human love experience. In much the same way that the essay permitted both self-analysis and personal comment, the sonnet does too. The sonnet began in Italy with Petrarch (and was later favored by Michelangelo) and travelled rapidly to England, where Wyatt and Surrey gave it a home and where it was adopted by poets throughout the Elizabethan period. It went to France, too, where the Pléiade (Ronsard, du Bellay, de Baïf) gave the Petrarchan sonnet its Gallic abode.

The literary criticism of the Renaissance also went back to the classics. Aristotle's *Poetics* was translated many times, but the most influential translation and exegesis was that of Castelvetro (1570), whose misinterpretation of Aristotle was responsible for many of the English and French "rules" concerning the drama. Perhaps the outstanding work of theory of the period, however, was that of Sidney, whose *Defense of Poesy*, constructed along the lines of a classical oration, defended poetry, analyzed the creative imagination, and helped raise the position of the poet from mere entertainer to expounder of moral truth.

Renaissance literature, then, finding much of worth in the classical past, combined it with the Medieval to create new literary forms that expressed contemporary humanist interests.

The Here and Now:
New Ordering of the Sciences

To Medieval man the world was a sacred text to be perused, studied for links to God. An apple stood for original sin, glass for the purity of Mary, a dog for fidelity. Logic reigned rather than experimentation, and classical precepts served instead of observation. It was not until the seventeenth century that modern science as we know it began to take shape; still, the Renaissance prepared the way. Direct observation slowly supplanted the symbolic interpretation of phenomena; classical precepts were used to encourage observation, the recording of sense data, rather than merely to supply dicta for belief.

The Renaissance became interested in the world *per se,* in nature, in the discovery of man's environment. And a newly ordered concept of the earth slowly emerged. Thanks to Aristotle and Ptolemy, man had long believed in a universe which revolved around the earth, at the center of which God had placed man. Copernicus, in his *On the Revolutions of the Celestial Spheres* (1543), gave strong evidence that the earth was not the center of the universe but a planet revolving around the sun. On this principle both Bruno and Galileo expounded. Giordano Bruno differentiated between the world and the universe, the former signifying the solar system and the fixed stars, and the latter a totality of worlds. Finally, Galileo's main contribution to Renaissance science (*Dialogue on the Two Chief Systems of the World,* published 1632, though written earlier), included a defense of the Copernican system and set up a wholly new scientific methodology based on experiment and observation. Ironically, even as man displaced himself from the center of the universe, his mastery of that universe became strengthened.

At the same time the heavens were being explored, man went about discovering areas closer to home. By 1600 the known surface of the earth was doubled, and such men as Columbus (1492), Vasco da Gama (1498), Amerigo Vespucci (1497-1504), and Magellan (1519-1522) were largely responsible. The means of discovery were also expanded, thanks mostly to the work of Mercator. His maps and globes were not only of vital importance to seamen, merchants, and statesmen but were also works of art in themselves. Expanded navigation, and the intense rivalries of colonizing nations, led to many advances in applied science— the refinement of the compass, for example.

Two of the most important technological innovations of the Renaissance were in printing and warfare. Printing, "the divine art," was invented about mid-fifteenth century in Germany, probably by Gutenberg—that is, printing from cast moveable type. Of course, the fact that production of paper made from linen had increased (vellum was entirely too expensive) helped popularize the new discovery. Printing revolutionized man's intellectual life, and again the Renaissance was responsible.

But the Renaissance's legacy was not benign only. The introduction of gunpowder made a new kind of warfare possible, new kinds of weapons, new means of exterminating recently awakened man.

But, not surprisingly, man became more interested in himself. Here the artist was a help. Leonardo was an avid student of anatomy (actually dissecting corpses in his quest for knowledge), and his drawings are amazingly accurate to this day. Vesalius' *Fabrica* (1543) introduced a

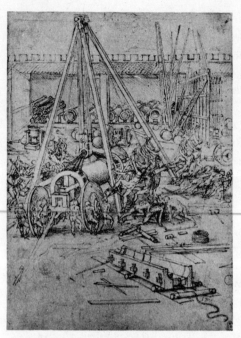

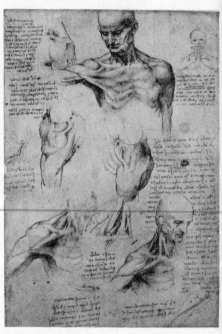

3. *A Large Cannon Being Raised on to a Gun Carriage,* Leonardo da Vinci.

4. *Anatomical Studies of a Man's Neck and Shoulders,* Leonardo da Vinci.

new era in anatomical studies; his work on the skeleton, on the brain, on muscles, on veins, on organs was the first systematic study of all parts of the body, almost overwhelming in its plan and scope. Medicine made great strides, particularly with Paracelsus (1493-1541), who was both healer and quack and who pioneered in the study of mental disease, iatrochemistry, and homeopathy; with the interest of Fracastoro of Verona in contagious diseases (his was the dubious honor of naming syphilis); and with William Harvey's studies of the action of the blood.

And the Renaissance had its pseudo-science, too, especially in the belief in astrology and alchemy. It was a long time before astrology and alchemy were separated from the sciences; indeed, one may still buy a horoscope at most newsstands, and the many times Brooklyn Bridge has been sold testifies to the enduring appeal of alchemy in one form or another. The Renaissance could not shake itself of superstition, but then neither can we.

A Trinity of Ideas:

New Ordering of Philosophy and Religion

If the Renaissance was credulous in some of its science, its handling of philosophy and religion was penetrating and profound. Philosophically, there were three currents of Renaissance thought: Humanism, Aristotelianism, and Platonism.

The study of Greek and Latin authors was the basis for Humanism, and there is no question that Humanism was the dominant intellectual current eddying through the Renaissance. In their rhetoric, history, poetry, and moral philosophy, classical authors stressed aesthetic form and earthly environment. The Humanists, children of the Renaissance, found in the classics both model and corrective. Such studies encouraged a revival of ancient philosophies other than Aristotle's.

Aristotelianism had survived into the Renaissance partly because of Aquinas' encyclopedic work. The Middle Ages were fascinated with Aristotle because he helped to provide a logical basis for Christian dogma. Early Italian Renaissance Aristotelians, particularly such men as Pompanazzi (1462-1525) and Zabarella (1532-1589), centered at the Universities of Padua and Bologna, continued the traditional interest in logic and method as well as in natural philosophy by stressing human values from points of view that were both scientific and naturalistic, but compared to its great Platonic rival, less personal and religious.

Marsilio Ficino's (1433-1499) Platonic Academy in a villa near Florence was the font from which flowed to many European countries the current of Neoplatonism. Priest, doctor, and scholar, Ficino was the most influential figure in the synthesis of Medieval philosophy and Greek Platonism. In the company of disciples such as Pico della Mirandola and Christoforo Landino, he made of Plato a philosopher of love and beauty, a contribution which profoundly influenced European humanists, intellectuals, and artists, including the Pléiade in France, the Oxford Reformers in England, the poets Sidney, Spenser, and Drayton, and the artists Cranach, Titian, and Michelangelo. In his major works, *Theologica Platonica* (1474) and *Convito* (1544), Ficino described a universe ordered by a benign, loving God who created man as the link between Himself and the world. Possessed of the exclusively human faculty of Reason, man occupied a pivotal position, capable of turning to either lower or higher realms of existence. But God preferred that man choose the latter, and provided him sure means for the ascent

31

heavenward—love. By infusing beauty in things natural and human, God lured man into becoming a lover through the contemplation and possession of beautiful things and persons and thus returned man to Himself. No wonder, then, society found so humanistic and congenial a philosophy, that had at its core the idea of love as motivation for Creator and created, attractive and compelling—particularly writers and artists. When schematized in words or pigments, Ficino's philosophy became a vast circle, the circle of love.

But the standard cliché about the Renaissance, that it was characteristically individual and creative, irreligious and pagan, needs clarification, particularly concerning religion. Certainly Renaissance man did not substitute the Olympian hierarchy for the Christian; but with increased secularization—first in Italy, then in other countries—religion inevitably underwent change. Perhaps for the first time in centuries, religious and theological matters competed with non-religious ones (scientific, social, political, and economic) in vitality and popular appeal. Although traditional Christian beliefs were neither challenged nor discarded, they were modified and transformed. The Church was forced to compete with emerging powers (the middle class, national states) and was hampered by the loss of authority which internal strife and papal wars engendered. Anti-clerical sentiment, rebellion against hierarchical authority and certain ritualistic aspects of Medieval religion marked the fourteenth and fifteenth centuries (note the heresies of Wycliff and Huss); the writings of Christian Humanists manifested both an increasing and an independent role played by laymen in influencing Christian thought.

In Italy, such Humanists as Lorenzo Valla (1406-1457) viewed traditional religious goals with deliberate skepticism and attempted to free themselves from bondage to Church dogma. When Aeneas Sylvius Piccolomini ascended the papal throne in 1458 as Pius II, he officially sanctioned an alliance between Humanism and the Church. In England, Erasmus and other Oxford Reformers attacked scholastic method and insisted upon a return to the sources of Christianity, the Scriptures, and patristic writings. When John Colet (1467-1519) returned to Oxford from Italy in 1496 and lectured on the Pauline Epistles, he broke with the traditional Medieval method of exegesis which demanded literal, allegorical, and figurative interpretations, and he interpreted important Biblical sources as a unified whole, the expression of a single, fundamental religious attitude. Thus the new religious spirit that had permeated Italy was carried into Northern Europe—the spirit that looked upon Christian writings not as repositories of dogmatic and theoretical knowledge concerning man's eternal destiny, but as inspiration for a reformation and revival of life itself.

Such a typically humanistic view regarding the critical examination of sacred texts, joined with the typically Renaissance notion that each individual is important enough and endowed with sufficient capacity to understand and make decisions concerning his own destiny in spite of established authority, led to the Protestant Revolt.

The Church had been elastic enough in theory and practice to accommodate the various reform movements of the Cluniac, Cistercian, and Franciscan monks of the late Middle Ages, but by the end of the fifteenth century, because of secularization in thought, and abuse and indifference in practice, it could not sustain the Humanism of Juan de Valdés (the Spanish Erasmian), or the mysticism of Thomas a Kempis, or the asceticism of the Florentine Savonarola, or the simple pietism of the German Brotherhood of the Common Life. Martin Luther (1483-1546), while proclaiming such humanistic notions as the priesthood of all believers who must be liberated from servitude to "good works," still held to the Medieval concern of the primacy of salvation. The ninety-five theses he pounded on the Cathedral door at Wittenberg adumbrated the Protestant program, one which the French John Calvin (1509-1564) and the Scottish John Knox (1505-1572) developed and refined.

The Reformation took shape both logically and naturally from the flurry of immediately preceding scientific, political, and religious ideas. Exploring and discovering in the realms of art, literature, geography, science, and philosophy, it became intimately related to the Renaissance.

The Renaissance and the Reformation, then, represented a new order, a new way of handling experience, a new way of viewing the universe, a new way for man to relate to his fellow man and to his God. Little that was completely new was revealed to man during the Renaissance, but filtering the classical past through the Medieval resulted in a synthesis that was new by virtue of arrangement, organization—order.

The old order changeth, but not much, and if the Renaissance was heavily dependent on its Medieval heritage, so are we, the children of the Renaissance. If the modern stress is secular rather than religious, so was that of the Renaissance; if science seems to be revealing a brave new universe, so it seemed in the Renaissance; if the modern preoccupa-

33

tion with the individual (man and state) seems to ignore ultimate questions, this too was the trademark of the Renaissance.

If we live today in a world forgotten by God where our choice seems to be between the absurd and a return to faith, between earthly as opposed to divine goals, perhaps we have here, too, to thank the Renaissance. What this period in history asked, we are still asking, but perhaps our answers will only come with a complete understanding of that time when man first turned to the here and now for his place in the universe—the Renaissance.

PART I

The Unraveled Tapestry:

New Ordering of
Political Science
and History

The Renaissance unraveled the tapestry of Church and State, and men chose to deal with secular rather than eternal problems. Political science focused on temporal rather than clerical power, and history was viewed as humanly rather than divinely ordered.

The authors on the following pages provide a spectrum of social belief: Shakespeare suggested the danger of tampering with the social and political order as established by God; to Marsilius of Padua religion, far from dominating the state, became mainly a part of that state and was integrated into it; his countryman, Machiavelli, chose to ignore religious issues altogether and decided instead to discuss realistically the nature of power and the means by which it is both attained and sustained; Montaigne was aware of the ephemeral and futile aspects of greatness; the shifting tides of power and of greatness, as well as their cost, became apparent in the histories Guicciardini so laboriously wrought; by the time of Holinshed, secular power was so much taken for granted that he could expend his historical efforts on propaganda supporting the Establishment; finally, Sir Thomas More offered the humanist's dream of man's earthly home.

WILLIAM SHAKESPEARE

DIVINE ORDER

> CANTERBURY. Therefore doth Heaven divide
> The state of man in divers functions,
> Setting endeavor in continual motion.
> To which is fixèd, as an aim or butt,
> Obedience. For so work the honeybees,
> Creatures that by a rule in nature teach

5. *Lorenzo de' Medici*, Verocchio.

The act of order to a peopled kingdom.
They have a King and officers of sorts,
Where some, like magistrates, correct at home,
Others, like merchants, venture trade abroad,
Others, like soldiers, armèd in their stings,
Make boot upon the summer's velvet buds,
Which pillage they with merry march bring home
To the tent royal of their Emperor.
Who, busied in his majesty, surveys
The singing masons building roofs of gold,
The civil citizens kneading up the honey,
The poor mechanic porters crowding in
Their heavy burdens at his narrow gate,
The sad-eyed Justice, with his surly hum,

Delivering o'er to executors pale
The lazy yawning drone. I this infer,
That many things, having full reference
To one consent, may work contrariously.
As many arrows, loosed several ways,
Come to one mark; as many ways meet in one town;
As many fresh streams meet in one salt sea;
As many lines close in the dial's center—
So many a thousand actions, once afoot,
End in one purpose, and be all well borne
Without defeat. . . .

(from *Henry V*)

ROSENCRANTZ. . . . The cease of majesty
Dies not alone, but like a gulf doth draw
What's near it with it. It is a massy wheel
Fixed on the summit of the highest mount,
To whose huge spokes ten thousand lesser things
Are mortised and adjoined; which, when it falls,
Each small annexment, petty consequence,
Attends the boisterous ruin. Never alone
Did the King sigh but with a general groan.

(from *Hamlet*)

KING RICHARD [To Northumberland]. We are amazed, and
thus long have we stood
To watch the fearful bending of thy knee,
Because we thought ourself thy lawful king.
And if we be, how dare thy joints forget
To pay their awful duty to our presence?
If we be not, show us the hand of God
That hath dismissed us from our stewardship;
For well we know no hand of blood and bone
Can gripe the sacred handle of our scepter
Unless he do profane, steal, or usurp.
And though you think that all, as you have done,
Have torn their souls by turning them from us,
And we are barren and bereft of friends,

Yet know my master, God Omnipotent,
Is mustering in His clouds on our behalf
Armies of pestilence; and they shall strike
Your children yet unborn and unbegot,
That lift your vassal hands against my head
And threat the glory of my precious crown.
Tell Bolingbroke—for yond methinks he stands—
That every stride he makes upon my land
Is dangerous treason. He is come to open
The purple testament of bleeding war.
But ere the crown he looks for live in peace,
Ten thousand bloody crowns of mothers' sons
Shall ill become the flower of England's face,
Change the complexion of her maid-pale peace
To scarlet indignation, and bedew
Her pastures' grass with faithful English blood.

(from *Richard II*)

KATHARINA. . . . Thy husband is thy lord, thy life, thy keeper,
Thy head, thy sovereign, one that cares for thee,
And for thy maintenance commits his body
To painful labor both by sea and land,
To watch the night in storms, the day in cold,
Whilst thou liest warm at home, secure, and safe;
And craves no other tribute at thy hands
But love, fair looks and true obedience,
Too little payment for so great a debt.
Such duty as the subject owes the prince
Even such a woman oweth to her husband,
And when she is froward, peevish, sullen, sour,
And not obedient to his honest will,
What is she but a foul contending rebel
And graceless traitor to her loving lord?
I am ashamed that women are so simple
To offer war where they should kneel for peace,
Or seek for rule, supremacy, and sway,
When they are bound to serve, love, and obey.
Why are our bodies soft and weak and smooth,
Unapt to toil and trouble in the world,

But that our soft conditions and our hearts
Should well agree with our external parts?
Come, come, you froward and unable worms!
My mind hath been as big as one of yours,
My heart as great, my reason haply more,
To bandy word for word and frown for frown;
But now I see our lances are but straws,
Our strength as weak, our weakness past compare,
That seeming to be most which we indeed least are.
Then vail your stomachs, for it is no boot,
And place your hands below your husband's foot;
In token of which duty, if he please,
My hand is ready, may it do him ease.

(from The Taming of the Shrew)

MARSILIUS OF PADUA

FROM DEFENSOR PACIS

The benefits and fruits of the tranquillity or peace of civil regimes were set forth by Cassiodorus in this passage of his first epistle. Exhibiting through these great goods the greatest good of man, sufficiency of life, which no one can attain without peace and tranquillity, Cassiodorus aimed thereby to arouse in men the desire to have peace with one another and hence tranquillity. In this aim he was in accord with what the blessed Job said in his twenty-second chapter: "Be at peace, and thereby thou shalt have the best fruits." . . .

Since, however, "contraries are [essentially] productive of contraries," from discord, the opposite of tranquillity, the worst fruits and troubles will befall any civil regime or state. This can readily be seen, and is obvious to almost all men, from the example of the Italian state. For while the inhabitants of Italy lived peacefully together, they experienced those sweet fruits of peace which have been mentioned above, and from and in those fruits they made such great progress that they brought the whole habitable world under their sway. But when discord and strife arose among them, their state was sorely beset by all kinds of hardships and troubles and underwent the dominion of hateful foreign nations.

And in the same way Italy is once again battered on all sides because of strife and is almost destroyed, so that it can easily be invaded by anyone who wants to seize it and who has any power at all. Nor is such an outcome astonishing, for, as Sallust attests, writing about Catiline: "By concord small things increase, by discord great things perish." . . .

Into this dire predicament, then, the miserable men are dragged because of their discord and strife, which, like the illness of an animal, is recognized to be the diseased disposition of the civil regime. Although strife has many original causes, almost all those which can emerge in the usual ways were described by the foremost of the philosophers in his *Civil Science*. Besides these, however, there is one singular and very obscure cause by which the Roman empire has long been troubled and is still troubled. This cause is very contagious and prone to creep up on all other cities and states; in its greediness it has already tried to invade most of them. Neither Aristotle nor any other philosopher of his time or before could have discerned the origin and species of this cause. For it was and is a certain perverted opinion (to be exposed by us below) which came to be adopted as an aftermath of the miraculous effect produced by the supreme cause long after Aristotle's time; an effect beyond the power of the lower nature and the usual action of causes in things. This sophistic opinion, wearing the guise of the honorable and beneficial, is utterly pernicious to the human race and, if unchecked, will eventually bring unbearable harm to every city and country.

The fruits of peace or tranquillity, then, are the greatest goods, as we have said, while those of its opposite, strife, are unbearable evils. Hence we ought to wish for peace, to seek it if we do not already have it, to conserve it once it is attained, and to repel with all our strength the strife which is opposed to it. To this end individual brethren, and in even greater degree groups and communities, are obliged to help one another, both from the feeling of heavenly love and from the bonds or law of human society. This admonition Plato also gives us, as Tully attests in the first book of his treatise *On Duties*, when he said: "We were not born for ourselves alone; to part of us our native land lays claim, and to part, our friends." To this sentence Tully adds: "And so, as the Stoics were wont to say, the things that grow in the earth are all created for the use of men; but men are born for the sake of men. In this we ought to follow the lead of nature, and to bring forth common utilities for all." But it would be no small common utility, indeed it is rather a necessity, to unmask the sophism of this singular cause of wars which threatens no small harm to all states and communities. Hence, whoever is willing and able to discern the common utility is obliged to give this matter his vigilant care and diligent efforts. For while this sophism remains concealed, this pestilence can in no way be avoided, nor its pernicious effect be completely uprooted from states or cities.

. . .

It is my purpose, therefore, with God's help, to expose only this singular cause of strife. For to reiterate the number and nature of those causes which were set forth by Aristotle would be superfluous; but this cause which Aristotle could not have known, and which no one after him who could know it has undertaken to investigate, we wish to unmask so that it may henceforth be readily excluded from all states or cities, and virtuous rulers and subjects live more securely in tranquillity. This is the desirable outcome which I propose at the beginning of this work; an outcome necessary for those who would enjoy civil happiness, which seems the best of the objects of desire possible to man in this world, and the ultimate aim of human acts.

. . .

The state, according to Aristotle in the *Politics*, Book I, Chapter 1, is "the perfect community having the full limit of self-sufficiency, which came into existence for the sake of living, but exists for the sake of living well." This phrase of Aristotle—"came into existence for the sake of living, but exists for the sake of living well"—signifies the perfect final cause of the state, since those who live a civil life not only live, which beasts or slaves do too, but live well, having leisure for those liberal functions in which are exercised the virtues of both the practical and the theoretic soul.

Having thus determined the end of the state to be living and living well, we must treat first of living and its modes. For this, as we have said, is the purpose for the sake of which the state was established, and which necessitates all the things which exist in the state and are done by the association of men in it. Let us therefore lay this down as the principle of all the things which are to be demonstrated here, a principle naturally held, believed, and freely granted by all: that all men not deformed or otherwise impeded naturally desire a sufficient life, and avoid and flee what is harmful thereto. This has been acknowledged not only with regard to man but also with regard to every genus of animals, according to Tully in his treatise *On Duties,* Book I, Chapter 3, where he says: "It is an original endowment which nature has bestowed upon every genus of living things, that it preserves itself, its body, and its life, that it avoids those things which seem harmful, and that it seeks and obtains all those things which are necessary for living." This principle can also be clearly grasped by everyone through sense induction.

But the living and living well which are appropriate to men fall into two kinds, of which one is temporal or earthly, while the other is usually called eternal or heavenly. However, this latter kind of living, the eternal, the whole body of philosophers were unable to prove by demonstration, nor was it self-evident, and therefore they did not concern themselves with the means thereto. But as to the first kind of living and living well or good life, that is, the earthly, and its necessary means, this the glorious philosophers comprehended almost completely through demonstration. Hence for its attainment they concluded the necessity of the civil community, without which this sufficient life cannot be obtained. Thus the foremost of the philosophers, Aristotle, said in his *Politics,* Book I, Chapter 1: "All men are driven toward such an association by a natural impulse." Although sense experience teaches this, we wish to bring out more distinctly that cause of it which we have indicated, as follows: Man is born composed of contrary elements, because of whose contrary actions and passions some of his substance is continually being destroyed; moreover, he is born "bare and unprotected" from excess of the surrounding air and other elements, capable of suffering and of destruction, as has been said in the science of nature. As a consequence, he needed arts of diverse genera and species to avoid the aforementioned harms. But since these arts can be exercised only by a large number of men, and can be had only through their association with one another, men had to assemble together in order to attain what was beneficial through these acts and to avoid what was harmful.

But since among men thus assembled there arise disputes and quarrels which, if not regulated by a norm of justice, would cause men to fight and separate and thus finally would bring about the destruction of the state, there had to be established in this association a standard of justice and a guardian or maker thereof. And since this guardian has to restrain excessive wrongdoers as well as other individuals both within and outside the state who disturb or attempt to oppress the community, the state had to have within it something by which to resist these. Again, since the community needs various conveniences, repairs, and protection of certain common things, and different things in time of peace and in time of war, it was necessary that there be in the community men to take care of such matters, in order that the common necessity might be relieved when it was expedient or needful. But beside the things which we have so far mentioned, which relieve only the necessities of the present life, there is something else which men associated in a civil community need for the status of the future world promised to the human race through God's supernatural revelation, and which is useful also for the status of the present life. This is the worship and honoring of God, and the giving of thanks both for benefits received in this world and for those to be received in the future one. For the teaching of these things and for the directing of men in them, the state had to designate certain teachers. The nature and qualities of all these and the other matters mentioned above will be treated in detail in the subsequent discussions.

Men, then, were assembled for the sake of the sufficient life, being able to seek out for themselves the necessaries enumerated above, and exchanging them with one another. This assemblage, thus perfect and having the limit of self-sufficiency, is called the state, whose final cause as well as that of its many parts has already been indicated by us in some measure, and will be more fully distinguished below. For since diverse things are necessary to men who desire a sufficient life, things which cannot be supplied by men of one order or office, there had to be diverse orders or offices of men in this association, exercising or supplying such diverse things which men need for sufficiency of life. But these diverse orders or offices of men are none other than the many and distinct parts of the state.

.　　.　　.

We have now completely listed the parts of the state, in whose perfect action and intercommunication, without external impediment, we have said that the tranquillity of the state consists. But he must now continue our discussion of them, since the fuller determination of these parts, with respect both to their functions or ends and to their other appropriate causes, will make more manifest the causes of tranquillity and of its opposite. Let us say, then, that the parts or offices of the state are of six kinds, as Aristotle said in the *Politics,* Book VII, Chapter 7: the agricultural, the artisan, the military, the financial, the priestly, and the judicial or deliberative. Three of these, the priestly, the warrior, and the judicial, are in the strict sense parts of the state, and in civil communities they are usually called the honorable class (*honorabilitatem*). The others are called parts only in the broad sense of the term, because they are offices necessary to the state according to the doctrine of Aristotle in the *Politics,* Book VII, Chapter 7. And the multitude belonging to these offices are usually called the common mass (*vulgaris*). These, then, are the more familiar parts of the city or state, to which all the others can appropriately be reduced.

.   .   .

In order to proportion all . . . actions and passions, and to fulfill them in that to which nature could not lead, there were discovered the various kinds of arts and other virtues, as we said above, and men of various offices were established to exercise these for the purpose of supplying human needs. These orders are none other than the parts of the state enumerated above. . . .

In order to moderate the actions and passions of our body caused by the impressions of the elements which externally surround us, there was discovered the general class of mechanics, which Aristotle in the *Politics,* Book VII, Chapter 6, calls the "arts." . . . concerning which Aristotle says in the *Politics,* Book IV, Chapter 3: "Of these arts some must exist from necessity, and others are for pleasure and living well." Under this class is also placed the practice of medicine, which is in some way architectonic to many of the above-mentioned arts.

In order to moderate the excesses of the acts deriving from the locomotive powers through knowledge and desire, which we have called transient acts and which can be done for the benefit or for the harm or injury of someone other than the doer for the status of the present world, there was necessarily established in the state a part or office by which the excesses of such acts are corrected and reduced to equality or due proportion. For without such correction the excesses of these acts would cause fighting and hence the separation of the citizens, and finally the destruction of the state and loss of the sufficient life. This part of the state, together with its subsidiaries, is called by Aristotle the "judicial" or "ruling" and "deliberative" part, and its function is to regulate matters of justice and the common benefit.

In addition, since the sufficient life cannot be led by citizens who are oppressed or cast into slavery by external oppressors, and also since the sentences of the judges against injurious and rebellious men within the state must be executed by coercive force, it was necessary to set up in the state a military or warrior part, which many of the mechanics also subserve. . . .

Again, since in some years on earth the harvests are large, and in others small; and the state is sometimes at peace with its neighbors, and sometimes not; and it is in need of various common services such as the construction and repair of roads, bridges, and other edifices, and similar things whose enumeration here would be neither appropriate nor brief—to provide all these things at the proper time it was necessary to establish in the state a treasure-keeping part, which Aristotle called the "money class." . . .

It remains for us to discuss the necessity of the priestly part. All men have not thought so harmoniously about this as they have about the necessity of the other parts of the state. The cause of this difference was that the true and primary necessity of this part could not be comprehended through demonstration, nor was it self-evident. All nations, however, agreed that it was appropriate to establish the priesthood for the worship and honoring of God, and for the benefit resulting therefrom for the status of the present or the future world. For most laws or religions promise that in the future world God will distribute rewards to those who do good and punishment to doers of evil.

However, besides these causes of the laying down of religious laws, causes which are believed without demonstration, the philosophers, including Hesiod, Pythagoras, and several others of the ancients, noted appropriately a quite different cause or purpose for the setting forth of divine laws or religions—a purpose which was in some sense necessary for the status of this world. This was to ensure the goodness of human acts both individual and civil, on which depend almost completely the quiet or tranquillity of communities and finally the sufficient life in the present world. For although some of the philosophers who founded such laws or religions did not accept or believe in human resurrection and that life which is called eternal, they nevertheless feigned and persuaded others that it exists and that in it pleasures and pains are in accordance with the qualities of human deeds in this mortal life, in order that they might thereby induce in men reverence and fear of God, and a desire to flee the vices and to cultivate the virtues. For there are certain acts which the legislator cannot regulate by human law, that is, those acts which cannot be proved to be present or absent to someone, but which never-theless cannot be concealed from God, whom these philosophers feigned to be the maker of such laws and the commander of their observance, under the threat or promise of eternal reward for doers of good and punishment for doers of evil. Hence, they said of the variously virtuous men in this world that they were placed in the heavenly firmament; and from this were perhaps derived the names of certain stars and constellations. These philosophers said that the souls of men who acted wrongly entered the bodies of various brutes; for example, the souls of men who had been intemperate eaters entered the bodies of pigs, those who were intemperate in embracing and making love entered the bodies of goats, and so on, according to the proportions of human vices to their con-demnable properties. So too the philosophers assigned various kinds of torments to wrongdoers, like perpetual thirst and hunger for intem-perate Tantalus: water and fruit were to be near him, but he was unable to drink or handle these, for they were always fleeing faster than he could pursue them. The philosophers also said that the infernal regions, the places of these torments, were deep and dark; and they painted all sorts of terrible and gloomy pictures of them. From fear of these, men eschewed wrongdoing, were instigated to perform virtuous works of piety and mercy, and were well disposed both in themselves and toward others. As a consequence, many disputes and injuries ceased in com-munities. Hence too the peace or tranquillity of states and the sufficient life of men for the status of the present world were preserved with less difficulty; which was the end intended by these wise men in laying down such laws or religions.

Such, then, were the precepts handed down by the gentile priests; and for the teaching of them they established in their communities temples in which their gods were worshiped. They also appointed teachers of these laws or doctrines, whom they called priests (*sacerdotes*), because they handled the sacred objects of the temples, like the books, vases, and other such things subserving divine worship.

These affairs they arranged fittingly in accordance with their beliefs and rites. For as priests they appointed not anyone at all, but only virtuous and esteemed citizens who had held military, judicial, or deliberative office, and who had retired from secular affairs, being excused from civil burdens and offices because of age. For by such men, removed from pas-sions, and in whose words greater credence was placed because of their age and moral dignity, it was fitting that the gods should be honored and their sacred objects handled, not by artisans or mercenaries who had exercised lowly and defiling offices. Whence it is said in the *Politics*, Book VII, Chapter 7: "Neither a farmer nor an artisan should be made a priest."

Now correct views concerning God were not held by the gentile laws or religions and by all the other religions which are or were outside the catholic Christian faith or outside the Mosaic law which preceded it or the beliefs of the holy fathers which in turn preceded this—and, in general, by all those doctrines which are outside the tradition of what is contained in the sacred canon called the Bible. For they followed the human mind or false prophets or teachers of errors. Hence too they did not have a correct view about the future life and its happiness or misery, nor about the true priesthood established for its sake. We have, nevertheless, spoken of their rites in order to make more manifest their difference from the true priesthood, that of the Christians, and the necessity for the priestly part in communities.

It remains now to discuss the final cause for which the true priesthood was established in communities of the faithful. This was in order to moderate human acts both immanent and transient controlled by knowledge and desire, according as the human race is ordered by such acts toward the best life of the future world. . . .

And for this reason the evangelical law is called the law of grace, both because through the passion and death of Christ the human race was redeemed from its guilt and from the penalty of losing eternal beatitude which it had incurred as a result of the fall or sin of its first parents; and also because, by observing this law and receiving the sacraments established with it and in it, we are given divine grace, after it is given it is strengthened in us, and when we lose it, it is restored to us. Through this grace, by the ordainment of God and the passion of Christ, our works come by a certain congruity (as we have said) to merit eternal happiness.

.   .   .

As teachers of this law, and as ministers of its sacraments, certain men in the communities were chosen, called priests and deacons or levites. It is their office to teach the commands and counsels of the Christian evangelical law, as to what must be believed, done, and spurned, to the end that a blessed status be attained in the future world, and the opposite avoided.

The end of the priesthood, therefore, is to teach and educate men in those things which, according to the evangelical law, it is necessary to believe, do, and omit in order to attain eternal salvation and avoid misery.

.   .   .

With respect to this chapter and the one following, we must understand that the causes of the offices of the state, in respect of each kind of cause, differ according as they are offices of the state and according as they are habits of the human body or mind. For according as they are habits of the human body or soul, their final causes are the functions which are immediately and essentially forthcoming from them. For example, the final cause of the shipbuilding part of the state is a ship; of the military part, the use of arms and fighting; of the priesthood, the preaching of the divine law and the administration of the sacraments in accordance with it; and so on with all the rest. But according as they are offices determined and established in the state, their final causes are the benefits and sufficiencies which perfect human actions and passions, and which are forthcoming from the functions of the aforesaid habits, or which cannot be had without them. For example, from fighting, which is the act or end of the military habit, freedom is forthcoming and is preserved for men in the state, and this freedom is the end of the acts and functions of the military. So too from the function or end of the housebuilding part, which is a house, there is forthcoming to men or to the state protection from the harmful impressions of the air, the hot, the cold, the wet, or the dry, which protection is the final cause for whose sake the housebuilding office was established in the state. In the same way, from observance of the divine law, which is the end of the priesthood, eternal happiness is forthcoming to men. Similar considerations apply to all the other parts or offices of the state. And the other kinds of causes of these offices—the material, formal, and efficient causes—are distinguished in the same or a similar manner. . . .

.   .   .

Law, then, is a "discourse" or statement "emerging from prudence and political "understanding," that is, it is an ordinance made by political prudence, concerning matters of justice and benefit and their opposites, and having "coercive force," that is, concerning whose observance there is given a command which one is compelled to observe, or which is made by way of such a command.

.   .   .

Let us say, then, in accordance with the truth and the counsel of Aristotle in the *Politics,* Book III, Chapter 6, that the legislator, or the primary and proper efficient cause of the law, is the people or the whole body of citizens, or the weightier part thereof, through its election or will expressed by words in the general assembly of the citizens, commanding or determining that something be done or omitted with regard to human civil acts, under a temporal pain or punishment. By the "weightier part" I mean to take into consideration the quantity and the quality of the persons in that community over which the law is made. The aforesaid whole body of citizens or the weightier part thereof is the legislator regardless of whether it makes the law directly by itself or entrusts the making of it to some person or persons, who are not and cannot be the legislator in the absolute sense, but only in a relative sense and for a particular time and in accordance with the authority of the primary legislator. And I say further that the laws and anything else established through election must receive their necessary approval by that same primary authority and no other, whatever be the case with regard to certain ceremonies or solemnities, which are required not for the being of the matters elected but for their well-being, since the election would be no less valid even if these ceremonies were not performed. Moreover, by the same authority must the laws and other things established through election undergo addition, subtraction, complete change, interpretation, or suspension, insofar as the exigencies of time or place or other circumstances make any such action opportune for the common benefit. And by the same authority, also, must the laws be promulgated or proclaimed after their enactment, so that no citizen or alien who is delinquent in observing them may be excused because of ignorance.

.   .   .

Again, and this is an abbreviation and summary of the previous demonstrations: The authority to make laws belongs only to the whole body of the citizens, as we have said, or else it belongs to one or a few men. But it cannot belong to one man alone for the reasons given [earlier]; for through ignorance or malice or both, this one man could make a bad law, looking more to his own private benefit than to that of the community, so that the law would be tyrannical. For the same reason, the authority to make laws cannot belong to a few; for they too could sin, as above, in making the law for the benefit of a certain few and not for the common benefit, as can be seen in oligarchies. The authority to make the laws belongs, therefore, to the whole body of citizens or to the weightier part thereof, for precisely the opposite reason. For since all the citizens must be measured by the law according to due proportion, and no one knowingly harms or wishes injustice to himself, it follows that all or most wish a law conducing to the common benefit of the citizens.

.   .   .

According to this reasoning, therefore, there is also a certain judge who has coercive authority over transgressors of divine law, which we have called the coercive standard of some human acts both immanent and transient. But this judge is one alone, Christ, and no one else. Whence in the fourth chapter of James: "There is one lawmaker and judge, that is able to destroy and to deliver." But this judge's coercive power is not exercised over anyone in this world, to punish or reward transgressors or observers of the law made immediately by him, which we have often called the evangelic law. For in his mercy Christ wished to give every person the opportunity to become deserving up to the very end of his life and to repent of sins committed against Christ's law, as will be shown below by the authorities of the holy Scripture.

But there is another judge according to the evangelic Scripture, who is analogous to the human law's judge in the first sense. This other judge is the priest, who is the teacher in this world of divine law and of its commands concerning what must be done or shunned in order to attain eternal life and avoid punishment. However, he has no coercive power in this world to compel anyone to observe these commands. For it would be useless for him to coerce anyone to observe them, since the person who observed them under coercion would be helped not at all toward eternal salvation, as we showed clearly in [a preceding chapter], through Chrysostom, or rather through the Apostle. Hence this judge is

6. *The Emperor and the Pope,* Anonymous. Political allegory relating to the meeting of the Pope and Frederick III. Woodcut.

properly likened to the physician, who is given the authority to teach, command, and predict or judge about the things which it is useful to do or omit in order to attain bodily health and avoid illness or death. It was for this reason, too, that Christ called himself a physician in and for the status of the present life, and not a ruler or a judge. Hence in the fifth chapter of Luke, which we also quoted in a preceding chapter, Christ spoke of himself to the Pharisees as follows: "They that are well do not need a physician, but they that are sick." For Christ did not ordain that anyone should be forced to observe in this world the law made by him, and for this reason he did not appoint in this world a judge having coercive power over transgressors of this law.

. . .

According to the truth, therefore, and the clear intention of the Apostle and the saints, who were the foremost teachers of the church or faith, it is not commanded that anyone, even an infidel, let alone a believer, be compelled in this world through pain or punishment to observe the commands of the evangelic law, especially by a priest; and hence the ministers of this law, the bishops or priests, neither can nor should judge anyone in this world by a judgment in the third sense, or compel an unwilling person, by any pain or punishment, to observe the commands of divine law, especially without authorization by the human legislator; for such coercive judgment in accordance with divine law must not be exercised or executed in this world, but only in the future one. Hence in the nineteenth chapter of Matthew: "But Jesus said to them," that is, to the apostles: " 'Verily I say unto you, that ye which have followed me, in the regeneration when the son of man shall sit on the throne of his glory, ye also shall sit upon twelve thrones, judging the twelve tribes of Israel.' " See then, when it was that the apostles were going to sit with Christ as judges in the third sense, namely, in the other world, not in this one. Whereon the gloss: " 'in the regeneration,' that is, when the dead will rise up alive again." Hence, according to the gloss: "There are two regenerations, the first from water and the holy spirit, the second in resurrection." Hence "ye also shall sit," and the gloss according to Augustine says: "When he who was in the guise of a servant and who was judged," that is, Christ, who was in this world judged by coercive judgment, and did not himself judge, "will exercise judiciary power," that is, in the resurrection, "you shall be judges with me." See, then, that according to Christ's words in the gospel and the exposition of the saints, Christ did not in this world exercise judiciary, that is, coercive power, which we called judgment in the third sense, but rather, in the guise of a servant, he underwent such judgment by another man; and when he will exercise such coercive judiciary power in the other world, then, and not before, will the apostles sit with him to make such judgments.

Hence it is indeed to be wondered why any bishop or priest, whoever he be, assumes for himself greater or other authority than that which Christ or his apostles wanted to have in this world. For they, in the guise of servants, were judged by the secular rulers. But their successors, the priests, not only refuse to be subject to the rulers, contrary to the example and command of Christ and of the apostles, but they even claim to be superior to the supreme rulers and powers in coercive jurisdiction. Christ, however, said in the tenth chapter of Matthew: "And ye shall be brought before governors and kings for my sake"; but he did not say: Ye shall be governors or kings. And further on he adds: "The disciple is not over his master, nor the servant above his lord." Therefore, no coercive judgment, rulership, or dominion can or ought to be exercised in this world by any priest or bishop as such. This was also clearly the view of the famous Philosopher in the *Politics,* Book IV, Chapter 12, for he said: "Hence not all those who are elected or chosen by lot are to be regarded as rulers. Consider the priests in the first place. These must be regarded as different from the political rulers. And also there are the masters of choruses and heralds, and also ambassadors who are elected. And of the superintendent functions some are political, being exercised over all the citizens with regard to some action." And a little below he adds: "And other offices are economic."

. . .

Concerning what we have said doubts may well arise. For if only the ruler by the legislator's authority has jurisdiction over all forms of compulsion in the present life, through coercive judgment and the infliction and exaction of penalties in property and in person, as was shown above, then it will pertain to this ruler to make coercive judgments over heretics or other infidels or schismatics, and to inflict, exact, and dispose of the penalties in property and in person. But this seems inappropriate. For it might seem that it pertains to the same authority to inquire into a crime and to judge and correct the crime; but since it pertains to the priest, the presbyter or bishop, and to no one else, to discern the crime of heresy, it would seem to follow that the coercive judgment or correction of this and similar crimes also pertains to the priest or bishop alone. Moreover, the judging and punishing of a criminal might seem to pertain to the person against whom or against whose law the criminal has sinned. But this person is the priest or bishop. For he is the minister or judge of divine law, against which essentially the heretic, schismatic or other infidel sins, whether this sinner be a group or an individual. It follows, therefore, that this judgment pertains to the priest, and not to the ruler. And this clearly seems to be the view of St. Ambrose in his first epistle to the Emperor Valentinian; but since he seems to adhere to this view throughout the whole epistle, I have omitted to quote from it for the sake of brevity.

But now let us say, in accordance with our previous conclusions, that any person who sins against divine law must be judged, corrected, and punished according to that law. But there are two judges according to it. One is a judge in the third sense, having coercive power to punish transgressors of this law; and this judge is Christ alone. . . . But Christ willed and decreed that all transgressors of this law should be coercively judged and punished in the future world only, not in this one, as the preceding chapter made sufficiently clear. There is another judge according to this law, namely, the priest or bishop, but he is not a judge in the third sense, and may not correct any transgressor of divine law in this world and punish him by coercive force; this was clearly shown in [earlier] chapters of this discourse by the authority and the invincible reasoning of the Apostle and the saints. However, the priest is a judge in the first sense of the word, and he has to teach, exhort, censure, and rebuke sinners or transgressors of divine law, and frighten them by a judgment of the future infliction of damnation and punishment upon them in the world to come by the coercive judge, Christ, as we showed [earlier in] this discourse, where the power of the priestly keys was discussed, and in [a] preceding chapter, where we compared the physician of bodies with the priests, "who are the physicians of souls," as Augustine said by the authority of the prophet and as the Master repeats in Book IV, Distinction 18, Chapter 9. Since, then, the heretic, the schismatic, or any other infidel is a transgressor of divine law, if he persists in this crime he will be punished by that judge to whom it pertains to correct transgressors of divine law as such, when he will exercise his judicial authority. But this judge is Christ, who will judge the living, the dead, and the dying, but in the future world, not in this one. For he has mercifully allowed sinners to have the opportunity of becoming deserving and penitent up to the very time when they finally pass from this world at death. But the other judge, namely, the pastor, bishop or priest, must teach and exhort man in the present life, must censure and rebuke the sinner and frighten him by a judgment or prediction of future glory or eternal damnation; but he must not coerce. . . .

Now if human law were to prohibit heretics or other infidels from dwelling in the region, and yet such a person were found there, he must be corrected in this world as a transgressor of human law, and the penalty fixed by that law for such transgression must be inflicted on him by the judge who is the guardian of human law by the authority of the legislator. . . . But if human law did not prohibit the heretic or other infidel from dwelling among the faithful in the same province, as heretics and

Jews are now permitted to do by human laws even in these times of Christian peoples, rulers, and pontiffs, then I say that no one is allowed to judge or coerce a heretic or other infidel by any penalty in property or in person for the status of the present life.

NICCOLÒ MACHIAVELLI

BECOMING A PRINCE BY VILLAINY

But as there are still two ways of becoming prince which cannot be attributed entirely either to fortune or to ability, they must not be passed over, although one of them could be more fully discussed if we were treating of republics. These are when one becomes prince by some nefarious or villainous means, or when a private citizen becomes the prince of his country through the favour of his fellow-citizen. And in speaking of the former means, I will give two examples, one ancient, the other modern, without entering further into the merits of this method, as I judge them to be sufficient for any one obliged to imitate them.

Agathocles the Sicilian rose not only from private life but from the lowest and most abject position to be King of Syracuse. The son of a potter, he led a life of the utmost wickedness through all the stages of his fortune. Nevertheless, his wickedness was accompanied by such vigour of mind and body that, having joined the militia, he rose through its ranks to be praetor of Syracuse. Having been appointed to this position, and having decided to become prince, and to hold with violence and without the support of others that which had been constitutionally granted him; and having imparted his design to Hamilcar the Carthaginian, who was fighting with his armies in Sicily, he called together one morning the people and senate of Syracuse, as if he had to deliberate on matters of importance to the republic, and at a given signal had all the senators and the richest men of the people killed by his soldiers. After their death he occupied and held rule over the city without any civil strife. And although he was twice beaten by the Carthaginians and ultimately besieged, he was able not only to defend the city, but leaving a portion of his forces for its defence, with the remainder he invaded Africa, and in a short time liberated Syracuse from the siege and brought the Carthaginians to great extremities, so that they were obliged to come to terms with him, and remain contented with the possession of Africa, leaving Sicily to Agathocles. Whoever considers, therefore, the actions and qualities of this man, will see few if any things which can be attributed to fortune; for, as above stated, it was not by the favour of any person, but through the grades of the militia, in which he had advanced with a thousand hardships and perils, that he arrived at the position of prince, which he afterwards maintained by so many courageous and perilous expedients. It cannot be called virtue to kill one's fellow-citizens, betray one's friends, be without faith, without pity, and without religion; by these methods one may indeed gain power, but not glory. For if the virtues of Agathocles in braving and overcoming perils, and his greatness of soul in supporting and surmounting obstacles be considered, one sees no reason for holding him inferior to any of the most renowned captains. Nevertheless his barbarous cruelty and inhumanity, together with his countless atrocities, do not permit of his being named among the most famous men. We cannot attribute to fortune or virtue that which he achieved without either.

In our own times, during the pontificate of Alexander VI, Oliverotto da Fermo had been left as a young fatherless boy under the care of his maternal uncle, Giovanni Fogliani, who brought him up, and sent him in early youth to soldier under Paolo Vitelli, in order that he might, trained in that hard school, obtain a good military position. On the death of Paolo he fought under his brother Vitellozzo, and in a very short time, being of great intelligence, and active in mind and body, he became one of the leaders of his troops. But deeming it servile to be under others, he resolved, with the help of some citizens of Fermo, who preferred servitude to the liberty of their country, and with the favour of the Vitelli, to occupy Fermo; he therefore wrote to Giovanni Fogliani, how, having been for many years away from home, he wished to come to see him and his city, and as far as possible to inspect his estates. And as he had only laboured to gain honour, in order that his fellow-citizens might see that he had not spent his time in vain, he wished to come honourably accompanied by one hundred horsemen, his friends and followers, and prayed him that he would be pleased to order that he should be received with honour by the citizens of Fermo, by which he would honour not only him, Oliverotto, but also himself, as he had been his pupil. Giovanni did not fail in any due courtesy towards his nephew; he caused him to be honourably received by the people of Fermo, and lodged him in his own houses. After waiting some days to arrange all that was necessary to his villainous projects, Oliverotto invited Giovanni Fogliani and all the principal men of Fermo to a grand banquet. After the dinner and the entertainments usual at such feasts, Oliverotto artfully introduced certain important matters of discussion, speaking of the greatness of Pope Alexander, and of his son Cesare, and of their enterprises. To which discourses Giovanni and others having replied, he all at once rose, saying that these matters should be spoken of in a more private place, and withdrew into a room where Giovanni and the other citizens followed him. They were no sooner seated than soldiers rushed out of hiding-places and killed Giovanni and all the others. After which massacre Oliverotto mounted his horse, rode through the town and besieged the chief magistrate in his palace, so that through fear they were obliged to obey him and form a government, of which he made himself prince. And all those being dead who, if discontented, could injure him, he fortified himself with new orders, civil and military, in such a way that within the year that he held the principality he was not only safe himself in the city of Fermo, but had become formidable to all his neighbours. And his overthrow would have been difficult, like that of Agathocles, if he had not allowed himself to be deceived by Cesare Borgia, when he captured the Orsini and Vitelli at Sinigaglia, as already related, where he also was taken, one year after the parricide he had committed, and strangled, together with Vitellozzo, who had been his teacher in ability and atrocity.

Some may wonder how it came about that Agathocles, and others like him could, after infinite treachery and cruelty, live secure for many years in their country and defend themselves from external enemies without being conspired against by their subjects; although many others have, owing to their cruelty, been unable to maintain their position in times of peace, not to speak of the uncertain times of war. I believe this arises from the cruelties being exploited well or badly. Well committed may be called those (if it is permissible to use the word well of evil) which are perpetuated once for the need of securing one's self, and which afterwards are not persisted in, but are exchanged for measures as useful to the subjects as possible. Cruelties ill committed are those which, although at first few, increase rather than diminish with time. Those who follow the former method may remedy in some measure their condition, both with God and man; as did Agathocles. As to the others, it is impossible for them to maintain themselves.

Whence it is to be noted, that in taking a state the conqueror must arrange to commit all his cruelties at once, so as not to have to recur to them every day, and so as to be able, by not making fresh changes, to reassure people and win them over by benefiting them. Whoever acts otherwise, either through timidity or bad counsels, is always obliged to stand with knife in hand, and can never depend on his subjects, because they, owing to continually fresh injuries are unable to depend upon him. For injuries should be done all together, so that being less tasted, they will give less offence. Benefits should be granted little by little, so that they may be better enjoyed. And above all, a prince must live with his subjects in such a way that no accident of good or evil fortune can deflect him from his course; for necessity arising in adverse times, you are not in time with severity, and the good that you do does not profit, as it is judged to be forced upon you, and you will derive no benefit whatever from it.

(from *The Prince*)

PRAISE AND BLAME

It now remains to be seen what are the methods and rules for a prince as regards his subjects and friends. And as I know that many have written of this, I fear that my writing about it may be deemed presumptuous, differing as I do, especially in this matter, from the opinions of others. But my intention being to write something of use to those who understand, it appears to me more proper to go to the real truth of the matter than to its imagination; and many have imagined republics and principalities which have never been seen or known to exist in reality; for how we live is so far removed from how we ought to live, that he who abandons what is done for what ought to be done, will rather learn to bring about his own ruin than his preservation. A man who wishes to make a profession of goodness in everything must necessarily come to grief among so many who are not good. Therefore it is necessary for a prince, who wishes to maintain himself, to learn how not to be good, and to use this knowledge and not use it, according to the necessity of the case.

Leaving on one side, then, those things which concern only an imaginary prince, and speaking of those that are real, I state that all men, and especially princes, who are placed at a greater height, are reputed for certain qualities which bring them either praise or blame. Thus one is

7. *The Ambassadors,* **Hans Holbein the Younger. Reproduced by courtesy of the** Trustees, The National Gallery, London.

considered liberal, another *misero* or miserly (using a Tuscan term, seeing that *avaro* with us still means one who is rapaciously acquisitive and *misero* one who makes grudging use of his own); one a free giver, another rapacious; one cruel, another merciful; one a breaker of his word, another trustworthy; one effeminate and pusillanimous, another fierce and high-spirited; one humane, another haughty; one lascivious, another chaste; one frank, another astute; one hard, another easy; one serious, another frivolous; one religious, another an unbeliever, and so on. I know that every one will admit that it would be highly praiseworthy in a prince to possess all the above-named qualities that are reputed good, but as they cannot all be possessed or observed, human conditions not permitting of it, it is necessary that he should be prudent enough to avoid the scandal of those vices which would lose him the state, and guard himself if possible against those which will not lose it him, but if not able to, he can indulge them with less scruple. And yet he must not mind incurring the scandal of those vices, without which it would be difficult to save the state, for if one considers well, it will be found that some things which seem virtues would, if followed, lead to one's ruin, and some others which appear vices result in one's greater security and well-being.

.   .   .

Alexander VI did nothing else but deceive men, he thought of nothing else, and found the occasion for it; no man was ever more able to give assurances, or affirmed things with stronger oaths, and no man observed them less; however, he always succeeded in his deceptions, as he well knew this aspect of things.

It is not, therefore, necessary for a prince to have all the above-named qualities, but it is very necessary to seem to have them. I would even be bold to say that to possess them and always to observe them is dangerous, but to appear to possess them is useful. Thus it is well to seem merciful, faithful, humane, sincere, religious, and also to be so; but you must have the mind so disposed that when it is needful to be otherwise you may be able to change to the opposite qualities. And it must be understood that a prince, and especially a new prince, cannot observe all those things which are considered good in men, being often obliged, in order to maintain the state, to act against faith, against charity, against humanity, and against religion. And, therefore, he must have a mind disposed to adapt itself according to the wind, and as the variations of fortune dictate, and, as I said before, not deviate from what is good, if possible, but be able to do evil if constrained.

A prince must take care that nothing goes out of his mouth which is not full of the above-named five qualities, and, to see and hear him, he should seem to be all mercy, faith, integrity, humanity, and religion. And nothing is more necessary than to seem to have this last quality, for men in general judge more by the eyes than by the hands, for every one can see, but very few have to feel. Everybody sees what you appear to be, few feel what you are, and those few will not dare to oppose themselves to the many, who have the majesty of the state to defend them; and in the actions of men, and especially of princes, from which there is no appeal, the end justifies the means. Let a prince therefore aim at conquering and maintaining the state, and the means will always be judged honourable and praised by every one, for the vulgar is always taken by appearances and the issue of the event; and the world consists only of the vulgar, and the few who are not vulgar are isolated when the many have a rallying point in the prince. A certain prince of the present time, whom it is well not to name, never does anything but preach peace and good faith, but he is really a great enemy to both, and either of them, had he observed them, would have lost him state or reputation on many occasions.

(from *The Prince*)

RELIGIOUS INFLUENCE

Princes and republics who wish to maintain themselves free from corruption must above all things preserve the purity of all religious observances, and treat them with proper reverence; for there is no greater indication of the ruin of a country than to see religion contemned. And this is easily understood, when we know upon what the religion of a country is founded; for the essence of every religion is based upon some one main principle. The religion of the Gentiles had for its foundation the responses of the oracles, and the tenets of the augurs and aruspices; upon these alone depended all their ceremonies, rites, and sacrifices. For they readily believed that the Deity which could predict their future good or ill was also able to bestow it upon them. Thence arose their temples, their sacrifices, their supplications, and all the other ceremonies; for the oracle of Delphos, the temple of Jupiter Ammon, and other celebrated oracles, kept the world in admiration and devoutness. But when these afterwards began to speak only in accordance with the wishes of the princes, and their falsity was discovered by the people, then men became incredulous, and disposed to disturb all good institutions. It is therefore the duty of princes and heads of republics to uphold the foundations of the religion of their countries, for then it is easy to keep their people religious, and consequently well conducted and united. And therefore everything that tends to favour religion (even though it were believed to be false) should be received and availed of to strengthen it; and this should be done the more, the wiser the rulers are, and the better they understand the natural course of things. Such was, in fact, the practice observed by sagacious men; which has given rise to the belief in the miracles that are celebrated in religions, however false they may be. For the sagacious rulers have given these miracles increased importance, no matter whence or how they originated; and their authority afterwards gave them credence with the people. Rome had many such miracles; and one of the most remarkable was that which occurred when the Roman soldiers sacked the city of Veii; some of them entered the temple of Juno, and, placing themselves in front of her statue, said to her, "Will you come to Rome?" Some imagined that they observed the statue make a sign of assent, and others pretended to have heard her reply, "Yes." Now these men, being very religious, as reported by Titus Livius, and having entered the temple quietly, they were filled with devotion and reverence, and might really have believed that they had heard a reply to their question, such as perhaps they could have presupposed. But this opinion and belief was favoured and magnified by Camillus and the other Roman chiefs.

And certainly, if the Christian religion had from the beginning been maintained according to the principles of its founder, the Christian states and republics would have been much more united and happy than what they are. Nor can there be a greater proof of its decadence than to witness the fact that the nearer people are to the Church of Rome, which is the head of our religion, the less religious are they. And whoever examines the principles upon which that religion is founded, and sees how widely different from those principles its present practice and application are, will judge that her ruin or chastisement is near at hand. But as there are some of the opinion that the well-being of Italian affairs depends upon the Church of Rome, I will present such arguments against that opinion as occur to me; two of which are most important, and cannot according to my judgment be controverted. The first is, that the evil example of the court of Rome has destroyed all piety and religion in Italy, which brings in its train infinite improprieties and disorders; for as we may presuppose all good where religion prevails, so where it is wanting we have the right to suppose the very opposite. We Italians then owe to the Church of Rome and to her priests our having become irreligious and bad; but we owe her a still greater debt, and one that will be the cause of our ruin, namely, that the Church has kept and still keeps our country divided. And certainly a country can never be united and happy, except when it obeys wholly one government, whether a republic or a monarchy, as is the case in France and in Spain; and the sole cause why Italy is not in the same condition, and is not governed by either one republic or one sovereign, is the Church; for having acquired and holding a temporal dominion, yet she has never had sufficient power or courage to enable her to seize the rest of the country and make herself sole sovereign of all Italy. And on the other hand she has not been so feeble that the fear of losing her temporal power prevented her from calling in the aid of a foreign power to defend her against such others as had become too powerful in Italy; as was seen in former days by many sad experiences, when through the intervention of Charlemagne she drove out the Lombards, who were masters of nearly all Italy; and when in our times she crushed the power of the Venetians by the aid of France, and afterwards with the assistance of the Swiss drove out in turn the French. The Church, then, not having been powerful enough to be able to master all Italy, nor having permitted any other power to do so, has been the cause why Italy has never been able to unite under one head, but has always remained under a number of princes and lords, which occasioned her so many dissensions and so much weakness that she became a prey not only to the powerful barbarians, but of whoever chose to assail her. This we other Italians owe to the Church of Rome, and to none other. And any one, to be promptly convinced by experiment of the truth of all this, should have the power to transport the court of Rome to reside, with all the power it has in Italy, in the midst of the Swiss, who of all peoples nowadays live most according to their ancient customs so far as religion and their military system are concerned; and he would see in a very little while that the evil habits of that court would create more confusion in that country than anything else that could ever happen there.

(from The Discourses)

HUMILITY AND INSOLENCE

We often see that humility not only is of no service, but is actually hurtful, especially when employed towards insolent men, who from jealousy or some other motive have conceived a hatred against you. Of

17. *The Tempest,* Giorgione.

nothing the effort for clear comprehension. You should make it seem
as though the sun shone through the clouds only thinly here and there
and diffused its light over the cities and mountains.

You should, moreover, render darkness, and let the cities be shadowed
by clouds, sometimes completely, sometimes only half; you should take
care that the mirrorlike surface of the water is not deprived of the colours
of the heavens; besides, it is pretty to let the dispersing clouds above
dissolve after the old fashion, and sometimes to show the sunshine.

You must also seek to portray with colours snow, hail, rainfall, frost,
rime, steaming, and dreary fogs, all the things that are necessary to
depict melancholy winter days, in such a way that the eye will not often
be drawn further than one can throw a stone, to see gateways, houses,
towns, and villages.

It is proper that our foreground should be strong, in order to let the other grounds recede, and that we take care to bring something large towards the front, as did Brueghel and other painters of great fame, to whom one may award the palm in what concerns landscape. For in the work of these men who are worthy of honour, there are often powerful tree trunks in the foreground. Let us follow them enthusiastically in this. . . .

There are few Italians who paint landscapes; these, however, are of consummate artistic skill and have almost no peers. They often let us see a vista of perspective effect and grounds firmly fitted into one another, and cities, as in what we see . . . in the especially great Titian, whose work in wood-engraving serves to instruct us here, also in what we see of the painter of Brescia [Geronimo Muzziano, 1528-92].

Besides these, I might name as a competitor with respect to beautiful colours and the artistic content of painting and engraving, the gifted Brueghel; in these pictures he shows us, when he was in the cragged Alps, how, without much trouble, to portray the view downward into valleys which make one dizzy, the sheer cliffs, the cloud-kissing pines, the far and distant prospects and rushing streams.

But in the happy time of spring one has to give attention to decorating in colours like the noble jewels, and to painting the earth carefully in emerald or sapphire green with their nuances, straight across the meandering curves of the crystal-clear, murmuring brooks, which flow between green and grassy banks.

On the one side sits Ceres with yellow ears of grain, on the other side the field of unripe oats in which Eurus moves in play, as he makes the field a sea of green billows and softly rustling movement. Here grows vetch, there buckwheat, yonder clover, red and blue flowers, wheat, and the wholesome flax with the colour of heaven.

Also ploughed fields with long furrows drawn across them or sometimes fields with harvested grain. Today the meadows and fields have canals, hedgerows, and curving paths, and then I do not know what kind of curious shepherds' huts and peasant villages we should build, with walls and roofs in hollow cliffs, and trees and tree trunks.

Do not make these huts of handsome red brick, but rather out of pieces of earth, rushes, straw, rags, and stonework, plastered and moss-grown in a special way, and towards the rear paint our blue shrubs which should seem to grow whiter on the blue ground, so that they stand out against the dry blue, as well as correctly drawn, light tree trunks turning inward, and one close behind the other.

18. *Self-Portrait*, Parmigianino.

19. *The Madonna with the Long Neck*, Parmigianino.

One should only stipple the smallest tree trunks. Yet before we hasten on to our trees in the foreground, let us climb a way up the steep cliffs, the cliffs moistened with wet lips by the drifting clouds which wash their highest summits. In general, their colour is light grey, and often they raise their bare peaks out of the midst of a dense forest of fir trees.

See how the stones hang like icicles on the rocks, irregular and green with moss, in this waterfall, and how the water rushes drunkenly through the twisting paths helter-skelter until it falls below; now you wise serpents of art, see how these mastic trees grow here and how strangely they lie! Who could dream of such a thing!

To paint the lovely structure of trees requires effort, whether it be a small shrub or a towering tree. Often they may be yellow, but sometimes green, also one should show the foliage turning upward from below. But to avoid dullness, you should not make the foliage too small, and when you paint your foliage, let it be so constructed as to be run through with little slender branches, some of which should be curved lightly upward and some downward.

It would be good if you would learn your story from books or poems beforehand—in whatever way pleases you—so as to arrange your landscape in accordance with it. Yet above all do not forget to place small figures next to the great trees, and to set your little world in motion, here to ploughing, there to mowing, there to loading a wagon, here and there to fishing, walking, running, and hunting.

LEONARDO DA VINCI

SCULPTURE AND PAINTING

I myself, having exercised myself no less in sculpture than in painting and doing both one and the other in the same degree, it seems to me that I can, without invidiousness, pronounce an opinion as to which of the two is of the greatest skill and difficulty and perfection. In the first place sculpture requires a certain light, that is, from above; a picture carries everywhere with it its own light and shade. Thus light and shade are essential to sculpture, and the sculptor is aided in this by the nature of the relief which produces these of its own accord, while the painter artificially creates them by his art in the place where nature would

20. *The Story of Jacob and Esau*, Lorenzo Ghiberti. Detail of bronze doors "Gates of Paradise." Florence, Baptistery.

21. *Prophet (Zuccone)*, Donatello.

normally produce them. The sculptor cannot diversify his work by the various natural colours of objects; painting is not defective in any particular. The sculptor when he uses perspective cannot make it in any way appear true; that of the painter can appear like a hundred miles beyond the picture itself. Their works have no aerial perspective whatever, they cannot represent transparent bodies, they cannot represent luminous bodies, nor reflected lights, nor lustrous bodies, as mirrors and the like polished surfaces, nor mists, nor dark skies, nor an infinite number of things which need not be told for fear of tedium. That which it has in advance is that it resists time better, but a picture painted on thick copper covered with white enamel on which it is painted with enamel colours and then put into the fire again and baked, exceeds sculpture in permanence. It may be said that if a mistake is made it is not easy to remedy it. This is but a poor argument to try to prove that a work be the nobler because errors are irremediable; I should rather say that it will be more difficult to mend the mind of the master who makes such mistakes than to mend the work he has spoilt. . . .

Andrea Palladio

from THE FOUR BOOKS OF ARCHITECTURE

The Author's Preface

My natural inclination leading me, from my very Infancy, to the Study of *Architecture*, I resolv'd to apply myself to it: And because I ever was of opinion, that the ancient *Romans* did far exceed all that have come after them, as in many other things so particularly in Building, I proposed to myself *Vitruvius* both as my Master and Guide, he being the only ancient Author that remains extant on this Subject. Then, I betook myself to the Search and Examination of such Ruins of ancient Structures as, in spight of Time and the rude Hands of *Barbarians,* are still remaining; and finding that they deserved a much more diligent Observation than I thought at first Sight, I began with the utmost Accuracy to measure even the minutest part by itself: And indeed, I became so scrupulous an Examiner of them (not discovering that any thing, of this kind, was perform'd, without the justest Reason and the finest Propor-

22. Title page of *Four Books of Architecture,* Andrea Palladio.

tion) that I afterwards, not once only, but very often, took Journies to several parts of *Italy,* and even out of it, that I might be able, from such Fragments, to comprehend what the whole must needs have been, and to make Draughts accordingly. Whereupon, considering how widely different the Building, commonly in use, is from the Observations I made on the said Edifices, and from what I read in *Vitruvius,* in *Leo Baptista Alberti,* and other excellent Writers since *Vitruvius*'s Time, as well as from Buildings of my own Performance, which raised my Reputation, and gave no small satisfaction to those who were pleased to employ me; I thought it an Undertaking worthy of a Man who considers that he was not born for himself only, but likewise for the good of others, to publish to the World the Designs (or Draughts) of those Edifices, which with equal Expence of Time and Danger to my Person, I have collected; and briefly to set down what seem'd to me most worthy to be consider'd in them; and further, to give those Rules which I have hitherto follow'd in Building, and which I still follow, to the end that they who shall read my Books, may be able to practise whatever they find useful in them, and to supply what is wanting, as many such things there may be. Thus Men, by degrees, will learn to lay aside the strange Abuses, the barbarous Inventions, the superfluous Expences and (what imports them more than all the rest) to avoid the various and continual Ruins which have happened in several Buildings. I have moreover apply'd myself to this Undertaking with the greater Alacrity, because at this time I see abundance of others become studious of this Profession, many of whom are worthily and honourably mentioned in the Books of that rare Painter and Architect, *George Vasari Arentino;* which makes me hope that the way of Building will be reduced to general Utility, and very soon arrive to that pitch of Perfection, which, in all Arts, is so much desired. We appear to come very near it, in this part of *Italy,* seeing that not only Venice (where all the polite Arts do flourish, and which City alone affords an Example of the Grandeur and Magnificence of the *Romans*) there begin to appear Fabricks of good taste, since that most celebrated Carver and Architect, *Giacomo Sansovino,* first introduced the true manner, as may be seen, not to mention his fine Performances in the new Palace of *Procuracy,* which is perhaps the most sumptuous and the most beautiful Edifice that has been erected since the time of the Ancients; but also in several other Places of less renown, and particularly in the City of *Vicenza,* which tho' of no great Extent, yet full of very refined Genius's and sufficiently abounds in Riches. There I had first occasion to put that in practice, which I now publish for the common Good. . . . But to return to our Subject, having designed to publish to the World the Fruits of those Labours, which, with the greatest Diligence from my Youth upwards, I have been collecting; as also the Searching and Measuring of those Ancient Buildings that any ways came to my Knowledge; and upon this occasion briefly to treat of Architecture in the most orderly and distinct method possible; I thought it most convenient to begin with the Houses of private Persons, as thinking it reasonable to believe, that these in time gave rise to publick Edifices, it being very probable that Men lived first asunder by themselves; and perceiving afterwards that they needed the Aid of others to make them happy, (if indeed there be any Happiness here) they naturally loved and desired the Company of other Men, whence, out of many Houses they made Villages, and out of many Villages Cities, in which they built publick Places and Edifices. Besides, as of all the parts of Architecture, none is more necessary than this for Mankind, nor any more frequently practised by them, I shall therefore in the first place treat of private Houses, and next of publick

23. The Belvedere Court, Donato Bramante. Rome, The Vatican.

Edifices. I shall briefly write of Streets, Bridges, publick Places, Prisons, *Basiliche,* or Courts of Justice; *Xisti* and *Palestre,* (which are Places design'd for bodily Exercises) of Temples, Theatres and Amphitheatres, of Arches, of publick Baths, of Aqueducts, and last of all, the manner of fortifying Cities and Havens. In all these I shall avoid superfluity of Words, and will barely remark such things as shall appear to me most necessary, using those Terms and Names that are in common use with our present Architects. And because I dare make no other boasts of myself than what flow merely from the long and earnest Study, great Diligence, strong Passion and Affection wherewith I have pursued the Knowledge and Practice of what I now offer to the World; if it please *God* that I have not *labour'd in vain,* I shall be thankful to his Goodness for it with all my heart; acknowledging myself obliged to those, who, from their fine Inventions and Experiments, have left us the Precepts of this Art; since thereby they have opened a more easy and expeditious way to the making of new Discoveries, and that by their means (which we ought thankfully to acknowledge) we are come to the Knowledge of many things, which otherwise had perhaps remain'd still unknown. This first part shall be divided into two Books; the first will contain the Preparation of the Materials, and being prepared, how, and in what form, to employ them from the Foundations up to the Roof: and here likewise will be contained those general Rules which are to be observed in all Edifices, as well publick as private. In the second I shall treat of the different Qualities of Buildings, so as to make them agreeable to Persons of different Conditions: First of Houses in the City, and next of the most convenient Situations for Country-houses, and how they ought to be most commodiously disposed. But since in this kind, we have but few ancient Originals, by which to be governed, I shall lay before you the Plans of several Houses I have built for Gentlemen in divers places; and lastly, the Ancients Designs of Country-houses, with those parts in them that were most remarkable, in the manner that *Vitruvius* has taught us, and that they themselves built them.

GIOVANNI DE' BARDI

DISCOURSE ON ANCIENT MUSIC AND GOOD SINGING

Since I think that I shall be doing a thing not unpleasing to you, my very dear Signor Giulio Caccini, if I collect one by one the countless discussions of music which we have had together in various places and at various times and bind them up, like a little sheaf gleaned from the field of your intellect, I shall do it in such a way that you may comprehend and consider them in one view, like a united and well-proportioned body. And I take pleasure in holding the present brief discourse, like those former ones, with you, for having been associated from your youth with so many noble and gifted members of the Florentine Academy, you have (not only in my opinion, but also in the opinion of those who understand the true and perfect music) reached such a point that there is not a man in Italy who surpasses you, nay, few—perhaps not one—who equals you.

I speak of that sort of music which today is sung to instruments, either in company with others, or alone. It would take too long and would perhaps become tedious to you and to him who reads this my discourse,

24. Teatro Olimpico, Andrea Palladio. Vicenza.

were I to treat one by one of its principles and of the great men who have taken part in it, of whom to my knowledge at least fifty became great philosophers or most polished reciters of poetry. Thus I shall not stop now to tell of the wealth of instruments that these great scholars had. But, in order that I may well express their ideas, I shall treat very briefly of who it was that defined this music, of the twenty-seven tunings that the ancients had, and of the seven modes that they called "harmonies," like the architect who, to finish the house that he had planned in his mind, first provides himself with everything he needs for his labor. Thus the beginning of my discourse will be the definition of this music. For just as one could have only a poor notion of what a man is if one did not know that a man is an animal rational, visible, and sociable, or of what a city is if one did not know that a city is a union of a number of houses and quarters situated in one place in order that men may live well and justly, so one cannot pass judgment on practical music and on good singing if one does not know what sort of thing this music is.

Music is defined by Plato in the third book of his *Republic,* where he

25. Interior of the Sistine Chapel showing Michelangelo's ceiling fresco and *The Last Judgment*.

says that it is a combination of words and harmony and rhythm. But in order that the terms "harmony" and "rhythm" may be thoroughly understood, we shall briefly define them as well as we can.

Harmony is a general term, and in speaking of it, Pythagoras says, and after him Plato, that the world is composed of it. But let us come to the particular and treat of the harmony of music as defined by Plato, which harmony, according to Pausanias, takes its name from Harmonia, the wife of Cadmus, at whose wedding the Muses sang. Harmony then is the proportion of the low and the high, and of words in rhythm, that is, well arranged with respect to the long and the short. And harmony is likewise in musical instruments, for in these too are the low, the high, and the intermediate, and also rhythm, that is, faster or slower movement of the long and the short. Again, harmony may be composed of all these things combined, that is, of words well sung and having, as their accompaniment, this or that instrument.

Rhythm is likewise a general term, and in defining it, Aristides Quintilianus says that it is a system of times arranged in certain orders, a system being simply an ordering of things. Discussing rhythm, Plato says that it is divided into three species, progressing either by harmony, or by bodily movement, or by words, bodily rhythm being manifest to the eye, the other two species to the ear. But let us come to the rhythm of music, which is simply giving time to words that are sung as long and short, and as fast and slow, likewise to musical instruments.

Taken all together, these considerations show that practical music is a combination of words arranged by a poet into verses made up of various metres with respect to the long and the short, these being in their movement now fast and now slow, now low, now high, and now intermediate, approaching the sound of the words of the human voice, now sung by that voice alone, now accompanied by a musical instrument, which in turn should accompany the words with the long and the short, with fast and slow movement, and with the low, the high, and the intermediate.

Now that we have given the definition of music according to Plato (a definition in which Aristotle and the other scholars concur) and have said what music is, . . . let us turn to the marvels of music, in discussing which Damon, the teacher of Socrates, says that, being chaste, it has the power of disposing our minds to virtue and, being the contrary, to vice. And Plato says that there are two disciplines—one for the body, which is gymnastics, and one for the good of the mind, which is music; he also tells us that Thales the Milesian sang so sweetly that he not only influenced the minds of certain persons, but also cured illness and the plague. And we read that Pythagoras cured drunkards with music, and Empedocles insane persons, and Socrates a man possessed. And Plutarch tells us that Asclepiades cured delirious persons with the symphony, which is simply a mixture of song and sound. And it is said that Ismenias cured sciatic persons and the fever with music. And Aulus Gellius writes that those who suffered from sciatic gout were healed with the sound of the tibia, likewise those who had been bitten by serpents.

But I should go far afield and beyond my intention if I were to give to music and all its marvels the praise that is their due, for my sole intention is to show you, as clearly as I can, how it is to be treated in practice. Thus, now that I have stated the definition of music and have said what rhythm is, and likewise harmony, both in general and in particular, it is fitting that I show you how many and of what sort are the divisions of music and what their virtues are, for without discussing these things it would be difficult for me to attain the end that I have set before me.

I say, therefore, that the music of our times has two divisions—one which is called counterpoint and another which we shall call the art of good singing. The first of these is simply a combination of several melodies and of several modes sung at the same time—a combination, that is, of the low, the high, and the intermediate, and of the various rhythms of the several melodies. To take an example, if a madrigal is composed in four parts, then the bass will sing one melody, the tenor another, and the alto and soprano still other ones, different from theirs and in different modes. This we have shown above—we have shown, that is, that in every one of our musical compositions there are, in the low, the intermediate, and the high, various octave-species, and various rhythms. And this, to take another example, because Messer Bass, soberly dressed in semibreves and minims, stalks through the ground-floor rooms of his palace while Soprano, decked out in minims and semiminims, walks hurriedly about the terrace at a rapid pace and Messers Tenor and Alto, with various ornaments and in habits different from the others, stray through the rooms of the intervening floors. For in truth it would seem a sin to the contrapuntists of today (may they be pardoned these mixtures of several melodies and several modes!)—it would seem, I say, a mortal sin if all the parts were heard to beat at the same time with the same notes, with the same syllables of the verse, and with the same longs and shorts; the more they make the parts move, the more artful

they think they are. This, is my opinion, is the concern of the stringed
instruments, for, there being no voice in these, it is fitting that the player,
in playing airs not suited to singing or dancing—it is fitting, I say, that
the player should make the parts move and that he should contrive
canons, double counterpoints, and other novelties to avoid wearying his
hearers. And I judge this to be the species of music so much condemned
by the philosophers, especially by Aristotle in the Eighth Book of his
Politics, where he calls it artificial and wholly useless, except as a con-
trast to its rivals, and unworthy of a free man for lacking the power to
move a man's mind to this or that moral quality. Elsewhere, speaking
of this same subject, he says that a man cannot be called a good musician
who lacks the power to dispose the mind of another with his harmony to
any moral quality.

But since we are so much in the dark, let us at least endeavor to give
poor unfortunate Music a little light, for from her decline until now,
and this means ever so many centuries, she has had not one artificer
who has at all considered her case, but has been treated in another way,
inimical to her, that of counterpoint. This light may be permitted to
reach her only little by little, just as a man who has been afflicted with
a very serious illness ought properly to be restored step by step to his
former state of health, taking little food, and that nourishing and easily
digestible.

For the present, the little food that we shall give to Music shall be
to endeavor not to spoil the verse, not imitating the musicians of today,
who think nothing of spoiling it to pursue their ideas or of cutting it to
bits to make nonsense of the words, like a man who does not mind that
the robe made from the cloth that he has is short and ill-fitting or even
that his large and conspicuous slippers happen to have been cut from
it. For, to take an example, while the soprano sings "Voi che ascoltate in
rime," the bass at the same time sings other words, thus mixing one idea
with another, which rightly considered is the torture and death of for-
saken Music. This subject is discussed by all the great scholars and in
particular by Plato, who says that the melody ought always to follow the
verse that the poet has composed, just as a good cook adds a little sauce
or condiment to a dish that he has well seasoned, to make it seem more
pleasing to his master.

In composing, then, you will make it your chief aim to arrange the
verse well and to declaim the words as intelligibly as you can, not letting
yourself be led astray by the counterpoint like a bad swimmer who lets

himself be carried out of his course by the current and comes to shore beyond the mark that he had set, for you will consider it self-evident that, just as the soul is nobler than the body, so the words are nobler than the counterpoint. Would it not seem ridiculous if, walking in the public square, you saw a servant followed by his master and commanding him, or a boy who wanted to instruct his father or his tutor? The divine Cipriano, toward the end of his life, was well aware how very grave an error this was in the counterpoint of his day. For this reason, straining every fibre of his genius, he devoted himself to making the verse and the sound of the words thoroughly intelligible in his madrigals, as may be seen in one of those for five voices, "Poichè m'invita amore," and in an earlier one, "Se bene il duolo," and in still another, "Di virtù, di costume, di valore"; also in those published very shortly before his death, in the one with the words "Un altra volta la Germania stride," in another beginning "O sonno, o della quiete umid'ombrosa," in "Schietto arbuscello," and in the rest, by no means composed at haphazard. For this great man told me himself, in Venice, that this was the true manner of composing and a different one, and if he had not been taken from us by death, he would in my opinion have restored the music combining several melodies to a degree of perfection from which others might easily have returned it little by little to that true and perfect music so highly praised by the ancients.

But perhaps we have made too long a digression. So we shall say that, besides not spoiling the words, you will likewise not spoil the verse. Thus, wishing to set to music a madrigal or canzone or any other poem, you will carefully commit it to memory and consider whether the content is, for example, magnificent or plaintive. If it is magnificent, you will take the Dorian mode, which begins on E *la mi,* and has a *la mi re* as its mese, giving the entire melody to the tenor and turning about the mese as much as you can, for (as we have said elsewhere) things that are sublime and magnificent are uttered in an agreeable and intermediate tone of voice. But if the content is plaintive, you will take the Mixolydian mode, which begins on b *mi* and has e *la mi* as its mese; about this you will turn as much as you can, giving the principal melody to the soprano part. And in this way you will continue to regulate matters according to the other contents expressed in the words, always bearing in mind the nature of the slow, the fast, and the intermediate. Having, for example, to set to music the canzone beginning "Italia mia, ben che'l parlar sia indarno," you will take the Dorian mode mentioned above, giving the principal

26. *A Concert,* Lorenzo Costa. Reproduced by courtesy
of the Trustees, The National Gallery, London.

melody to the tenor, turning about the mese, and so adapting the
rhythm, that is, the long and the short, that it will be neither too slow
nor too fast but will imitate the speech of a man magnificent and serious.
And in considering other cases, you will proceed just as we have directed
in this one.

But since it is the usual thing nowadays to enliven musical performances by adding to the voice the delicate melody of instruments, it
will not be inappropriate if with all possible brevity I say something
about these. I say, then, that musical instruments are of two sorts, being
either wind instruments or stringed instruments; of those like the drum
I find no science, for in them there is no musical sound, only a per-
cussion.

113

Wind instruments, as more nearly imitating the human voice, are given preference over the others by Aristotle in his *Problems*. But to discuss this point is not to our purpose. We shall simply say that among the wind instruments there are some for playing compositions that are low-pitched and somnolent—these are the trombones; others apt for playing those that are high-pitched and lively, such as the *cornetti;* still others apt for playing those usual ones that lie in the intermediate register, such as the flutes and *pifferi allemani*. But seeing that I have not sufficient grasp of the wind instruments to use suitably those that I know, I defer to the judgment of those who are skilled in this profession.

Next come the stringed instruments, their strings worked in two sorts, although we use them in many forms. For part of them are of brass or of some other metal; the others, taken from animals, we call gut. Strings of gut are used for the viols and harps, also for the lute and such other instruments as are similar to it, and as more nearly resembling the human voice, they will be the better suited to the intermediate modes, like the Dorian; the same may be said of the viols, which have much of the grave and the magnificent. Strings of metal are used for the *gravicembali* and citherns, and as more effective in the higher harmonies than the above, can be played in the low, the high, and the intermediate.

Besides this, it is necessary to take great care in combining these instruments, for not all of them are tuned according to the same tuning, the viol and lute being tuned according to the tuning of Aristoxenus, the harp and *gravicembalo* making their modulations with other intervals. And more than once I have felt like laughing when I saw musicians struggling to put a lute or viol into proper tune with a keyboard instrument, for aside from the octave these instruments have few strings in common that are in unison, a circumstance that may detract from their usefulness, since until now this highly important matter has gone unnoticed or, if noticed, unremedied. In your consorts, then, you will as far as possible avoid combining lutes or viols with keyboard instruments or harps or other instruments not tuned in unison, but in various ways.

Before concluding my discussion of instruments, I have thought to make known to you an idea that has often occurred to me. Since you are to be the source of an unparalleled music, I would have you skilled in playing upon an instrument some beautiful melody partaking of the sublime and magnificent, perhaps one such as that composed by the philosopher Memphis, to the sound of which Socrates illustrated all the precepts of the Pythagorean philosophy without speaking a word. I add that, just as among Moors and Spanish women one may see shameless and wanton customs represented in music and dancing, so the virtuous and perfect musician can represent the contrary, that is, songs and dances filled with majesty and continence, as we read of that never-sufficiently-to-be-praised musician who for so many years maintained the resolution of Penelope and preserved her from the importunity of her suitors until the wise and cunning Ulysses returned from his long exile to his native land.

But let us leave the sort of practical music that consists in good composing and playing and come to the sort that is used in good singing. This has two divisions—singing in company and singing alone. Thus, to bring our discussion to an end, we must again place before our eyes all that we have discussed thus far, for this is the foundation upon which our palace is to stand firm. Let us recall, then, that the tunings were devised by the ancient philosophers with the greatest care and in a determined number, since each sound in singing must fit its place exactly; that the same may be said of the highness and the lowness of the modes and of their quality, and of the distinctions of the octaves with their various semitones, and of the force of the harmonies that are low, intermediate, and high; that the Dorian mode, lying in the center of the sounds suited to human speech, was prized and revered more highly than the rest, while the lower and higher harmonies were less prized, the one being too sluggish, the other too agitated. We have shown that the verse is made up of the long and the short and that, in the opinion of Plato and others, the sound and the counterpoint (as we choose to call it) should follow the speech and not the contrary, and we have defined music, harmony, and rhythm.

Let us now speak of the great distinction that should be made between singing alone and singing in company and of how one should not imitate those who, when they sing in parts, as though the whole company had come only to hear their creaking, think only of making their own voices heard, not knowing or perhaps not remembering that good part-singing is simply joining one's voice with the voices of others and forming one body with these; the same may be said of those others who, to complete their passages, disregard the time, so breaking and stretching it that they make it altogether impossible for their colleagues to sing properly. The singer ought also to take care to enter softly after a rest, not imitating those who enter so noisily that they seem to be finding fault with you for some mistake, or those others who, to avoid the bass parts, sing so loudly in the high register that they seem like criers auctioning off the pledges of the unfortunate, like little snarling dogs stealing silently through the streets of others and imagining that they are making no end of noise.

When singing alone, whether to the lute or *gravicembalo* or to some other instrument, the singer may contract or expand the time at will, seeing that it is his privilege to regulate the time as he thinks fit. To make divisions upon the bass is not natural, for (as we have said) this part is by nature slow, low, and somnolent. Yet it is the custom to do this. I know not what to say of it and am not eager to praise or to blame it, but I would counsel you to do it as little as possible and, when you do, at least to make it clear that you do it to please someone, also taking care never to pass from the tenor to the bass, seeing that with its passages the bass takes away whatever magnificence and gravity the tenor, with its majesty, has bestowed.

Besides this, it is necessary to sing accurately and well, to give each tone and semitone its proper place, and to connect the sounds exactly. Rejecting the improper practices employed today by those who search for unusual sounds, you will seek to use only a few, turning about the mese of the mode and employing it as often as you can, bearing in mind that, in speaking, man seeks to use few sounds and seldom, perhaps never uses wide leaps unless stirred up by anger or some other violent passion. In this you will imitate the great musician Olympus, who, in the many hundreds of songs that he gave to the world, never touched more than four strings in the principal part.

Then you will bear in mind that the noblest function a singer can perform is that of giving proper and exact expression to the canzone as set down by the composer, not imitating those who aim only at being thought clever (a ridiculous pretension) and who so spoil a madrigal with their ill-ordered passages that even the composer himself would not recognize it as his creation.

Finally, the nice singer will endeavor to deliver his song with all the suavity and sweetness in his power, rejecting the notion that music must be sung boldly, for a man of this mind seems among other singers like a plum among oranges or like a man of fierce appearance showing the *giaro* among city dwellers and well-bred people. Speaking on this topic, Aristotle says in his *Politics* that youths should be taught music as a thing seasoned with great sweetness; and Plato, that Thales the Milesian cured illness with his sweet manner of singing; and Macrobius, that, on leaving the body, the soul returns to its origin, which is heaven, through the sweetness of music; and the poet:

Musica dulcisono coelestia numina cantu

with the rest of the passage; and Petrarch:

Sweet song, O ladies virtuous and fair

and at another time:

Here sweetly sang and here sat down;

and the divine poet Dante, in the second canto of his *Purgatorio,* in which he meets Casella, an excellent musician of his time:

Then he began so sweetly
That the sweetness still sounds within me

and in his *Paradiso,* in the twenty-third canto:

Then they remained there in my sight,
Singing *Regina coeli* so sweetly
That it has never left my heart

and again in the twenty-seventh canto:

To Father, Son, and Holy Ghost
All Paradise took up the Glory
So that the sweet song intoxicated me.

From these things one may gather that music is pure sweetness and that he who would sing should sing the sweetness music and the sweetest modes well ordered in the sweetest manner.

Beyond this—and this will be the end of my discourse—you will bear in mind that in company a man ought always to be mannerly and courteous, not insisting on his own wishes but yielding to those of others, giving satisfaction to the best of his ability as often as he is called on, not imitating those who always grumble and, if they perform a service, perform it so grudgingly and disagreeably that their compliance becomes a mortification and a burden. Thus your manners will be pleasing and gentle, always at the command of others. When you sing you will take care to stand in a suitable posture, so much like your usual one that your hearers will question whether the sound is coming from your lips or from those of someone else. And you will not imitate those who, with much ado, begin tuning their voices and recounting their misfortunes, saying that they have caught cold, that they have not slept the night before, that their stomach is not right, and other things of this sort, so tedious that before they begin to sing they have canceled the pleasure with their exasperating excuses.

I have come to the end of what I undertook to discuss. May God grant that it may be as helpful and pleasing to you as it was troublesome to me. And I have no doubt at all that it will prove of great service to you if you will be on your guard against those three horrible monsters that prey on virtue—Adulation, Envy, and Ignorance. Of Adulation, Dante says (through the person of Interminelli) in the eighteenth canto of his *Inferno:*

> Down to this have sunk me the flatteries
> Of which my tongue was never weary;

of Envy, gentle Petrarch says:

> O envy, enemy of virtue,
> By nature hostile to fair principles;

and of the Ignorant, Dante sings, in the third canto of his *Inferno,* as follows:

> These have not hope of death,
> And their blind life is so base
> That they are envious of every other fate;
>
> Report of them the world allows not to exist;
> Mercy and Justice disdain them;
> Let us not speak of them, but look and pass.

EDMUND SPENSER

FROM THE FAERIE QUEENE

> *Her faithfull knight faire Vna brings*
> *to house of Holinesse,*
> *Where he is taught repentance, and*
> *the way to heauenly blesse.*

What man is he, that boasts of fleshly might,
And vaine assurance of mortality,

Which all so soone, as it doth come to fight,
Against spirituall foes, yeelds by and by,
Or from the field most cowardly doth fly?
Ne let the man ascribe it to his skill,
That thorough grace hath gained victory.
If any strength we haue, it is to ill,
But all the good is Gods, both power and eke will.

By that, which lately hapned, *Vna* saw,
That this her knight was feeble, and too faint;
And all his sinews woxen weake and raw,
Through long enprisonment, and hard constraint,

Which he endured in his late restraint,
That yet he was vnfit for bloudie fight:
Therefore to cherish him with diets daint,
She cast to bring him, where he chearen might,
Till he recouered had his late decayed plight.

There was an auntient house not farre away,
Renownd throughout the world for sacred lore,
And pure vnspotted life: so well they say
It gouernd was, and guided euermore,
Through wisedome of a matrone graue and hore;
Whose onely ioy was to relieue the needes
Of wretched soules, and helpe the helpelesse pore:
All night she spent in bidding of her bedes,
And all the day in doing good and godly deedes.

Dame *Caelia* men did her call, as thought
From heauen to come, or thither to arise,
The mother of three daughters, well vpbrought
In goodly thewes, and godly exercise:
The eldest two most sober, chast, and wise,
Fidelia and *Speranza* virgins were,
Though spousd, yet wanting wedlocks solumnize;
But faire *Charissa* to a louely fere
Was lincked, and by him had many pledges dere.

Arriued there, the dore they find fast lockt;
For it was warely watched night and day,
For feare of many foes: but when they knockt,
The Porter opened vnto them streight way:

He was an aged syre, all hory gray,
 With lookes full lowly cast, and gate full slow,
 Wont on a staffe his feeble steps to stay,
 Hight *Humiltá*. They passe in stouping low;
For streight and narrow was the way, which he did show.

.   .   .

Thence forward by that painfull way they pas,
 Forth to an hill, that was both steppe and hy
 On top whereof a sacred chappell was,
 And eke a litle Hermitage thereby,
 Wherein an aged holy man did lye,
 That day and night said his deuotion,
 Ne other worldly busines did apply;
 His name was heauenly *Contemplation;*
Of God and goodnesse was his meditation.

.   .   .

Thrise happy man, said then the father graue,
 Whose staggering steps thy steady hand doth lead,
 And shewes the way, his sinfull soule to saue.
 Who better can the way to heauen aread,
 Then thou thy selfe, that was both borne and bred
 In heauenly throne, where thousand Angels shine?
 Thou doest the prayers of the righteous sead
 Present before the majestie diuine,
And his auenging wrath to clemencie incline.

Yet since thou bidst, thy pleasure shalbe donne.
 Then come thou man of earth, and see the way,
 That neuer yet was seene of Faeries sonne,
 That neuer leads the traueiler astray,
 But after labours long, and sad delay,
 Brings them to ioyous rest and endlesse blis.
 But first thou must a season fast and pray,
 Till from her bands the spright assoiled is,

And haue her strength recur'd from fraile infirmitis.

That done, he leads him to the highest Mount;
   Such one, as that same mighty man of God,
   That bloud-red billowes like a walled front
   On either side disparted with his rod,
   Till that his army dry-foot through them yod,
   Dwelt fortie dayes vpon; where writ in stone
   With bloudy letters by the hand of God,
   The bitter doome of death and balefull mone
He did receiue, whiles flashing fire about him shone.

Or like that sacred hill, whose head full hie,
   Adornd with fruitfull Oliues all arownd,
   Is, as it were for endlesse memory
   Of that deare Lord, who oft thereon was fownd,
   For euer with a flowring girlond crownd:
   Or like that pleasaunt Mount, that is for ay
   Through famous Poets verse each where renownd,
   On which the thrise three learned Ladies play
Their heauenly notes, and make full many a louely lay.

From thence, far off he vnto him did shew
   A litle path, that was both steepe and long,
   Which to a goodly Citie led his vew;
   Whose wals and towres were builded high and strong
   Of perle and precious stone, that earthly tong
   Cannot describe, nor wit of man can tell;
   Too high a ditty for my simple song;
   The Citie of the great king hight it well,
Wherein eternall peace and happinesse doth dwell.

·   ·   ·

    Guyon, by Palmers gouernance,
     passing through perils great,
    Doth ouerthrow the Bowre of blisse,
     and Acrasia defeat.

   Now gins this goodly frame of Temperance
     Fairely to rise, and her adorned hed

To pricke of highest praise forth to aduance,
Formerly grounded, and fast setteled
On firme foundation of true bountihed;
And this braue knight, that for that vertue fights,
Now comes to point of that same perilous sted,
Where Pleasure dwelles in sensuall delights,
Mongst thousand dangers, and ten thousand magick mights.

Two dayes now in that sea he sayled has,
Ne euer land beheld, ne liuing wight,
Ne ought saue perill, still as he did pas:
Tho when appeared the third *Morrow* bright,
Vpon the waues to spred her trembling light,
An hideous roaring farre away they heard,
That all their senses filled with affright,
And streight they saw the raging surges reard
Vp to the skyes, that them of drowning made affeard.

Said then the Boteman, Palmer stere aright,
And keepe an euen course; for yonder way
We needes must passe (God do vs well acquight,)
That is the *Gulfe of Greedinesse,* they say,
That deepe engorgeth all this worldes pray:
Which hauing swallowd vp excessiuely,
He soone in vomit vp againe doth lay,
And belcheth forth his superfluity,
That all the seas for feare do seeme away to fly.

.   .   .

Thence passing forth, they shortly do arriue,
Whereas the *Bowre of blisse* was situate;
A place pickt out by choice of best aliue,
That natures worke by art can imitate:
In which what euer in this wordly state
Is sweet, and pleasing vnto liuing sense,
Or that may dayntiest fantasie aggrate,
Was poured forth with plentifull dispence,
And made there to abound with lauish affluence.

Goodly it was enclosed round about,
    Aswell their entred guestes to keepe within,
    As those vnruly beasts to hold without;
    Yet was the fence thereof but weake and thin;
    Nought feard their force, that fortilage to win,
    But wisedomes powre, and temperaunces might,
    By which the mightiest things efforced bin:
    And eke the gate was wrought of substaunce light,
Rather for pleasure, then for battery or fight.

.   .   .

The wanton Maidens him espying, stood
    Gazing a while at his vnwonted guise;
    Then th'one her selfe low ducked in the flood,
    Abasht, that her a straunger did a vise:
    But th'other rather higher did arise,
    And her two lilly paps aloft displayd,
    And all, that might his melting hart entise
    To her delights, she vnto him bewrayd:
The rest hid vnderneath, him more desirous made.

.   .   .

On which when gazing him the Palmer saw,
    He much rebukt those wandring eyes of his,
    And counseld well, him forward thence did draw.
    Now are they come nigh to the *Bowre of blisse*
    Of her fond fauorites so nam'd amis:
    When thus the Palmer; Now Sir, well auise;
    For here the end of all our trauell is:
    Here wonnes *Acrasia*, whom we must surprise,
Else she will slip away, and all our drift despise.

.   .   .

Vpon a bed of Roses she was layd,
    As faint through heat, or dight to pleasant sin,

And was arayd, or rather disarayd,
All in a vele of silke and siluer thin,
That hid no whit her alabaster skin,
But rather shewd more white, if more might bee:
More subtile web *Arachne* cannot spin,
Nor the fine nets, which oft we wouen see
Of scorched deaw, do not in th'aire more lightly flee.

.   .   .

The young man sleeping by her, seemd to bee
~~Some goodly swayne of honourable place,~~
That certes it great pittie was to see
Him his nobilitie so foule deface;
A sweet regard, and amiable grace,
Mixed with manly sternnesse did appeare
Yet sleeping, in his well proportiond face,
And on his tender lips the downy beare
Did now but freshly spring, and silken blossomes beare.

His warlike armes, the idle instruments
Of sleeping praise, were hong vpon a tree,
And his braue shield, full of old moniments,
Was fowly ra'st, that none the signes might see;
Ne for them, ne for honour cared hee,
Ne ought, that did to his aduauncement tend,
But in lewd loues, and wastfull luxuree,
His dayes, his goods, his bodie he did spend:
O horrible enchantment, that him so did blend.

The noble Elfe, and carefull Palmer drew
Sonigh them, minding nought, but lustfull game,
That suddein forth they on them rusht, and threw
A subtile net, which onely for the same
The skilfull Palmer formally did frame.
So held them vnder fast, the whiles the rest
Fled all away for feare of fowler shame.
The faire Enchauntresse, so vnwares opprest,
Tryde all her arts, and all her sleights, thence out to wrest.

124

And eke her louer stroue: but all in vaine;
  For that same net so cunningly was wound,
  That neither guile, nor force might it distraine.
  They tooke them both, and both them strongly bound
  In captiue bandes, which there they readie found:
  But her in chaines of adamant he tyde;
  For nothing else might keepe her safe and sound;
  But *Verdant* (so he hight) he soone vntyde,
And counsell sage insteed thereof to him applyde.

But all those pleasant bowres and Pallace braue,
  Guyon broke downe, with rigour pittilesse;
  Ne ought their goodly workmanship might saue
  Them from the tempest of his wrathfulnesse,
  But that their blisse he turn'd to balefulnesse:
  Their groues he feld, their gardins did deface,
  Their arbers spoyle, their Cabinets suppresse,
  Their banket houses burne, their buildings race,
And of the fairest late, now made the fowlest place.

Then led they her away, and eke that knight
  They with them led, both sorrowfull and sad:
  The way they came, the same retourn'd they right,
  Till they arriued, where they lately had
  Charm'd those wild-beasts, that rag'd with furie mad.
  Which now awaking, fierce at them gan fly,
  As in their mistresse reskew, whom they lad;
  But them the Palmer soone did pacify.
Then *Guyon* askt, what meant those beastes, which there
    did ly.

Said he, These seeming beasts are men indeed,
  Whom this Enchauntresse hath transformed thus,
  Whylome her louers, which her lusts did feed,
  Now turned into figures hideous,
  According to their mindes like monstruous.
  Sad end (quoth he) of life intemperate,
  And mournefull meed of ioyes delicious:
  But Palmer, if it mote thee so aggrate,
Let them returned be vnto their former state.

27. *Vision of a Young Knight,* Raphael.

Streight way he with his vertuous staffe them strooke,
   And streight of beasts they comely men became;
   Yet being men they did vnmanly looke,
   And stared ghastly, some for inward shame,
   And some for wrath, to see their captiue Dame:
   But one aboue the rest in speciall,
   That had an hog beene late, hight *Grille* by name
   Repined greatly, and did him miscall,
That had from hoggish forme him brought to naturall.

Said *Guyon,* See the mind of beastly man,
   That hath so soone forgot the excellence
   Of his creation, when he life began,
   That now he chooseth, with vile difference,
   To be a beast, and lacke intelligence.
   To whom the Palmer thus, The donghill kind
   Delights in filth and foule incontinence:
   Let *Grill* be *Grill,* and haue his hoggish mind,
But let vs hence depart, whilest wether serues and wind.

126

PETRARCH

SONNETS

Wherein Petrarch Confesses His Folly

Voi ch' ascoltate in rime sparse il suono

O ye that hear in vagrant rhymes the sighing
On which the headlong heart of youth went feeding,
When, still unseasoned, still at folly's leading
I turned from fears in sudden terror flying
To hopes whose glitter proved no less a lying—
As variously related for your reading—
If ever from Love's arrow ye fled bleeding,
Pity, and pardon me this anguished crying!
But well I know how I must walk derided,
A jest, a syllable in tavern chatter;
By self-reproach my self-deceit goes chided,
And shame is all the fruit my follies scatter—
Shame and a sense of pleasures that have glided
Like ghosts in a dream too trivial to matter.

Wherein He Sings the Birthplace of Laura

Quel ch' infinita providenza et arte

He who revealed such infinite care and pride
In His miraculous activity;
Who ordered hemispheres melodiously,
Lit Jupiter softly, poured a ruddier tide
Through Mars; who came on earth to open wide
The secret Scriptures and prove prophecy;
Took John and Peter from the nets at sea
And stationed each to stand, a starry guide,
Choosing the lowliest—so, for His birth
Humility honoured not imperial Rome,
But gentle little Judea, gem of earth!
And now from such another humble home
He hangs an equal star with equal grace—
Praise Him for such a birth in such a place!

Wherein He Recounts His State When Laura Is Present and When She Leaves Him

Piovommi amare lagrime dal viso

Tears, bitter tears fall in a bitter rain,
And my heart trembles with a storm of sighs
When on your beauty bend my burning eyes,
For whose sole sake the world seems flat and vain.
But ah, when I can see that smile again,
That chaste, sweet, delicate smile, then passion dies
Withered in its own flaming agonies:
Gazing upon you, passion is lost and pain.
But all too soon my very soul is rocked
When you depart and with your passing dear
Pluck from my perilous heaven my stars, O Sweet!
Then at the last, by Love's own keys unlocked,
My soul from out my body leaping clear
On wings of meditation finds your feet.

To Pandolfo Malatesta, Lord of Rimini

L' aspettata vertú, che 'n voi fioriva

The seed of virtue shed its blossom deep
Within thy heart when Love found lodging there;
And like the flower, the fruit is also fair:
The hopes I cherished long, I richly reap.
Wherefore my spirit into song must leap
To deck with praise the mighty name you bear:
For proudest marble never can declare
More than the flesh that withers in a sleep.
Think you Marcellus or the purple name
Of Caesar, Paulus, Scipio spring to flame
By anvil's heat or hammer's nervous thrust?
No, my Pandolfo, stone dissolves in dust:
Only the poet's pure immortal plan
Outwits the swift mortality of man.

Wherein He Expatiates Upon Love's Paradoxes

Pace non trovo e non ho da far guerra

I find no peace, yet from all wars abstain me;
I fear, I hope, I burn—and straightway wizen;
I mount above the wind, yet stay unrisen;
Grasp the world—thus—yet nothing does it gain me.
Love neither lets me go, nor will detain me;
Gives me no leave, nor yet keeps me in prison:
I am not held, and yet the hard chain is on
The heart; he yields no death, yet will he chain me.
Sightless, I see; and without tongue, I sorrow;
I cling to life, and yet would gladly perish;
Detest myself, and yet another cherish;
Feed upon grief; from grief my laughter borrow,
Death is a spear and life a poisoned arrow,
And in delight my fears take root and flourish.

A Catechism of His Lady's Charms—
with No Answers

Onde tolse Amor l' oro e di qual vena

From what source could Love suck the gold, what vein
Packed ore into those tresses? What thorn gave
That rose up? And what meadow could so lave
With white dew those locks dropping gold again
And yet again? What pearl-paved grottoes rain
Such lustre on that mouth whence murmurs grave
And golden move like bells beneath a wave?
Whence came those graces like some starry stain?
Ah, what fierce angels lead, what spheres can sway
The heavenly song that ravishes away
The senses dead to lesser harmonies?
What sun poured light into those eyes that freeze
The heart with hostile heat or, in a jest,
Put it on fire with the false hope of rest?

Wherein He Finds No Respite

La vita fugge e non s'arresta un' ora

Life rushes by on proud impatient feet,
And Death pursues her with a massive stride;
Ills past and present tear the soul aside,
With pain the future threatens to repeat:
I look before and after—pain I meet;
A thousand menaces my peace deride;
Ah, were not pity so involved with pride,
Long, long ago I should have found death sweet!
If ever any joy this heart has known,
Memory on it broods while, tempest-battered,
The winds still howl, the sinister heavens frown;
Even in port no truce prevents this war:
My pilot faint, mast split and sails all shattered,
And sunk forever my accustomed star.

Wherein Her Death Has Left Him Only the Philosophy of Despair

Soleasi nel mio cor star bella e viva

She stepped into my heart so vividly,
A thing of light and warmth!—as, all unknown,
A princess, having wandered from her throne,
Might crowd a peasant's hut with courtesy.
And she is dead!—and dead my soul in me;
She storms the stars!—and I could turn a stone
To blood and tears of blood: but there is none
To tell love's pain and my soul's poverty.
These plead too deep for any ears save mine,
Who sing, with equal emptiness oppressed,
As moans the bird about a barren nest.
Ah, we are shadows crying for a sign!
Ah, sick and sightless stares the human will!
Ah, hope is a mirage that cheats us still!

Wherein to Recall the Past Is to Augment the Despair of the Present

Quand io mi volgo in dietro a mirar gli anni

When I look back upon the fugitive time
Which swept my noblest ecstasies to doom,
And spilled the fire and trampled the white plume
And weighted down with tears the wings of rhyme;
And when I see Love turned to pantomime,
The dream derided, and the double bloom
Of flesh and spirit betrayed—half to the tomb,
And half to heaven—O cruel celestial crime!—
Then like one drugged and rifled, I awake,
And still in stupour, feel the wind and stare
At both my hands and body stripped, and quake,
Remembering lutes and sleep with purple hair . . .
O Stars like stone! O Death! Black Day! Blind Fate!
How you have done me to this dark estate!

Wherein a Grieving Bird Reminds Him of His Own Heavier Anguish

Vago augelletto che cantando vai

Sweet wandering bird, that on the branch you swing to
Pour such impartial music or in phrases
Darkened with imminent winter mourn dead graces
As song dies with the summer that you sing to—
Ah could you guess the bitter bough I cling to,
Your golden grief would find in mine clear traces
Of kinship! In my heart your singing space is;
One song is ours, one measure we both ring to.
And yet who knows? The grief you give a name to
May not endure: some bough she could not leap to,
A bruised wing, maybe, holds the mate you weep to;
Not so my theme, my sweet I pour this flame to:
Death and this bleak day, thoughts my soul must keep to,
Prompt me to call what Death alone has claim to.

28. *Fête Champêtre,* Giorgione.

PIERRE DE RONSARD

SONNETS

Quand vous serez bien vieille, au soir à la chandelle

When you are very old, by the hearth's glare,
 At candle-time, spinning and winding thread,
 You'll sing my lines, and say, astonishéd:
Ronsard made these for me, when I was fair.

Then not a servant even, with toil and care
 Almost out-worn, hearing what you have said,
 Shall fail to start awake and lift her head
And bless your name with deathless praise fore'er.

My bones shall lie in earth, and my poor ghost
 Take its long rest where Love's dark myrtles thrive.
 You, crouching by the fire, old, shrunken, grey,

Shall rue your proud disdain and my love lost. . . .
   Nay, hear me, love! Wait not to-morrow! Live,
   And pluck life's roses, oh! to-day, to-day.

Le soir qu' Amour vous fist en la salle descendre

That evening when love bade you take the floor
   to tread his brilliant ballet of Things Tender,
your eyes, though it was night, did day restore,
   those stars that took the ballroom with their splendour.
O what a proud pavane, now less, now more,
   breaking, rejoining, now in circled wonder
first mixing, then dividing, till I swore
   no dance it was but the bent stream Meander.
Now the ring formed, dissolved, now it was narrow,
   now in a pointed triangle it lifted
sharp as the migrant squadron of the crane.
I lie. You did not dance. Your foot—an arrow—
   flew over earth, while your light body drifted,
   assuming for the night the god again.

Adieu, cruelle adieu, je te suis ennuyeux

Cruel, farewell, since I do but annoy thee,
   and love in song grows tedious unrequited.
I go, and let who will or can enjoy thee,
   though never will he match the love you slighted.
In fifteen months love taught me tricks and fashion,
   planting within my brain the seeds of verse.
Now reason school the lunacies of passion
   and brings me to her side and makes me hers.
Feed not this child, who gnaws upon the heart,
   the angler catching fools upon the string,
the comedy, the perfect liar's art,
   a hundred pains and one joy vanishing.
Nay, let's be sure, however things may seem,
   that man is doomed who sups upon a dream.

MICHELANGELO

POEMS

To Giovanni, the one from Pistoia

I've developed a goirre, in this chagrin,
As if I had, like cats in Lombardy,
Drunk dirty water in large quantity,—
Which makes the stomach bulge up to the chin.
Beard to the stars, and a nape that I pin
On the shoulders, a harpy's breast—that's *me;*
And, dripping still, the brush, as you can see,
Has made my face a floor stained out and in.

Into the belly have entered my hips,
And with the seat I counterpoise the hunch
And, as I cannot look, in vain I march.
In front, my skin is taut, and almost flips,
But in the back the wrinkles make a bunch,
And I am bent like an Assyrian arch.

That is why, bent and smirched
Even my thought emerges from my head:
Shooting a crookéd harquebus is bad.

Defend my painting dead,
Giovanni, and my honor which grows fainter:
This place is bad; besides, I am no painter.

.   .   .

Simply because the sun does not embrace
With lucent arms this cold and humid globe,
They thought of calling "night" his other face,
That second sun they fail to know and prove.
Oh, but so frail is night, that one quick blaze
Of torch can rend her life, and can disrobe her;
And so foolish is she, that the swift trace
Of a gunshot can make her bleed and throb.

If something she must be, she doubtless is
The daughter of the sun and of the earth:

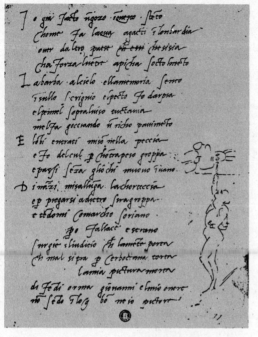

29. Sonnet with illustration,
Michelangelo.

One gives her life, the other holds her here.
Wrong are all those who praise her qualities:
She is so dark, lost, lonely, that the birth
Of one small firefly can make war on her.

.   .   .

I feel constrained and blocked as is the marrow
Into its bone, right here, so poor and lonely,
And as some spirit in a vial narrow.

And this grave-dungeon is so small, that only
Arachne dwells with webs and all her clients,
Each hardly finding room to spin so cunningly.

Around the door I have mountains of giants;
Those who eat grapes or take some medicine,
They all come here to place their putrid viands.

So I have learned to recognize the urine
And its emitting pipes: those many holes
Still rouse me with their morning overturing.

Carcasses, cats, foul vessels, stinking bowls
For fertilizer, or just laid right there,—
These are the things that greet whoever calls.

My soul would profit from my body, I swear,
For, should it come right out and smell this stench,
My bread and cheese it could no longer bear.

My cough and cold, I gather, cannot quench it;
But, if they do, it must escape through the rear,
Since through the mouth my breath can hardly venture.

Hernia, lumbago, lameness—oh so weary
Am I from all my work. Death is an inn
In which I live and eat my food in fear.

My gladness is but sadness, my one kin,
And my repose is discomfort and trouble:
Who wants all this—let hell soon grab him in!

If the Three Kings who traveled to the stable
Should return, passing many a wealthy house,
They would come, I am sure, to this my rubble.

My long-dead heart—no flame of love can rouse;
If a great sorrow makes a small one dull,
My soul has lost its wings and cannot rise.

I have a buzzing wasp within my skull,
And in a leather sack keep nerves and bones,
And three hard pills of pitch float in my gall.

My eyes are sand which has been ground of stones,
My teeth are keys of some old instrument
Which, as they move, make jarring sounds and drones.

My face makes people scared and diffident;
To save the seeds, my clothes, without a stick,
Would scare away all black crows fraudulent.

A spider, in one ear, has spun a thick

Web; in the other sings a cricket all night;
No sleep, no snore, but a catarrhous trick.

All my love verses, all my drawings bright,
Have gone to fold guitars, wrap meat for stews,
And to embellish cesspools with their sight.

To paint so many puppets—what's the use,
If it will make me finish like the one
Who crossed the sea to drown in his own mucus?

Art, which I once have honored, and has done
Me honor for some time, gives me such boon:
A poor old man who must serve everyone.

Ah, I am finished, if I don't die soon!

.　　.　　.

If my rough hammer gives a human face
To this or that of all hard blocks that wait,
It is another smith makes me create,
Controlling each my motion, each my pace.
But that high hammer beyond stars and space
Makes self, and others, with each stroke, more great
And bright; and since the first must generate
All hammers, *that* gives life to all, always.

And since the most effective is that blow
Which falls from highest in the smithy, mine
Shall fall no more—my hammer having flown.
Now here am I, unskilled, and do not know
How to go on, unless the smith divine
Teaches me how, who am on earth alone.

.　　.　　.

When all my past returns to grieve my mind,—
And every hour it does—
Deceitful world, I know how love is wrong
On earth, and recognize how wrong was I.
The heart that, ah, swears by
Your flatteries and lures,

Gives to the soul a thousand moans and woes.
How well I know that you
Promise that peace which you yourself have not,
And which you never knew.
Therefore, long life is long unhappiness:
He sooner goes to God, who dwells here less.

. . .

I feel more precious, I am more than one,
For, since you held my heart, my worth grew more:
A marble block, when carving has been done,
Is not the rough, cheap stone it was before.
As paper painted or just written on
No longer is a rag one can ignore,
So, since you looked at me, and I was won,
My value has increased for evermore.

Now, with your splendor printed on my face,
I go like one who, dressed with every kind
Of amulets and arms, can dare all wars.
I can walk on the ocean, brave all blaze,
Give in your name the light to all the blind,
And my saliva heals all poisonous sores.

Sir Thomas Wyatt

SONNETS

Description of the Contrarious
Passions in a Lover

I find no peace, and all my war is done.
I fear and hope, I burn and freeze like ice.
I fly aloft, yet can I not arise;
And nought I have, and all the world I season.
That locks nor loseth holdeth me in prison
And holds me not, yet can I scape nowise;

Nor lets me live nor die at my devise,
And yet of death it geveth me occasion.
Without eye I see, without tongue I plain.
I wish to perish, yet I ask for health;
I love another, and thus I hate myself.
I feed me in sorrow and laugh in all my pain.
Lo! thus displeaseth me both death and life,
And my delight is causer of this strife.

The Lover Compareth His State to a Ship in Perilous Storm Tossed on the Sea

My galley charged with forgetfulness
Through sharp seas in winter nights doth pass
Tween rock and rock; and eke my foe, alas,
That is my lord, steereth with cruelness.
And every [oar] a thought in readiness,
As though that death were light in such a case;
An endless wind doth tear the sail apace
Of forced sighs and trusty fearfulness.
A rain of tears, a cloud of dark disdain,
Have done the wearied cords great hinderance,
Wreathed with error and with ignorance.
The stars be hid that led me to this pain.
Drown'd is reason that should be my comfort,
And I remain, dispearing of the port.

MICHAEL DRAYTON

Since There's No Help

Since there's no help, come, let us kiss and part.
Nay, I have done, you get no more of me,
And I am glad, yea glad with all my heart
That thus so cleanly I myself can free;
Shake hands forever, cancel all our vows,
And when we meet at any time again
Be it not seen in either of our brows

That we one jot of former love retain.
Now at the last gasp of Love's latest breath,
When, his pulse failing, Passion speechless lies,
When Faith is kneeling by his bed of death
And Innocence is closing up his eyes,
   Now if thou would'st, when all have given him over,
   From death to life thou might'st him yet recover.

GIOVANNI BOCCACCIO

FROM THE DECAMERON

*Masetto da Lamporecchio feigns to be dumb, and obtains a
gardener's place at a convent of women, who with one accord
make haste to lie with him.*

Fairest ladies, not a few there are both of men and of women, who are
so foolish as blindly to believe that, so soon as a young woman has been
veiled in white and cowled in black, she ceases to be a woman, and is no
more subject to the cravings proper to her sex, than if, in assuming the
garb and profession of a nun, she had put on the nature of a stone: and
if, perchance, they hear of aught that is counter to this their faith, they
are no less vehement in their censure than if some most heinous and unnatural crime had been committed; neither bethinking them of themselves, whom unrestricted liberty avails not to satisfy, nor making due
allowance for the prepotent forces of idleness and solitude. And likewise
not a few there are that blindly believe that, what with the hoe and the
spade and coarse fare and hardship, the carnal propensities are utterly
eradicated from the tillers of the soil, and therewith all nimbleness of
wit and understanding. But how gross is the error of such as so suppose, I, on whom the queen has laid her commands, am minded, without
deviating from the theme prescribed by her, to make manifest to you by
a little story.

In this very country-side of ours there was and yet is a convent of
women of great repute for sanctity—name it I will not, lest I should in
some measure diminish its repute—the nuns being at the time of which I
speak but nine in number, including the abbess, and all young women.
Their very beautiful garden was in charge of a foolish fellow, who, not

30. *The Month of April,* detail, Francesco del Cossa.

being content with his wage, squared accounts with their steward, and hied him back to Lamporecchio, whence he came. Among others who welcomed him home was a young husbandman, Masetto by name, a stout and hardy fellow, and handsome for a contadino, who asked him where he had been so long. Nuto, as our good friend was called, told him. Masetto then asked how he had been employed at the convent, and Nuto answered:—"I kept their large and beautiful garden in good trim, and, besides, I sometimes went to the wood to fetch the faggots, I drew water, and did some other trifling services; but the ladies gave so little wage that it scarce kept me in shoes. And moreover they are all young, and, I think, they are one and all possessed of the devil, for 'tis impossible to do anything to their mind; indeed, when I would be at work in the kitchen-garden, 'put this here,' would say one, 'put that here,' would say another, and a third would snatch the hoe from my hand, and say, 'that is not as it should be'; and so they would worry me until I would give up work-ing and go out of the garden; so that, what with this thing and that, I was minded to stay there no more, and so I am come hither. The steward asked me before I left to send him any one whom on my return I might find fit for the work, and I promised; but God bless his loins, I shall be at no pains to find out and send him any one."

As Nuto thus ran on, Masetto was seized by such a desire to be with these nuns that he quite pined, as he gathered from what Nuto said that his desire might be gratified. And as that could not be, if he said nothing to Nuto, he remarked:—"Ah! 'twas well done of thee to come hither. A man to live with women! he might as well live with so many devils: six times out of seven they know not themselves what they want." There the conversation ended; but Masetto began to cast about how he should proceed to get permission to live with them. He knew that he was quite competent for the services of which Nuto spoke, and had therefore no fear of failing on that score; but he doubted he should not be received, because he was too young and well-favoured. So, after much pondering, he fell into the following train of thought:—The place is a long way off, and no one there knows me; if I make believe that I am dumb, doubtless I shall be admitted. Whereupon he made his mind up, laid a hatchet across his shoulder, and saying not a word to any of his destination, set forth, intending to present himself at the convent in the character of a destitute man. Arrived there, he had no sooner entered than he chanced to encounter the steward in the courtyard, and making signs to him as dumb folk do, he let him know that of his charity he craved something to eat, and that, if need were, he would split firewood. The steward promptly gave him to eat, and then set before him some logs which Nuto had not been able to split, all which Masetto, who was very strong, split in a very short time. The steward, having occasion to go to the wood, took him with him, and there set him at work on the lopping; which done he placed the ass in front of him, and by signs made him understand that he was to take the loppings back to the convent. This he did so well that the steward kept him for some days to do one or two odd jobs. Whereby it so befell that one day the abbess saw him, and asked the steward who he was. "Madam," replied the steward, "'tis a poor deaf mute that came here a day or two ago craving alms, so I have treated him kindly, and have let him make himself useful in many ways. If he knew how to do the work of the kitchen-garden and would stay with us, I doubt not we should be well served; for we have need of him, and he is strong, and would be able for whatever he might turn his hand to; besides which you would have no cause to be apprehensive lest he should be cracking his jokes with your young women." "As I trust in God," said the abbess, "thou sayst sooth; find out if he can do the garden work, and if he can, do all thou canst to keep him with us; give him a pair of shoes, an old hood, and speak him well, make much of him, and let him be well fed." All which the steward promised to do.

Masetto, meanwhile, was close at hand, making as if he were sweeping the courtyard, and heard all that passed between the abbess and the steward, whereat he gleefully communed with himself on this wise:—Put

me once within there, and you will see that I will do the work of the
kitchen-garden as it never was done before. So the steward set him to
work in the kitchen-garden, and finding that he knew his business excellently well, made signs to him to know whether he would stay, and he
made answer by signs that he was ready to do whatever the steward
wished. The steward then signified that he was engaged, told him to take
charge of the kitchen-garden, and shewed him what he had to do there.
Then, having other matters to attend to, he went away, and left him
there. Now, as Masetto worked there day by day, the nuns began to tease
him, and make him their butt (as it commonly happens that folk serve
the dumb) and used bad language to him, the worst they could think of,
supposing that he could not understand them: all which passed scarce
heeded by the abbess, who perhaps deemed him as destitute of virility as
of speech. Now it so befell that after a hard day's work he was taking a
little rest, when two young nuns, who were walking in the garden, approached the spot where he lay, and stopped to look at him, while he
pretended to be asleep. And so the bolder of the two said to the other:—
"If I thought thou wouldst keep the secret, I would tell thee what I have
sometimes meditated, and which thou perhaps, mightest also find agreeable." The other replied:—"Speak thy mind freely and be sure that I
will never tell a soul." Whereupon the bold one began:—"I know not if
thou hast ever considered how close we are kept here, and that within
these precincts dare never enter any man, unless it be the old steward or
this mute: and I have often heard from ladies that have come hither,
that all the other sweets that the world has to offer signify not a jot in
comparison of the pleasure that a woman has in connexion with a man.
Whereof I have more than once been minded to make experiment with
this mute, no other man being available. Nor, indeed, could one find
any man in the whole world so meet therefor; seeing that he could not
blab if he would; thou seest that he is but a dull clownish lad, whose size
has increased out of all proportion to his sense; wherefore I would fain
hear what thou hast to say to it." "Alas!" said the other, "what is 't thou
sayst? Knowest thou not that we have vowed our virginity to God?"
"Oh," rejoined the first, "think but how many vows are made to Him all
day long, and never a one performed: and so, for our vow, let Him find
another or others to perform it." "But," said her companion, "suppose
that we conceived, how then?" "Nay but," protested the first, "thou goest
about to imagine evil before it befalls thee: time enough to think of
that when it comes to pass; there will be a thousand ways to prevent its

ever being known, so only we do not publish it ourselves." Thus reassured, the other was now the more eager of the two to test the quality of the male human animal. "Well then," she said, "how shall we go about it?" and was answered:—"Thou seest 'tis past noon; I make no doubt but all the sisters are asleep, except ourselves; search we through the kitchen-garden, to see if there be any there, and if there be none, we have but to take him by the hand and lead him hither to the hut where he takes shelter from the rain; and then one shall mount guard while the other has him with her inside. He is such a simpleton that he will do just whatever we bid him." No word of this conversation escaped Masetto, who, being disposed to obey, hoped for nothing so much as that one of them should take him by the hand. They, meanwhile, looked carefully all about them, and satisfied themselves that they were secure from observation: then she that had broached the subject came close up to Masetto, and shook him; whereupon he started to his feet. So she took him by the hand with a blandishing air, to which he replied with some clownish grins. And then she led him into the hut, where he needed no pressing to do what she desired of him. Which done, she changed places with the other, as loyal comradeship required; and Masetto, still keeping up the pretence of simplicity, did their pleasure. Wherefore before they left, each must needs make another assay of the mute's powers of riding; and afterwards, talking the matter over many times, they agreed that it was in truth not less but even more delightful than they had been given to understand; and so, as they found convenient opportunity, they continued to go and disport themselves with the mute.

Now it so chanced that one of their gossips, looking out of the window of her cell, saw what they did, and imparted it to two others. The three held counsel together whether they should not denounce the offenders to the abbess, but soon changed their mind, and came to an understanding with them, whereby they became partners in Masetto. And in course of time by divers chances the remaining three nuns also entered the partnership. Last of all the abbess, still witting nought of these doings, happened one very hot day, as she walked by herself through the garden, to find Masetto, who now rode so much by night that he could stand very little fatigue by day, stretched at full length asleep under the shade of an almond-tree, his person quite exposed in front by reason that the wind had disarranged his clothes. Which the lady observing, and knowing that she was alone, fell a prey to the same appetite to which her nuns had yielded: she aroused Masetto, and took him with her to her chamber,

31. *Shepherd and Shepherdess,* Titian.

where, for some days, though the nuns loudly complained that the gardener no longer came to work in the kitchen-garden, she kept him, tasting and re-tasting the sweetness of that indulgence which she was wont to be the first to censure in others. And when at last she had sent him back from her chamber to his room, she must needs send for him again and again, and made such exorbitant demands upon him, that Masetto, not being able to satisfy so many women, bethought him that his part of mute, should he persist in it, might entail disastrous consequences. So one night, when he was with the abbess, he cut the tongue-string, and thus broke silence:—"Madam, I have understood that a cock may very well serve ten hens, but that ten men are sorely tasked to satisfy a single woman; and here am I expected to serve nine, a burden quite beyond my power to bear; nay, by what I have already undergone I am now so reduced that my strength is quite spent; wherefore either bid me Godspeed, or find some means to make matters tolerable." Wonder-struck to hear the supposed mute thus speak, the lady exclaimed:—"What means this? I took thee to be dumb." "And in sooth, Madam, so was I," said Masetto, "not indeed from my birth, but through an illness which took from me the power of speech, which only this very night have I recovered; and so I praise God with all my heart." The lady believed him; and asked him what he meant by saying that he had nine to serve. Masetto told her how things stood; whereby she perceived that of all her nuns there was not any but was much wiser than she; and lest, if Masetto were sent away, he should give the convent a bad name, she discreetly determined to arrange matters with the nuns in such sort that he might remain there. So, the steward having died within the last few days, she assembled all the nuns; and their and her own past errors being fully avowed, they by common consent, and with Masetto's concurrence, resolved that the neighbours should be given to understand that by their prayers and the merits of their patron saint, Masetto, long mute, had recovered the power of speech; after which they made him steward, and so ordered matters among themselves that he was able to endure the burden of their service. In the course of which, though he procreated not a few little monastics, yet 'twas all managed so discreetly that no breath of scandal stirred, until after the abbess's death, by which time Masetto was advanced in years and minded to return home with the wealth that he had gotten; which he was suffered to do as soon as he made his desire known. And so Masetto, who had left Lamporecchio with a hatchet on his shoulder, returned thither in his old age rich and a father, having by the wisdom with which he employed his youth, spared himself the pains and expense of rearing children, and averring that such was the measure that Christ meted out to the man that set horns on his cap.

> *Two young men lodge at an inn, of whom the one lies with the host's daughter, his wife by inadvertence lying with the other. He that lay with the daughter afterwards gets into her father's bed and tells him all, taking him to be his comrade. They bandy words: whereupon the good woman, apprehending the circumstances, gets her to bed with her daughter, and by divers apt words re-establishes perfect accord.*

Calandrino as on former occasions, so also on this, moved the company to laughter. However, when the ladies had done talking of his doings, the queen called for a story from Pamfilo, who thus spoke:—Worshipful ladies, this Niccolosa, that Calandrino loved, has brought to my mind a story of another Niccolosa; which I am minded to tell you, because 'twill shew you how a good woman by her quick apprehension avoided a great scandal.

In the plain of Mugnone there was not long ago a good man that furnished travellers with meat and drink for money, and, for that he was in poor circumstances, and had but a little house, gave not lodging to every comer, but only to a few that he knew, and if they were hard bested. Now the good man had to wife a very fine woman, and by her had two children, to wit, a pretty and winsome girl of some fifteen or sixteen summers, as yet unmarried, and a little boy, not yet one year old, whom the mother suckled at her own breast. The girl had found favour in the eyes of a goodly and mannerly young gentleman of our city, who was not seldom in those parts, and loved her to the point of passion. And she, being mightily flattered to be loved by such a gallant, studied how to comport herself so debonairly as to retain his regard, and while she did so, grew likewise enamoured of him; and divers times, by consent of both, their love had had its fruition, but that Pinuccio—such was the gallant's name—shrank from the disgrace that 'twould bring upon the girl and himself alike. But, as his passion daily waxed apace, Pinuccio, yearning to find himself abed with her, bethought him that he were best contrive to lodge with her father, deeming, from what he knew of her father's economy, that, if he did so, he might effect his purpose, and never a soul be the wiser: which idea no sooner struck him, than he set about carrying it into effect.

So, late one evening Pinuccio and a trusty comrade, Adriano by name, to whom he had confided his love, hired two nags, and having set upon them two valises, filled with straw or suchlike stuff, sallied forth of Florence, and rode by a circuitous route to the plain of Mugnone, which they reached after nightfall; and having fetched a compass, so that it might seem as if they were coming from Romagna, they rode up to the good man's house, and knocked at the door. The good man, knowing them both very well, opened to them forthwith: whereupon:—"Thou must even put us up to-night," quoth Pinuccio; "we thought to get into Florence, but, for all the speed we could make, we are but arrived here, as thou seest, at this hour." "Pinuccio," replied the host, "thou well knowest that I can but make a sorry shift to lodge gentlemen like you; but yet, as night has overtaken you here, and time serves not to betake you elsewhere, I will gladly give you such accommodation as I may." The two gallants then dismounted and entered the inn, and having first looked to their horses, brought out some supper that they had carried with them, and supped with the host.

32. *Bathsheba,* Cornelis
Cornelisz van
Haarlem.

Now the host had but one little bedroom, in which were three beds,
set, as conveniently as he could contrive, two on one side of the room,
and the third on the opposite side, but, for all that, there was scarce
room enough to pass through. The host had the least discomfortable of
the three beds made up for the two friends; and having quartered them
there, some little while afterwards, both being awake, but feigning to be
asleep, he caused his daughter to get into one of the other two beds,
while he and his wife took their places in the third, the good woman
setting the cradle, in which was her little boy, beside the bed. Such, then,
being the partition made of the beds, Pinuccio, who had taken exact
note thereof, waited only until he deemed all but himself to be asleep,
and then got softly up and stole to the bed in which lay his beloved,
and laid himself beside her; and she according him albeit a timorous yet
a gladsome welcome, he stayed there, taking with her that solace of which
both were most fain.

Pinuccio being thus with the girl, it chanced that certain things, being
overset by a cat, fell with a noise that aroused the good woman, who, fear-

ing that it might be a matter of more consequence, got up as best she might in the dark, and betook her to the place whence the noise seemed to proceed. At the same time Adriano, not by reason of the noise, which he heeded not, but perchance to answer the call of nature, also got up, and questing about for a convenient place, came upon the cradle beside the good woman's bed; and not being able otherwise to go by, took it up, and set it beside his own bed, and when he had accomplished his purpose, went back, and giving never a thought to the cradle got him to bed. The good woman searched until she found that the accident was no such matter as she had supposed; so without troubling to strike a light to investigate it further, she reproved the cat, and returned to the room, and groped her way straight to the bed in which her husband lay asleep; but not finding the cradle there, quoth she to herself:—Alas! blunderer that I am, what was I about? God's faith! I was going straight to the guest's bed; and proceeding a little further, she found the cradle, and laid herself down by Adriano in the bed that was beside it, taking Adriano for her husband; and Adriano, who was still awake, received her with all due benignity, and tackled her more than once to her no small delight.

Meanwhile Pinuccio fearing lest sleep should overtake him while he was yet with his mistress, and having satisfied his desire, got up and left her, to return to his bed; but when he got there, coming upon the cradle, he supposed that 'twas the host's bed; and so going a little further, he laid him down beside the host, who thereupon awoke. Supposing that he had Adriano beside him:—"I warrant thee," quoth Pinuccio to the host, "there was never so sweet a piece of flesh as Niccolosa: by the body of God, such delight have I had of her as never had man of woman; and, mark me, since I left thee, I have gotten me up to the farm some six times." Which tidings the host being none too well pleased to learn, said first of all to himself:—What the Devil does this fellow here? Then, his resentment getting the better of his prudence:—" 'Tis a gross affront thou hast put upon me, Pinuccio," quoth he; "nor know I what occasion thou hast to do me such a wrong; but by the body of God I will pay thee out." Pinuccio, who was not the most discreet of gallants, albeit he was now apprised of his error, instead of doing his best to repair it, retorted: —"And how wilt thou pay me out? What canst thou do?" "Hark what high words our guests are at together!" quoth meanwhile the host's wife to Adriano, deeming that she spoke to her husband. "Let them be," replied Adriano with a laugh: "God give them a bad year: they drank too much yestereve." The good woman had already half recognized her husband's angry tones, and now that she heard Adriano's voice, she at once knew where she was and with whom. Accordingly, being a discreet woman, she started up, and saying never a word, took her child's cradle, and, though there was not a ray of light in the room, bore it, divining rather than feeling her way, to the side of the bed in which her daughter slept; and then, as if aroused by the noise made by her husband, she called him, and asked what he and Pinuccio were bandying words about. "Hearest thou not," replied the husband, "what he says he has this very night done to Niccolosa?" "Tush! he lies in the throat," returned the good woman: "he has not lain with Niccolosa; for what time he might have done so, I laid me beside her myself, and I have been wide awake ever since; and thou art a fool to believe him. You men take so many cups before going to bed that then you dream, and walk in your sleep, and imagine wonders. 'Tis a great pity you do not break your necks. What does Pinuccio there? Why keeps he not in his own bed?"

Whereupon Adriano, in his turn, seeing how adroitly the good woman cloaked her own and her daughter's shame:—"Pinuccio," quoth he, "I have told thee a hundred times that thou shouldst not walk about at night; for this thy bad habit of getting up in thy dreams and relating thy dreams for truth will get thee into a scrape some time or another: come back, and God send thee a bad night." Hearing Adriano thus confirm what his wife had said, the host began to think that Pinuccio must be really dreaming; so he took him by the shoulder, and fell a-shaking him, and calling him by his name, saying:—"Pinuccio, wake up, and go back to thy bed." Pinuccio, taking his cue from what he had heard, began as a dreamer would be like to do, to talk wanderingly; whereat the host laughed amain. Then, feigning to be aroused by the shaking, Pinuccio uttered Adriano's name, saying:—"Is't already day, that thou callest me?" "Ay, 'tis so," quoth Adriano: "come hither." Whereupon Pinuccio, making as if he were mighty drowsy, got him up from beside the host, and back to bed with Adriano. On the morrow, when they were risen, the host fell a-laughing and making merry touching Pinuccio and his dreams. And so the jest passed from mouth to mouth, while the gallants' horses were groomed and saddled, and their valises adjusted: which done, they drank with the host, mounted and rode to Florence, no less pleased with the manner than with the matter of the night's adventure. Nor, afterwards, did Pinuccio fail to find other means of meeting Niccolosa, who assured her mother that he had unquestionably dreamed. For which cause the good woman, calling to mind Adriano's embrace, accounted herself the only one that had watched.

MARGUERITE DE NAVARRE

THE BOATWOMAN

There was in the port of Coulon, near Niort, a boatwoman, who did nothing day and night but convey people from point to point. Two Cordeliers of Niort crossed the river alone with her. As it was one of the widest ferries in France, they took it into their heads to make love to her, for fear she should grow dull by the way. She gave no more ear to them than they deserved, but the good fathers, who were neither fatigued by the labor of the passage, nor chilled by the coldness of the water, nor abashed by the woman's refusal, resolved to force her, or throw her into the river if she was refractory.

But she was as good and as shrewd as they were wicked and witless, and said to them, "I am not so ill-natured as you might suppose; only grant me two things I have to beg of you, and you will see I am not less willing to satisfy you than you are to be satisfied." The Cordeliers swore by their good St. Francis there was nothing they would not grant her to have from her what they wanted. "Well, then," she said, "I ask you, in the first place, to promise and vow that living man shall never know from you what passes between us." This they did with great readiness. "The second thing I ask is, that you will have to do with me one by one, for I should be too much ashamed if it was done in the presence of you both. Settle between yourselves which is to have me first." The Cordeliers thought that fair enough, and the younger of them yielded precedence to the elder.

Running the boat ashore at a little island, she said to the younger one, "Say your prayers there whilst your comrade and I go to another island. If he is satisfied with me when we come back, we will leave him, and you and I will go away together." The younger friar jumped ashore at once, and the boatwoman rowed away with his companion to another island. When they reached it, she pretended to be making her boat fast, whilst she said to the monk, "See if you can find a convenient spot."

The Cordelier, like a booby, stepped out of the boat to do as she told him, and no sooner was he ashore than, setting her foot against a tree, she shot the boat out into the stream, and left the two good fathers in the lurch. "Wait there, my masters," said she, "till God's angel comes to console you, for you will get nothing from me." The duped Cordeliers went down on their knees, and begged her, for Heaven's sake, not to serve them so, but take them to the port, upon their solemn oath they would ask nothing of her. "A pretty fool I should be," she replied, still rowing away, "to put myself into your hands again once I have got out of them."

When she got home to the village, she told her husband what had occurred, and applied to the ministers of justice to come and capture those two wolves from whose fangs she had contrived to escape. The ministers of justice set out for the purpose, well accompanied, for there was no one, great or small, but was bent on taking part in this hunt. The poor friars, seeing such a multitude coming after them, hid themselves each on his island, as Adam did from the sight of God when he had eaten the apple.

Half dead with shame and the fear of punishment, they were caught and led away prisoners, amid the jeers and hootings of men and women. "These good fathers," said one, "preach chastity to us and want to foul our wives." "They dare not touch money," said the husband, "but they are ready enough to handle women's thighs, which are far more dangerous." "They are sepulchres," said others, "whitened without, but full of rottenness within." "By their fruits you shall know the nature of these trees."

In short, all the passages of Scripture against hypocrites were cast in the teeth of the poor prisoners. At last the warden came to the rescue. They were given up to him at his request, upon his assuring the magistrate that he would punish them more severely than secular justice itself could do, and that, by way of reparation to the offended parties, they should say as many masses and prayers as might be desired. As he was a worthy man, they were chaptered in such a manner that they never afterwards passed over a river without crossing themselves, and beseeching God to keep them out of all temptation.

MIGUEL DE CERVANTES

THE ADVENTURE OF THE WINDMILLS

At this point they caught sight of thirty or forty windmills which were standing on the plain there, and no sooner had Don Quixote laid eyes upon them than he turned to his squire and said, "Fortune is guiding our affairs better than we could have wished; for you see there before you, friend Sancho Panza, some thirty or more lawless giants with whom I mean to do battle. I shall deprive them of their lives, and with the spoils from this encounter we shall begin to enrich ourselves; for this is righteous warfare, and it is a great service to God to remove so accursed a breed from the face of the earth."

"What giants?" said Sancho Panza.

"Those that you see there," replied his master, "those with the long arms some of which are as much as two leagues in length."

"But look, your Grace, those are not giants but windmills, and what appear to be arms are their wings which, when whirled in the breeze, cause the millstone to go."

"It is plain to be seen," said Don Quixote, "that you have had little experience in this matter of adventures. If you are afraid, go off to one side and say your prayers while I am engaging them in fierce, unequal combat."

Saying this, he gave spurs to his steed Rocinante, without paying any heed to Sancho's warning that these were truly windmills and not giants that he was riding forth to attack. Nor even when he was close upon them did he perceive what they really were, but shouted at the top of his lungs, "Do not seek to flee, cowards and vile creatures that you are, for it is but a single knight with whom you have to deal!"

At that moment a little wind came up and the big wings began turning.

"Though you flourish as many arms as did the giant Briareus," said Don Quixote when he perceived this, "you still shall have to answer to me."

He thereupon commended himself with all his heart to his lady Dulcinea, beseeching her to succor him in this peril; and, being well covered with his shield and with his lance at rest, he bore down upon them at a full gallop and fell upon the first mill that stood in his way, giving a thrust at the wing, which was whirling at such a speed that his lance was broken into bits and both horse and horseman went rolling over the plain, very much battered indeed. Sancho upon his donkey came hurrying to his master's assistance as fast as he could, but when he reached the spot, the knight was unable to move, so great was the shock with which he and Rocinante had hit the ground.

"God help us!" exclaimed Sancho, "did I not tell your Grace to look well, that those were nothing but windmills, a fact which no one could fail to see unless he had other mills of the same sort in his head?"

"Be quiet, friend Sancho," said Don Quixote. "Such are the fortunes of war, which more than any other are subject to constant change. What is more, when I come to think of it, I am sure that this must be the work of that magician Frestón, the one who robbed me of my study and my books, and who has thus changed the giants into windmills in order to deprive me of the glory of overcoming them, so great is the enmity that he bears me; but in the end his evil arts shall not prevail against this trusty sword of mine."

"May God's will be done," was Sancho Panza's response. And with the aid of his squire the knight was once more mounted on Rocinante, who stood there with one shoulder half out of joint. And so, speaking of the adventure that had just befallen them, they continued along the Puerto Lápice highway; for there, Don Quixote said, they could not fail to find many and varied adventures, this being a much traveled thoroughfare. The only thing was, the knight was exceedingly downcast over the loss of his lance.

"I remember," he said to his squire, "having read of a Spanish knight by the name of Diego Pérez de Vargas, who, having broken his sword in battle, tore from an oak a heavy bough or branch and with it did such feats of valor that day, and pounded so many Moors, that he came to be known as Machuca, and he and his descendants from that day forth have been called Vargas y Machuca. I tell you this because I too intend to provide myself with just such a bough as the one he wielded, and with it I propose to do such exploits that you shall deem yourself fortunate to have been found worthy to come with me and behold and witness things that are almost beyond belief."

"God's will be done," said Sancho. "I believe everything that your Grace says; but straighten yourself up in the saddle a little, for you seem to be slipping down on one side, owing, no doubt, to the shaking-up that you received in your fall."

"Ah, that is the truth," replied Don Quixote, "and if I do not speak of my sufferings, it is for the reason that it is not permitted knights-errant to complain of any wound whatsoever, even though their bowels may be dropping out."

"If that is the way it is," said Sancho, "I have nothing more to say; but, God knows, it would suit me better if your Grace did complain when something hurts him. I can assure you that I mean to do so, over the least little thing that ails me—that is, unless the same rule applies to squires as well."

Don Quixote laughed long and heartily over Sancho's simplicity, telling him that he might complain as much as he liked and where and when he liked, whether he had good cause or not; for he had read nothing to the contrary in the ordinances of chivalry. Sancho then called his master's attention to the fact that it was time to eat. The knight replied that he himself had no need of food at the moment, but his squire might eat whenever he chose. Having been granted this permission, Sancho seated himself as best he could upon his beast, and, taking out from his saddle-bags the provisions that he had stored there, he rode along leisurely behind his master, munching his victuals and taking a good, hearty swig now and then at the leather flask in a manner that might well have caused the biggest-bellied tavernkeeper of Málaga to envy him. Between draughts he gave not so much as a thought to any promise that his master might have made him, nor did he look upon it as any hardship, but rather as good sport, to go in quest of adventures however hazardous they might be.

The short of the matter is, they spent the night under some trees, from one of which Don Quixote tore off a withered bough to serve him as a lance, placing it in the lance head from which he had removed the broken one. He did not sleep all night long for thinking of his lady Dulcinea; for this was in accordance with what he had read in his books, of men of arms in the forest or desert places who kept a wakeful vigil, sustained by the memory of their ladies fair. Not so with Sancho, whose stomach was full, and not with chicory water. He fell into a dreamless slumber, and had not his master called him, he would not have been awakened either by the rays of the sun in his face or by the many birds who greeted the coming of the new day with their merry song.

Upon arising, he had another go at the flask, finding it somewhat more flaccid than it had been the night before, a circumstance which grieved his heart, for he could not see that they were on the way to remedying the deficiency within any very short space of time. Don Quixote did not wish any breakfast; for, as has been said, he was in the habit of nourishing himself on savorous memories. They then set out once more along the road to Puerto Lápice, and around three in the afternoon they came in sight of the pass that bears that name.

"There," said Don Quixote as his eyes fell upon it, "we may plunge our arms up to the elbow in what are known as adventures. But I must warn you that even though you see me in the greatest peril in the world, you are not to lay hand upon your sword to defend me, unless it be that

155

33. *St. Martin and the Beggar,* El Greco.

those who attack me are rabble and men of low degree, in which case you may very well come to my aid; but if they be gentlemen, it is in no wise permitted by the laws of chivalry that you should assist me until you yourself shall have been dubbed a knight."

"Most certainly, sir," replied Sancho, "your Grace shall be very well obeyed in this; all the more so for the reason that I myself am of a peaceful disposition and not fond of meddling in the quarrels and feuds of others. However, when it comes to protecting my own person, I shall not take account of those laws of which you speak, seeing that all laws, human and divine, permit each one to defend himself whenever he is attacked."

"I am willing to grant you that," assented Don Quixote, "but in this matter of defending me against gentlemen you must restrain your natural impulses."

"I promise you I shall do so," said Sancho. "I will observe this precept as I would the Sabbath day."

As they were conversing in this manner, there appeared in the road in front of them two friars of the Order of St. Benedict, mounted upon dromedaries—for the she-mules they rode were certainly no smaller than that. The friars wore travelers' spectacles and carried sunshades, and behind them came a coach accompanied by four or five men on horseback and a couple of muleteers on foot. In the coach, as was afterwards learned, was a lady of Biscay, on her way to Seville to bid farewell to her husband, who had been appointed to some high post in the Indies. The religious were not of her company although they were going by the same road.

The instant Don Quixote laid eyes upon them he turned to his squire. "Either I am mistaken or this is going to be the most famous adventure that ever was seen; for those black-clad figures that you behold must be, and without any doubt are, certain enchanters who are bearing with them a captive princess in that coach, and I must do all I can to right this wrong."

"It will be worse than the windmills," declared Sancho. "Look you, sir, those are Benedictine friars and the coach must be that of some travelers. Mark well what I say and what you do, lest the devil lead you astray."

"I have already told you, Sancho," replied Don Quixote, "that you know little where the subject of adventures is concerned. What I am saying to you is the truth, as you shall now see."

With this, he rode forward and took up a position in the middle of the road along which the friars were coming, and as soon as they appeared to be within earshot he cried out to them in a loud voice, "O devilish and monstrous beings, set free at once the highborn princesses whom you bear captive in that coach, or else prepare at once to meet your death as the just punishment of your evil deeds."

The friars drew rein and sat there in astonishment, marveling as much as Don Quixote's appearance as at the words he spoke. "Sir Knight," they answered him, "we are neither devilish nor monstrous but religious of the Order of St. Benedict who are merely going our way. We know nothing of those who are in that coach, nor of any captive princesses either."

"Soft words," said Don Quixote, "have no effect on me. I know you for what you are, lying rabble!" And without waiting for any further parley he gave spur to Rocinante and, with lowered lance, bore down upon the first friar with such fury and intrepidity that, had not the fellow tumbled from his mule of his own accord, he would have been hurled to the ground and either killed or badly wounded. The second religious, seeing how his companion had been treated, dug his legs into his she-mule's flanks and scurried away over the countryside faster than the wind.

Seeing the friar upon the ground, Sancho Panza slipped lightly from his mount and, falling upon him, began stripping him of his habit. The two mule drivers accompanying the religious thereupon came running up and asked Sancho why he was doing this. The latter replied that the friar's garments belonged to him as legitimate spoils of the battle that his master Don Quixote had just won. The muleteers, however, were lads with no sense of humor, nor did they know what all this talk of spoils and battles was about; but, perceiving that Don Quixote had ridden off to one side to converse with those inside the coach, they pounced upon Sancho, threw him to the ground, and proceeded to pull out the hair of his beard and kick him to a pulp, after which they went off and left him stretched out there, bereft at once of breath and sense.

Without losing any time, they then assisted the friar to remount. The good brother was trembling all over from fright, and there was not a speck of color in his face, but when he found himself in the saddle once more, he quickly spurred his beast to where his companion, at some little distance, sat watching and waiting to see what the result of the encounter would be. Having no curiosity as to the final outcome of the fray, the two of them now resumed their journey, making more signs of the cross than the devil would be able to carry upon his back.

Meanwhile Don Quixote, as we have said, was speaking to the lady in the coach.

"Your beauty, my lady, may now dispose of your person as best may please you, for the arrogance of your abductors lies upon the ground, overthrown by this good arm of mine; and in order that you may not pine to know the name of your liberator, I may inform you that I am Don Quixote de la Mancha, knight-errant and adventurer and captive of the peerless and beauteous Doña Dulcinea del Toboso. In payment of the favor which you have received from me, I ask nothing other than that you return to El Toboso and on my behalf pay your respects to this lady, telling her that it was I who set you free."

One of the squires accompanying those in the coach, a Biscayan, was listening to Don Quixote's words, and when he saw that the knight did not propose to let the coach proceed upon its way but was bent upon having it turn back to El Toboso, he promptly went up to him, seized his lance, and said to him in bad Castilian and worse Biscayan, "Go, *caballero,* and bad luck go with you; for by the God that created me, if you do not let this coach pass, me kill you or me no Biscayan."

Don Quixote heard him attentively enough and answered him very mildly, "If you were a *caballero,* which you are not, I should already have chastised you, wretched creature, for your foolhardiness and your impudence."

"Me no *caballero?*" cried the Biscayan. "Me swear to God, you lie like a Christian. If you will but lay aside your lance and unsheath your sword, you will soon see that you are carrying water to the cat! Biscayan on land, gentleman at sea, but a gentleman in spite of the devil, and you lie if you say otherwise."

" ' "You shall see as to that presently," said Agrajes,' " Don Quixote quoted. He cast his lance to the earth, drew his sword, and, taking his buckler on his arm, attacked the Biscayan with intent to slay him. The latter, when he saw his adversary approaching, would have liked to dismount from his mule, for she was one of the worthless sort that are let for hire and he had no confidence in her; but there was no time for this, and so he had no choice but to draw his own sword in turn and make the best of it. However, he was near enough to the coach to be able to snatch a cushion from it to serve him as a shield; and then they fell upon each other as though they were mortal enemies. The rest of those present sought to make peace between them but did not succeed, for the Biscayan with his disjointed phrases kept muttering that if they did not let him finish the battle then he himself would have to kill his mistress and anyone else who tried to stop him.

The lady inside the carriage, amazed by it all and trembling at what she saw, directed her coachman to drive on a little way; and there from a distance she watched the deadly combat, in the course of which the Biscayan came down with a great blow on Don Quixote's shoulder, over the top of the latter's shield, and had not the knight been clad in armor, it would have split him to the waist.

Feeling the weight of this blow, Don Quixote cried out, "O lady of my soul, Dulcinea, flower of beauty, succor this your champion who out of gratitude for your many favors finds himself in so perilous a plight!" To utter these words, lay hold of his sword, cover himself with his buckler, and attack the Biscayan was but the work of a moment; for he was now resolved to risk everything upon a single stroke.

As he saw Don Quixote approaching with so dauntless a bearing, the Biscayan was well aware of his adversary's courage and forthwith determined to imitate the example thus set him. He kept himself protected with his cushion, but he was unable to get his she-mule to budge to one side or the other, for the beast, out of sheer exhaustion and being, moreover, unused to such childish play, was incapable of taking a single step. And so, then, as has been stated, Don Quixote was approaching the wary Biscayan, his sword raised on high and with the firm resolve of cleaving his enemy in two; and the Biscayan was awaiting the knight in the same posture, cushion in front of him and with uplifted sword. All the bystanders were trembling with suspense at what would happen as a result of the terrible blows that were threatened, and the lady in the coach and her maids were making a thousand vows and offerings to all the images and shrines in Spain, praying that God would save them all and the lady's squire from this great peril that confronted them.

But the unfortunate part of the matter is that at this very point the author of the history breaks off and leaves the battle pending, excusing himself upon the ground that he has been unable to find anything else in writing concerning the exploits of Don Quixote beyond those already set forth. It is true, on the other hand, that the second author of this work could not bring himself to believe that so unusual a chronicle would have been consigned to oblivion, nor that the learned ones of La Mancha were possessed of so little curiosity as not to be able to discover in their archives or registry offices certain papers that have to do with this famous knight. Being convinced of this, he did not despair of coming upon the end of this pleasing story, and Heaven favoring him, he did find it, as shall be related in the second part.

(from *Don Quixote*)

THE KNIGHT OF LA MANCHA

In the first part of this history we left the valorous Biscayan and the famous Don Quixote with swords unsheathed and raised aloft, about to let fall furious slashing blows which, had they been delivered fairly and squarely, would at the very least have split them in two and laid them wide open from top to bottom like a pomegranate; and it was at this doubtful point that the pleasing chronicle came to a halt and broke off, without the author's informing us as to where the rest of it might be found.

I was deeply grieved by such a circumstance, and the pleasure I had had in reading so slight a portion was turned into annoyance as I thought of how difficult it would be to come upon the greater part which it seemed to me must still be missing. It appeared impossible and contrary to all good precedent that so worthy a knight should not have had some scribe to take upon himself the task of writing an account of these unheard-of exploits; for that was something that had happened to none of the knights-errant who, as the saying has it, had gone forth in quest of adventures, seeing that each of them had one or two chroniclers, as if ready at hand, who not only had set down their deeds, but had depicted their most trivial thoughts and amiable weaknesses, however well concealed they might be. The good knight of La Mancha surely could not have been so unfortunate as to have lacked what Platir and others like him had in abundance. And so I could not bring myself to believe that this gallant history could have remained thus lopped off and mutilated, and I could not but lay the blame upon the malignity of time, that devourer and consumer of all things, which must either have consumed it or kept it hidden.

On the other hand, I reflected that inasmuch as among the knight's books had been found such modern works as *The Disenchantments of Jealousy* and *The Nymphs and Shepherds of Henares*, his story likewise must be modern, and that even though it might not have been written down, it must remain in the memory of the good folk of his village and the surrounding ones. This thought left me somewhat confused and more than ever desirous of knowing the real and true story, the whole story, of the life and wondrous deeds of our famous Spaniard, Don Quixote, light and mirror of the chivalry of La Mancha, the first in our age and in these calamitous times to devote himself to the hardships and exercises of knight-errantry and to go about righting wrongs, succoring widows, and protecting damsels—damsels such as those who, mounted upon their palfreys and with riding-whip in hand, in full possession of their virginity, were in the habit of going from mountain to mountain and from valley to valley; for unless there were some villain, some rustic with an ax and hood, or some monstrous giant to force them, there were in times past maiden ladies who at the end of eighty years, during all which time they had not slept for a single day beneath a roof, would go to their graves as virginal as when their mothers had borne them.

If I speak of these things, it is for the reason that in this and in all other respects our gallant Quixote is deserving of constant memory and praise, and even I am not to be denied my share of it for my diligence and the labor to which I put myself in searching out the conclusion of this agreeable narrative; although if heaven, luck, and circumstance had not aided me, the world would have had to do without the pleasure and the pastime which anyone may enjoy who will read this work attentively for an hour or two. The manner in which it came about was as follows:

I was standing one day in the Alcaná, or market place, of Toledo when a lad came up to sell some old notebooks and other papers to a silk weaver who was there. As I am extremely fond of reading anything, even though it be but the scraps of paper in the streets, I followed my natural inclination and took one of the books, whereupon I at once perceived that it was written in characters which I recognized as Arabic. I recognized them, but reading them was another thing; and so I began looking around to see if there was any Spanish-speaking Moor near by who would be able to read them for me. It was not very hard to find such an interpreter, nor would it have been even if the tongue in question had been an older and a better one. To make a long story short, chance brought a fellow my way; and when I told him what it was I wished and placed the book in his hands he opened it in the middle and began reading and at once fell to laughing. When I asked him what the cause of his laughter was, he replied that it was a note which had been written in the margin.

I besought him to tell me the content of the note, and he, laughing still, went on, "As I told you, it is something in the margin here: 'Thi

Dulcinea del Toboso, so often referred to, is said to have been the best hand at salting pigs of any woman in all La Mancha.' "

No sooner had I heard the name Dulcinea del Toboso than I was astonished and held in suspense, for at once the thought occurred to me that those notebooks must contain the history of Don Quixote. With this in mind I urged him to read me the title, and he proceeded to do so, turning the Arabic into Castilian upon the spot: *History of Don Quixote de la Mancha, Written by Cid Hamete Benengeli, Arabic Historian.* It was all I could do to conceal my satisfaction and, snatching them from the silk weaver, I bought from the lad all the papers and notebooks that he had for half a real; but if he had known or suspected how very much I wanted them, he might well have had more than six reals for them.

The Moor and I then betook ourselves to the cathedral cloister, where I requested him to translate for me into the Castilian tongue all the books that had to do with Don Quixote, adding nothing and subtracting nothing; and I offered him whatever payment he desired. He was content with two arrobas of raisins and two fanegas of wheat and promised to translate them well and faithfully and with all dispatch. However, in order to facilitate matters, and also because I did not wish to let such a find as this out of my hands, I took the fellow home with me, where in a little more than a month and a half he translated the whole of the work just as you will find it set down here.

In the first of the books there was a very lifelike picture of the battle between Don Quixote and the Biscayan, the two being in precisely the same posture as described in the history, their swords upraised, the one covered by his buckler, the other with his cushion. As for the Biscayan's mule, you could see at the distance of a crossbow shot that it was one for hire. Beneath the Biscayan there was a rubric which read: "Don Sancho de Azpeitia," which must undoubtedly have been his name; while beneath the feet of Rocinante was another inscription: "Don Quixote." Rocinante was marvelously portrayed: so long and lank, so lean and flabby, so extremely consumptive-looking that one could well understand the justness and propriety with which the name of "hack" had been bestowed upon him.

Alongside Rocinante stood Sancho Panza, holding the halter of his ass, and below was the legend: "Sancho Zancas." The picture showed him with a big belly, a short body, and long shanks, and that must have been where he got the names of Panza y Zancas by which he is a number of times called in the course of the history. There are other small details that might be mentioned, but they are of little importance and have nothing to do with the truth of the story—and no story is bad so long as it is true.

If there is any objection to be raised against the veracity of the present one, it can be only that the author was an Arab, and the nation is known for its lying propensities; but even though they be our enemies, it may readily be understood that they would more likely have detracted from, rather than added to, the chronicle. So it seems to me, at any rate; for whenever he might and should deploy the resources of his pen in praise of so worthy a knight, the author appears to take pains to pass over the matter in silence; all of which in my opinion is ill done and ill conceived, for it should be the duty of historians to be exact, truthful, and dispassionate, and neither interest nor fear nor rancor nor affection should swerve them from the path of truth, whose mother is history, rival of time, depository of deeds, witness of the past, exemplar and adviser to the present, and the future's counselor. In this work, I am sure, will be found all that could be desired in the way of pleasant reading; and if it is lacking in any way, I maintain that this is the fault of that hound of an author rather than of the subject.

But to come to the point, the second part, according to the translation, began as follows:

As the two valorous and enraged combatants stood there, swords upraised and poised on high, it seemed from their bold mien as if they must surely be threatening heaven, earth, and hell itself. The first to let fall a blow was the choleric Biscayan, and he came down with such force and fury that, had not his sword been deflected in mid-air, that single stroke would have sufficed to put an end to this fearful combat and to all our knight's adventures at the same time; but fortune, which was reserving him for greater things, turned aside his adversary's blade in such a manner that, even though it fell upon his left shoulder, it did him no other damage than to strip him completely of his armor on that side, carrying with it a good part of his helmet along with half an ear, the headpiece clattering to the ground with a dreadful din, leaving its wearer in a sorry state.

Heaven help me! Who could properly describe the rage that now entered the heart of our hero of La Mancha as he saw himself treated in this fashion? It may merely be said that he once more reared himself in the stirrups, laid hold of his sword with both hands, and dealt the

Biscayan such a blow, over the cushion and upon the head, that, even so good a defense proving useless, it was as if a mountain had fallen upon his enemy. The latter now began bleeding through the mouth, nose, and ears; he seemed about to fall from his mule, and would have fallen, no doubt, if he had not grasped the beast about the neck, but at that moment his feet slipped from the stirrups and his arms let go, and the mule, frightened by the terrible blow, began running across the plain, hurling its rider to the earth with a few quick plunges.

Don Quixote stood watching all this very calmly. When he saw his enemy fall, he leaped from his horse, ran over very nimbly, and thrust the point of his sword into the Biscayan's eyes, calling upon him at the same time to surrender or otherwise he would cut off his head. The Biscayan was so bewildered that he was unable to utter a single word in reply, and things would have gone badly with him, so blind was Don Quixote in his rage, if the ladies of the coach, who up to then had watched the struggle in dismay, had not come up to him at this point and begged him with many blandishments to do them the very great favor of sparing their squire's life.

To which Don Quixote replied with much haughtiness and dignity, "Most certainly, lovely ladies, I shall be very happy to do that which you ask of me, but upon one condition and understanding, and that is that this knight promise me that he will go to El Toboso and present himself in my behalf before Doña Dulcinea, in order that she may do with him as she may see fit."

Trembling and disconsolate, the ladies did not pause to discuss Don Quixote's request, but without so much as inquiring who Dulcinea might be they promised him that the squire would fulfill that which was commanded of him.

"Very well, then, trusting in your word, I will do him no further harm, even though he has well deserved it."

(from Don Quixote)

FRANÇOIS RABELAIS

FROM GARGANTUA AND PANTAGRUEL

The Author's Prologue
Hail, O Most Valiant and Illustrious Drinkers! Your health, my

precious pox-ridden comrades! To you alone, I dedicate my writings. Suffer me, therefore to draw your attention to a dialogue of Plato's called *The Banquet*.

In this work, Alcibiades, praising his master Socrates (undoubtedly the prince of philosophers) happens, among other things, to liken him to sileni.

Sileni, in the days of yore, were small boxes such as you may see nowadays at your apothecary's. They were named for Silenus, foster-father to Bacchus. The outside of these boxes bore gay, fantastically painted figures of harpies, satyrs, bridled geese, hares with gigantic horns, saddled ducks, winged goats in flight, harts in harness and many other droll fancies. They were pleasurably devised to inspire just the sort of laughter Silenus, Bacchus' master, inspired.

But inside these sileni, people kept priceless drugs such as balsam of Mecca, ambergris from the sperm whale, amomum from the cardamon, musk from the deer and civet from the civet's arsehole—not to mention various sorts of precious stones, used for medical purposes, and other invaluable possessions.

Well, Alcibiades likened Socrates to these boxes, because, judging by his exterior, you would not have given an onion skin for him. He was ill-shaped, ridiculous in carriage, with a nose like a knife, the gaze of a bull and the face of a fool. His ways stamped him a simpleton, his clothes a bumpkin. Poor in fortune, unlucky when it came to women, hopelessly unfit for all office in the republic, forever laughing, forever drinking neck to neck with his friends, forever hiding his divine knowledge under a mask of mockery. . . .

Yet had you opened this box, you would have found in it all sorts of priceless, celestial drugs: immortal understanding, wondrous virtue, indomitable courage, unparalleled sobriety, unfailing serenity, perfect assurance and a heroic contempt for whatever moves humanity to watch, to bustle, to toil, to sail ships overseas and to engage in warfare.

Alcibiades? Socrates? The sileni? Why all this introductory flourish? Let me explain to you only, O my beloved disciples, and to such other idlers and idiots as read my works. Having noted the flippant titles of certain books of my invention—*Gargantua, Pantagruel, Drownbottle, The Dignity of Codpieces and Trouserflies, Of Peas and Bacon, with Tables and Sauce Material, etc.*—you jump to the conclusion that these tomes are filled with mere jests, vulgarities and buffoonery. Alas! you leap at the outward and visible sign; you swallow the title in a spirit of levity and derision without pausing to make further inquiry. How unseemly to consider so frivolously the works of humankind! Is it you who profess that clothes do not make the man nor robes the monk? Do I quote you when I declare that a fellow most monasterially apparelled may turn out to be a downright infidel whereas another, draped in a Spanish cloak, may possess every virtue on earth except Castilian pride and daring? Well then, you see why you should look beyond my title, open my book and seriously weigh its subject matter. The spice secreted within the box is more precious, far, than its exterior promised. In other words, the topics treated are not so foolish as the title suggested at first hand.

.   .   .

How Gargamelle, Bigswoln with Gargantua, ate an Abundance of Tripe.

The occasion and manner of Gargamelle's delivery were as I am about to relate; if you do not believe me, may your vent-peg slip, may your stopper fail your (rectal) organ, your fundament fall and your flue pipe collapse!

This is exactly what happened to Gargamelle, on February third, after dinner. And why? Because she had eaten too abundantly of tripe . . . of that tripe which comes from beeves . . . from beeves which are fatted in their stalls and put to graze in meadows . . . in meadows which bear two crops of grass each year. . . .

Three hundred and sixty-seven thousand and fourteen of these fat beeves had been slaughtered. They were to be salted on Shrove Tuesday so that there would be pressed beef aplenty that spring for the invocation of thirst and its subsequent exorcization by wine.

There was abundance of tripe, as you may imagine, such succulent tripe, too, that every one licked his fingers with glee. But there was a rub—and a four-devil power rub at that! Alas, the tripe could not be kept on hand long or it would spoil—a most disagreeable thought! They therefore decided to guzzle it all down to the last scrap. For fear of leaving any, they summoned all the citizenry of Sinais, Seuilly, La Roche Chermault and Vaugaudry, without forgetting their friends from Coudray-Montpensier and Gué de Vède and other neighbors, all accomplished tosspots, debonair fellows and ha! fine cuedrivers, skilled tailpushers, all!

That dear man Grangousier, mightily pleased at their company, ordered meat by the ton, wine by the thousand gallons. No pains were spared to honor his guests. But he *did* caution his wife to eat sparingly, since she was near her time, and in her condition tripe was not exactly the most suitable diet.

"Whoever eats the skins of these chitterlings," he announced, "is an unparalleled turdchewer!"

Despite his warnings, Gargamelle consumed sixteen quarters, two bushels and six pecks; in cases, barrels and pots. La! the sweet fecality that must have swelled up within her!

After dinner, they all made helter-skelter for La Saussaie, a meadow planted with willow trees. Here, on the soft greensward, they danced so gleefully to the tune of airy flutes and melodious bagpipes that to watch them was a most heavenly pastime.

.   .   .

A few moments later she began to groan, lament and cry out. Suddenly crowds of midwives came rushing up from all directions. Feeling and groping her below, they found certain loose shreds of skin, of a rather unsavory odor, which they took to be the child. It was, on the contrary, her fundament which had escaped with the mollification of her right intestine (you call it the bùmgut) because she had eaten too much tripe, as I explained above.

Thereupon, a grimy old baggage of the company, who had come from Brisepaille near St. Genou threescore years before, and was reputed to be a great she-physician, administered an astringent. So horrible was this restrictive medicine that it obstructed and contracted the sphincters of Gargamelle's vents and flues, until you could barely have pried them open with your teeth. A truly revolting thought, this, but one suggested by the story of the Devil at St. Martin's Mass noting down the chatter of two trollops and with his teeth stretching the parchment he wrote on, in a vain effort to keep up with them.

As a result of Gargamelle's discomfort, the cotyledons of the placenta of her matrix were enlarged. The child, leaping through the breech and entering the hollow vein, ascended through her diaphragm to a point above her shoulders. Here the vein divides into two; the child accordingly worked his way in a sinistral direction, to issue, finally, through the left ear.

No sooner born, he did not, like other babes, cry: "Whaay! Whaay!" but in a full, loud voice bawled: "Drink, drink, drink!" as though inviting the company to fall to. What is more, he shouted so lustily that

4. *The Garden of Delights*, Hieronymus Bosch. Center panel.

he was heard throughout the regions of Beuxe (pronounced "booze") and Bibarois, (which in sound evokes bibbers and is how the Gascons pronounce "Vivarais").

Now I suspect that you do not thoroughly believe this strange nativity. If you do not, I care but little, though an honest and sensible man always believes what he is told and what he finds written. Does not Solomon say in *Proverbs* (XIII, 15): "*Innocens credit omni verbo,* the innocent believeth every word," and does not St. Paul (*I Corinthians,* 13) declare: "*Charitas omnia credit,* Charity believeth all."

Why should you not believe what I tell you? Because, you reply, there is no evidence. And I reply in turn that for this very reason you should believe with perfect faith. For the gentlemen of the Sorbonne say that faith is the argument of non-evident truths.

Is anything I have related beyond our law or faith, contrary to our reason, or opposed to Divine Scriptures? For my part, I find nothing in the Holy Bible that stands against it. And if such had been the will of God, would you affirm that He could not accomplish it? Ha, I pray you, do not ambiguembrangle your minds with such vain conceits. I tell you that nothing is impossible to God and, if He but pleased, women would henceforth give birth to their children through the left ear.

Was not Bacchus engendered out of the very thigh of Jupiter? Was not Roquetaillade or Cleftrock ushered into the world through his mother's heel? Did not Croquemouche or Craunchfly first see the light out of his nurse's slipper? Was not Minerva progenerated out of the brain and through the ear of Jupiter? Was not the bark of a myrrh tree brought to bed of Adonis? And did not an eggshell, laid and hatched by Leda, extravasate Castor and Pollux into being?

You would be infinitely more surprised and stunned were I presently to expose to you the entire chapter in which Pliny deals with fantastic and unnatural births, yet I am not nearly so accomplished a liar as he was. Read his *Natural History,* Book VII, Chapter III, yourselves and do not plague me further with the subject.

.   .   .

*How Gargantua came by his Name and how he
Swilled Down the Wine.*

That excellent man Grangousier was drinking and making merry with the others, when he heard a horrible tumult. It was his son emerging into the light of this world, bellowing, "Drink, drink, drink!"

At once Grangousier exclaimed: *"Que grand tu as le gousier"* or "What a great gullet you have!" Hearing this, the company declared that the child should indeed be named *"grand tu as"*: Gargantua or Great-gullet. Were these not the first sounds the father had uttered after the child's birth? And was this not an ancient Hebrew custom well worth following? Grangousier assented; Gargamelle was delighted with the idea.

Next, to quiet the babe, they made him drink till his throat almost burst. Then, carrying him to the font, they baptized him, as is the custom among all good Christians.

Shortly after, they appointed seventeen thousand nine hundred and thirteen cows from Pontille and Bréhémont to furnish him with milk in ordinary, for, considering his enormous needs, it was impossible to find a satisfactory nurse in all the country. Nevertheless, certain learned doctors, disciples of Duns Scotus, have affirmed that his own mother suckled him. She could, they say, draw from her breasts two thousand one hundred and three hogsheads and eighteen pints at one time. This seems scarcely probable. Indeed, this point has been condemned by the Sorbonne as mammarily scandalous and reeking with heresy.

Gargantua was thus looked after until he was twenty-two months old. Then, on the advice of the physicians, they began to carry him, and Jean Denyau built a special ox-drawn cart for him. They drove him about in it here, there and everywhere with the greatest pleasure; and a fine sight he was, too, with a great, open face and almost eighteen chins! He cried very little but he beshitted himself at all times. For he was wondrously phlegmatic of bum, as much by natural complexion as from an accidental predisposition, due to exaggerated quaffing of the juices of Septembral mash. Yet he never touched a drop without good reason; for whenever he happened to be out of sorts, vexed, angry or melancholy, if he stamped, wept or shouted, they brought him a drink. This invariably restored his native good humor and at once made him as quiet and happy as before.

One of his governesses told me on oath what a rooted habit this tippling had become. Indeed, the mere clinking of pints and flagons sent him off into the ecstasy of one who tastes the joys of Paradise. Accordingly, in view of this divine character, they used to delight him every morning by making music on glasses with knives, on bottles with their stoppers, and on pots with their lids. At this he would turn gay, thrill with joy, wag his head and rock from side to side, monochording with his fingers and barytoning through his tail.

.   .   .

How Gargantua was Taught Latin by a Theologian and Sophist.

The excellent Grangousier was rapt with admiration as he listened to his son talking. Truly this lad was marvellously gifted! What a vast intelligence, what cogent understanding! Turning to the governesses:

"Philip, King of Macedon," he declared, "recognized the sound judgment of Alexander, his son, when he saw how skilfully the lad managed his horse. This beast Bucephalus was so fierce and unruly that it threw all its riders. It cracked one man's neck, smashed another's legs, brained a third, and crushed the jawbone of a fourth. No one, then, dared mount it. Alexander happened to be in the hippodrome watching them breaking in and training the horses; he noticed at once that the beast's frenzy came from fright at its own shadow. He therefore made short shrift of vaulting upon its back and heading it towards the sun. There, its shadow falling behind it, he easily mastered it. Philip, by this token, realized the divine insight rooted in his son's intelligence and had him most carefully reared by Aristotle, then the most renowned philosopher in Greece.

"For my part, the brief conversation I have just had with Gargantua in your presence suffices to convince me that his mind is illumined by the divine spark. How else, pray, could he have proved so acute, so subtle, so profound and withal so serene? Give the boy proper schooling, say I, and he will attain a supreme degree of wisdom! Accordingly, I intend to trust him to some scholar who will instruct him to his capacity. What is more, I shall spare no cost."

The name of Master Tubal Holofernes, a great sophist and Doctor of Theology, was proposed to Grangousier. Subsequently this savant taught Gargantua his A B C so thoroughly that he could say it by heart backwards. This took five years and three months. A succession of standard texts followed; the *Facet* (a treatise of puerile moral precepts) the *Ars Grammatica* of Actius Donatus, the fourth-century grammarian; the *Theodolet* (in which Theodulus, Bishop of Syria in the fifth century, exposed in Latin the falsity of mythology and the truth of Holy Scripture) and the *Alanus in Parabolis* (a series of moral quatrains by Alanus of Lille, a thirteenth-century worthy). It took Gargantua thirteen years, six months and two weeks to master these authorities.

It is only fair to add, however, that Gargantua, in the process, learned to write in Gothic characters. (Printing had not yet been invented and the young student had to write out his own texts.)

He had, therefore, to carry in front of him a tremendous writing apparatus that weighed more than seven hundred thousand pounds. The pencase was as large and as tall as the great columns of the Church of St. Martin of Ainay in Lyons; the inkhorn was suspended to it by great iron chains wide enough to hold five cubic yards of merchandise.

Another book, *De Modis Significandi*—a work of speculative grammar by Thomas Aquinas, or Albert of Saxony or probably Duns Scotus—was Gargantua's next reading, together with comments by Hurtebize or Windjammer, by Fasquin or Roadheaver, by Tropditeux or Toomany-such, by Gualehault or Galahad, by Jean Le Veau or John Calf, by Billonio or Lickspittle, by Brelinguandus or Timeserver, and by a rabble of others. This took more than eighteen years and eleven months, but Gargantua knew the texts so well that at examinations he could recite them by heart backwards. And he could prove to his mother on his fingers' ends that *de modis significandi non erat scientia,* grammar was no science.

Next he read the *Compost* or *Popular Calendar,* and had spent sixteen years and two months at it, when suddenly, in 1420, his tutor died of the pox.

Holofernes' successor was another wheezy old pedant named Master Jobelin Bridé or Jolter Clotpoll, who read him the *Liber Derivationum* or *Latin Vocabulary* of Hugutio of Pisa, thirteenth-century Bishop of Ferrara . . . the *Grecism* by Everard de Béthune, a philological lexicon illustrating the Latin words derived from the Greek . . . *De Octo Partibus Orationis* or *Of the Eight Parts of Speech* . . . the *Quid Est?* or *What is it?* a school manual in the form of questions and answers . . . the *Supplementum,* a collection of commentaries . . . the *Mammotreptus,* a monkish or monkeyish commentary on the Psalter and the Saints . . . the *Libellus de Moribus in Mensa Servandis* or *Essay on Manners in Serving at Table,* a rhymed treatise on youthful propriety and morals by Sulpizio de Veroli . . . Seneca's *De Quatuor Virtutibus Cardinalibus* or *Of the Four Cardinal Virtues,* a moral work by Martin de Braga, Bishop of Mondonedo in the sixth century . . . the *Specchio della vera Penitenza* or *Mirror of True Penitence* by Jacobo Passaventi, the Florentine monk of the sixteenth century—with its inevitable commentary! . . . a book of sermons, *Dormi Secure* or *Sleep in Peace,* a collection designed to save the preacher the pains of composing his sermons . . . and finally, other stuff of the same ilk, feather, kidney and broth. . . .

Indeed, Gargantua grew as even as any down ever smoothed, as full of matter as any goose liver ever crammed!

· · ·

How Gargantua ate Six Pilgrims in a Salad.

We must now relate what happened to six pilgrims who were returning from St. Sebastien-d'Aigne, near Nantes. Afraid of the enemy, they sought shelter that night in the garden, crouched among the cabbage, lettuce and peas.

Gargantua, being somewhat thirsty, asked for some lettuce salad. When they told him the lettuce in that garden was the greatest and finest in the land (some heads were tall as plum trees or walnut trees) he determined to pick it himself. Plucking what he thought good, he also carried off in the hollow of his hand the six pilgrims, who were too terrified to cough, let alone to speak.

While Gargantua was washing the heads of lettuce in the fountain, the pilgrims plucked up their courage and held a whispered consultation.

"What can we do?"

"We're drowning in all this lettuce!"

"Dare we speak?"

"If we speak, he'll kill us for spies."

Amid their deliberations, Gargantua put them with the lettuce in a bowl of Grangousier's large as the tun at the Abbey of Cîteaux, in Burgundy, a fine huge cask reputed to hold three hundred hogsheads. Then he doused the leaves (and pilgrims) with salt, vinegar and oil, and, for refreshment before supper, began to eat. He had already swallowed five pilgrims and the sixth lay under a leaf, completely invisible save for his staff, when Grangousier pointed to the latter.

"Look, Gargantua, that's a snail's horn. Don't eat it!"

"Why not? Snails are good this month."

Picking up staff and pilgrim, he swallowed them neat, then drank a terrific draught of red Burgundy while awaiting his supper.

The pilgrims thus devoured crept out of his gullet as best they could, avoiding the millstones of his teeth. They believed they had been cast into the pit of the lowest dungeon in a prison. When Gargantua downed his wine, they all but drowned; the crimson torrent almost swept them down again into the abyss of his belly. However, leaping on their staffs as the Mont St. Michel pilgrims do, they found shelter in the chinks between his teeth. Unhappily one of them, sounding the lay of the land with his staff to ascertain its safety, struck hard into the cavity of a sore tooth and hit the mandibulary nerve. Gargantua screamed with pain, then, for relief, reached for his toothpick. Strolling out towards the great walnut tree in the garden, he proceeded to dislodge our six gentlemen

35. *Land of Cockaigne*, Pieter Brueghel.

pilgrims. He jerked one out by the legs, another by the shoulders, a third by his scrip, a fourth by his pouch, a fifth by his neckerchief and the last, the poor devil who had hurt him, he pulled out by the codpiece. This turned out to be a piece of great good fortune for the pilgrim, since Gargantua in the process broke a chancre that had been torturing him since they left Ancenis on the Loire.

The pilgrims, thus dislodged, scurried away, at top speed. Gargantua's toothache subsided, just as Eudemon announced dinner.

"Very well," said Gargantua. "I shall piss away my misfortune."

Which he proceeded to do so copiously that the pilgrims' road was washed away and they were forced to wade through this vast, foamy salt lake. Skirting a small wood, all but Fournillier were swept off their feet into a trap set for wolves. But they finally escaped, thanks to the industry of Fournillier, who broke all the snares and ropes. Free once again, they spent the rest of the night in a hut near Le Coudray, where they drew comfort in their misfortune from the words of one of their number, Lasdaller or Dogweary, who reminded them that this adventure had been foretold by the prophet David in his *Psalms*.

Cum exergerent homines in nos, forte vivos deglutissent nos, then had they swallowed us up when their wrath was kindled against us (in other words, when we were eaten in salad with salt, oil and vinegar) . . . *cum*

irascaretur furore eorum in tuos forsitan aqua absorbuisset nos, then the
waters had overwhelmed us, the stream gone over our soul (that was
when he took the deep draught of wine) . . . *forsitan pertransisset anima
nostra aquam intolerabilem,* then the proud waters had gone over our
soul (that was when he took the piss!) . . . *Benedictus Dominus qui non
dedit in captionem dentibus eorum,* blessed be the Lord who hath not
not given us as a prey to their teeth (alas, the mandibulary nerve we
struck!) . . . *Anima nostra sicut passer erepta est de laqueo venantium,*
our soul is escaped as a bird out of the snare of the fowlers (when we fell
into the trap!) . . . *laqueus contritus est a Fournillier et nos liberati
sumus,* the snare is broken by Fournillier and we are escaped . . . *Ad-
jutorum nostrum,* etc.; Our help is in the name of The Lord, etc.

·   ·   ·

Why Monks are Pariahs and why some have Bigger Noses than Others.

"By my faith as a Christian," said Eudemon, "I wonder and marvel as
I consider this friar's excellence. God bless the honest fellow, for he delights us all! How then can you explain that any decent company ex-
cludes monks? Why are they considered death's heads? Why do we drive
them from our midst as bees drive drones far from their hives? Recall
old Maro's *Georgics:*

> *Ignavum fucos pecus a praesipibus arcent*
> *Drive in the drones, lazy herd, from the field."*

Gargantua interposed:
"Frock and cowl obviously attract opprobrium, insult and malediction
as surely as the wind Cecias, from the northeast, attracts the clouds. My
Lords Aristotle, Pliny, Gellius and Erasmus vouch for my climatology.
Do you know the peremptory reason why humanity eschews monks? I'll
tell you: it's because they eat the turds of the world, or, if you prefer, because they batten upon the sins of the people. That is pretty disgusting!
Can you wonder, therefore, that they are banished to the privies—or, as
they call them, convents and monasteries? Are we wrong to cut them off
from our polite intercourse? If so, then let us place our lavatories next
to our dining rooms.
"Take the ape. Can you explain why a monkey is invariably scoffed
at and teased? Well then, you understand why monks are invariably given
wide room by old and young. The monkey does not watch the house like

a dog, draw the plow like the ox, yield milk like the cow or give wool like the sheep, nor, let me add, bear burdens like the horse. What, pray, does he do? He spills shit over everything and befouls it: there lies the reason for the mockery and beatings we allot him.

"By the same token, take a monk, I mean a lazy, timeserving monklet. He does not plow like the peasant, defend his country like the soldier, heal the sick like the doctor, preach and elevate like the teacher, nor, let me add, handle essential commodities like the merchant. Very good: there lies the reason for the hatred and revulsion we allot him!"

"One moment!" Grangousier broke in. "Monks pray to God on our behalf!"

"Right!" Gargantua conceded. "They make life hideous everywhere with their eternal jangling of bells!"

"But a mass, a matin, a vesper well rung are already half said," Friar John protested.

"They mumble a quantity of litanies and psalms which they do not begin to understand. Automatically and without the slightest comprehension, they say countless paternosters, interlarded with interminable aves. I call that flouting God, not worshipping Him. I will go further. So help me God, if they pray for us, do you know why? Because they're terrified of losing their white bread and savory stews. All true Christians of all classes and conditions always and everywhere send up their prayers to the Creator; the Holy Spirit intercedes on their behalf and God is gracious to them. Now Friar John of the Funnels is just such a Christian; therefore we welcome him in our midst and prize him. Is he a bigot or dissenter? No—Friar John is downright, straightforward, happy, merry, and good company. He works hard, defends the oppressed, comforts the afflicted, succors the ailing and guards the abbey's close."

"I do more," said the monk. "Let me tell you. While we are dispatching our matins and memorial masses in the choir, I am also busy making crossbow strings, polishing arrows, cleaning weapons, lacing nets and snares to catch rabbits. By God, I am not idle one second of the livelong day. . . . But ho there! fill my glass, pour on! And pass me some fruit. Cheers! here are chestnuts from Estroc near Fontenay and a brisk new wine to wash them down with. Bottoms up, lads, and that liquor will make your bums produce an Oratorio. You are not yet half-shot; by God! like a horse in heat, I drink at all fords."

"Suppose, my dear Friar," Gymnastes ventured, "you wipe the snot dangling from your nostrils?"

"Pooh!" the monk countered. "Must I drown because there's water over my mouth? A thousand times no. *Quare? quia?* wherefore and how? Water drips out, granted: but have you seen any go in? And why not? Because, my friends, wine acts as antidote. A man with winter boots of that leather can fish for oysters with impunity: no water will leak *in!*"

"Why has Friar John of the Funnels such a beautiful nose?" Gargantua asked the company.

"Because God wills it so," Grangousier explained. "God moulds us like a potter his vessels in such shape and to such an end as please His divine judgment."

"Because," Ponocrates explained, "Friar John was among the first to reach the Nose Market. He therefore chose the biggest and the most handsome."

"Pooh!" cried the monk, "go further into it. True monastical philosophy can prove the point. My nose is large because my wetnurse had billowy soft milkers; when she gave me suck, my nostrils sank into them as into butter. Hard bubs make pug-nosed children. But la, la! *ad formam nasi cognoscitur* . . . *ad te levavi,* by their noses shall ye know them . . . unto Thee lift I up mine noselike erection. . . .

"I loathe sweet things; jam is for others. Page, bring me liquor now and food, to boot."

.   .   .

How Pantagruel in Paris received a Letter from his Father Gargantua.

As you may suppose, Pantagruel studied very hard and profited much by his study, for his intelligence was naturally active and his memory as full as twelve casks of olives. While in Paris, he received the following letter from his father:

My beloved Son,

Among the gifts, graces and prerogatives with which our sovereign Creator, God Almighty, blessed and enriched humanity from the beginning, there is one that I deem supreme. By its means, though we be mortal, we can yet achieve a sort of immortality; through it, we may, in the course of our transitory lives, yet perpetuate our name and race.

To be sure, what we gain by a progeny born of lawful wedlock cannot make up for what we lost through the sin of our first parents. Adam and Eve disobeyed the commandments of the Lord their God: mortality was

*their punishment. By death the magnificent mould in which Man was
fashioned vanished into the dust of oblivion.*

*However, thanks to seminal propagation, what a man loses his children
revive and, where they fail, their children prevail. So it has gone, and so
it shall be, from generation to generation, until the Day of Judgment,
when Christ shall restore to God the Father his kingdom pacified, secured and cleansed of all sin. Then all generation and corruption shall
cease, for the elements will have completed their continuous transmuta-
tions. The peace humanity has craved so anxiously will have been attained; all things will have been reduced to their appointed end and
period.*

*I therefore have reason to give thanks to God, my Saviour, for having
granted me the joy of beholding my old age blossom anew in your youth.
When, by His pleasure, which rules and orders everything, my soul must
abandon this human habitation, I shall not believe I am dying utterly,
but rather passing from one place to another. For in you my visible image
will continue to live on earth; by you, I shall go on frequenting honorable men and true friends, as I was wont to do.*

*My associations have not been without sin, I confess. We all transgress
and must continually beseech God to forgive us our trespasses. But they
have been without reproach in the eyes of men.*

*That is why if, beside my bodily image, my soul did not likewise shine
in you, you would not be accounted worthy of guarding the precious immortality of my name. In that case, the least part of me (my body) would
endure. Scant satisfaction, that, when the best part (my soul, which should
keep my name blessed among men) had degenerated and been bastard-
ized. I say this not through any doubt as to your virtue, which I have
already often tested, but to encourage you to go on doing ever better and
profiting by your constant improvement.*

*My purpose is not so much to keep you absolutely on your present
virtuous course as to make you rejoice that you have kept and are keeping on it. I seek to quicken your heart with resolutions for the future. To
help you make and carry these out, remember that I have spared nothing.
I have helped you as though my sole treasure on earth were once in my
lifetime to see you well-bred and accomplished in honesty and valor as
well as in knowledge and civility. Ay, I have longed to leave you after my
death as a mirror of your father's personality. The reflection may not
prove perfect in practice, but certainly I could not more studiously wish
for its perfection.*

My late father Grangousier, of blessed memory, made every effort that I might achieve mental, moral and technical excellence. The fruit of my studies and labors matched, indeed surpassed, his dearest wish. But you can realize that conditions were not as favorable to learning as they are today. Nor had I such gifted teachers as you. We were still in the dark ages; we still walked in the shadow of the dark clouds of ignorance; we suffered the calamitous consequences of the destruction of good literature by the Goths. Now, by God's grace, light and dignity have been restored to letters, and I have lived to see it. Indeed, I have watched such a revolution in learning that I, not erroneously reputed in my manhood the leading scholar of the century, would find it difficult to enter the bottom class in a grammar school.

I tell you all this not through boastfulness, though in writing to you I might be proud with impunity. Does not Marcus Tullius authorize it in his book Of Old Age, *and Plutarch in* How a Man May Praise Himself Without Envy? *Both authors recognize that such pride is useful in fostering the spirit of emulation. No—I do it simply to give you a proof of my love and affection.*

To-day, the old sciences are revived, knowledge is systematized, discipline reëstablished. The learned languages are restored: Greek, without which a man would be ashamed to consider himself educated; Hebrew, Chaldean and Latin. Printing is now in use, an art so accurate and elegant that it betrays the divine inspiration of its discovery, which I have lived to witness. Alas! Conversely, I was not spared the horror of such diabolic works as gunpowder and artillery.

To-day, the world is full of learned men, brilliant teachers and vast libraries: I do not believe that the ages of Plato, Cicero or Papinian afforded such facilities for culture. From now on, it is unthinkable to come before the public or move in polite circles without having worshipped at Minerva's shrine. Why, the robbers, hangmen, adventurers and jockeys of to-day are infinitely better educated than the doctors and preachers of my time. More, even women and girls aspire to the glory, the heavenly manna of learning. Thus, at my advanced age, I have been forced to take up Greek. Not that I had despised it, like Cato; I never had the opportunity to learn it. Now I delight in reading Plutarch's Morals, *Plato's noble* Dialogues, *the* Monuments of Pausanias *and the* Antiquities of Athenaeus, *as I await the hour when it shall please God, my Creator, to call me back to His bosom.*

That is why, my dear son, I urge you to spend your youth making the most of your studies and developing your moral sense. You are in Paris, which abounds in noble men upon whom to pattern yourself; you have Epistemon, an admirable tutor, who can inspire you by direct oral teaching. But I demand more of you. I insist you learn languages perfectly! Greek first, as old Quintilian prescribes; then Latin; then Hebrew for the sake of the Holy Scripture; then Chaldee and Arabic, too. Model your Greek style on Plato, your Latin on Cicero. Let no history slip your memory; cultivate cosmography, for you will find its texts helpful.

As for the liberal arts of geometry, arithmetic and music, I gave you a taste of them when you were a little lad of five or six. Proceed further in them yourself, learning as much as you can. Be sure to master all the rules of astronomy; but dismiss astrology and the divinatory art of Lullius as but vanity and imposture. Of civil law, I would have you know the texts of the Code by heart, then compare them with philosophy.

A knowledge of nature is indispensable, devote yourself to this study with unflagging curiosity. Let there be no sea, river or fountain but you know the fish that dwell in it. Be familiar with all the shrubs, bushes and trees in forest or orchard, all the plants, herbs and flowers that grow on the ground, all the birds of the air, all the metals in the bowels of earth, all the precious stones in the orient and the south. In a word, be well informed in everything that concerns the physical world we live in.

Then carefully consult the works of Greek, Arabian and Latin physicians, without slighting the Jewish doctors, Talmudists and Cabbalists. By frequent exercises in dissection, acquire a perfect knowledge of that other world, which is man.

Devote a few hours a day to the study of Holy Writ. Take up the New Testament and the Epistles in Greek; then, the Old Testament in Hebrew. Strive to make your mind an inexhaustible storehouse of knowledge. For you are growing to manhood now: soon you will have to give up your studious repose to lead a life of action. You will have to learn to bear arms, to achieve knighthood, so as to defend my house and help our allies frustrate the attacks of evildoers.

Further, I wish you soon to test what profit you have gained from your education. This you can best do by public discussion and debate on all subjects against all comers, and by frequenting learned men both in Paris and elsewhere.

But remember this. As Solomon says, wisdom entereth not into a malicious soul, and science without conscience spells but destruction of the spirit. Therefore serve, love and fear God, on Him pin all your thoughts

181

and hopes; by faith built of charity, cling to Him so closely that never a sin can come between you. Hold the abuses of the world in just suspicion. Set not your heart upon vanity, for this life is a transitory thing, but the Word of God endureth forever. Be serviceable to your neighbor, love him as you do yourself. Honor your teachers. Shun the company of all men you would not wish to resemble; receive not in vain the favors God has bestowed upon you.

When you realize that you have acquired all the knowledge Paris has to offer, come back so I may see you and give you my blessing before I die. My son, the peace and grace of Our Lord be with you. Amen.

Your father,

Gargantua

From Utopia, the seventeenth day of September.

Having read this letter, Pantagruel, greatly encouraged, strove more ardently than ever to profit in his work. Had you seen him studying vigorously, practically and tirelessly, you would have compared his spirit moving among his books to flames blazing through a bonfire of dry branches.

MICHEL DE MONTAIGNE

THE PASSIONS OF THE SOUL

One of our gentlemen who was wondrously subject to the gout, on being urged by the doctors to give up entirely the use of salt meats, used to answer them very humorously that in the agonies and torments of the illness he wanted to have something to blame, and by crying out and cursing now the sausage, now the ox tongue and the ham, he felt just that much relieved. But in all seriousness, just as when the arm is raised to strike, it hurts us if the blow does not land and is wasted on the air; also as the sight, to make a pleasant view, must not be lost and led away in the vague reaches of the air, but must have some bound to sustain it at a reasonable distance;

> As wind loses its strength, diffused in empty space,
> Unless some strong dense wood resists its forward pace;
>
> Lucan

so it seems that the soul, once stirred and set in motion, is lost in itself unless we give it something to grasp; and we must always give it an object to aim at and act on. Plutarch says of those who grow fond of monkeys and little dogs that the loving part that is in us, lacking a legitimate object, rather than remain idle, thus forges itself a false and frivolous one. And we see that the soul in its passions will sooner deceive itself by setting up a false and fantastical object, even contrary to its own belief, than not act against something.

Thus animals are carried away by their rage to attack the stone or the metal that has wounded them and to take revenge tooth and nail on themselves for the pain they feel.

> So the Pannonian bear, made fiercer by the sting,
> When struck by the dart from the Lybian hunter's sling,
> Turns on the wound enraged, attacks the buried spear,
> Which whirls as she whirls after, flees as she draws near.
>
> Lucan

What causes do we not invent for the misfortunes that befall us? On what do we not place the blame, rightly or wrongly, so as to have something at which to thrust? It is not those blond tresses that you are tearing, nor the whiteness of that bosom that in your anger you beat so cruelly, that have made you lose by an unlucky bullet that well-loved brother: place the blame elsewhere. Livy, speaking of the Roman army in Spain after the loss of two brothers, their great captains, says: *Immediately all began to weep and beat their heads.* It is a common practice. And was it not amusing of the philosopher Bion to say about that king who was tearing his hair for grief, "Does this man think that baldness relieves grief?" Who has not seen people chew and swallow the cards or stuff themselves with a set of dice to avenge the loss of their money? Xerxes whipped the waters of the Hellespont, put irons on it and had a thousand insults hurled at it, and wrote a challenge to Mount Athos. Cyrus wasted a whole army's time for several days taking vengeance on the river Gyndus for the fright he had had crossing it. And Caligula ruined a very beautiful house for the displeasure that his mother had had there.

In my youth the people used to say that one of our neighboring kings, having received a beating from God, swore to take revenge; and ordered that for ten years no one should pray to God, or speak of him, or, as far as the king's authority could prevent it, believe in him. By which they wanted to portray not so much the folly as the vainglory natural to the nation about whom the story was told. These are vices that always go together; but in truth such actions spring from presumption even more than from stupidity.

Augustus Caesar, having been battered by a tempest at sea, set about defying the god Neptune, and in the celebration of the circus games had his image removed from the place where it was among the other gods, to take vengeance on him. Wherein he is still less excusable than the preceding ones, and less than he was later, when, having lost a battle under Quintilius Varus in Germany, he went about in anger and despair banging his head against the wall and crying: "Varus, give me back my soldiers." For those surpass all madness who, adding impiety to folly, turn their blame against God himself, or against Fortune, as if she had ears susceptible to our assault; like the Thracians who, when there is thunder or lightning, start shooting at the heavens with a Titan's vengeance, to bring God to reason by arrow shots. Now, as that ancient poet says in Plutarch,

> Anger at things that happen shows small wit;
> For all our wrath concerns them not a bit.
> Author Unknown

But we shall never heap enough insults on the unruliness of our mind.

FRANCIS BACON

OF STUDIES

Studies serve for Delight, for Ornament, and for Ability. Their chiefe use for Delight is in privatenesse and retiring; for Ornament, is in discourse; & for Ability, is in the judgement and disposition of Businesse. For expert men can execute, & perhaps judge of particulars, one by one; but the generall counsels, and the plots, and marshalling of affaires, come best from those that are Learned. To spend too much time in Studies, is sloth; to use them too much for ornament, is affectation; to make judgement wholly by their rules is the humour of a Scholler. They perfect Nature, and are perfected by Experience: for naturall abilities are like naturall plants, that need proyning by Study: and Studies them-

selves doe give forth directions too much at large, except they be bounded
in by experience. Crafty men contemne Studies; simple men admire
them; and wise men use them: for they teach not their owne use; but
that is a wisdome without them, and above them, won by observation.
Reade not to contradict and confute; nor to beleeve and take for granted;
nor to finde talke and discourse; but to weigh and consider. Some Bookes
are to be tasted, others to be swallowed, and some few to be chewed and
digested: that is, some Bookes are to be read onely in parts; others to be
read but not curiously; and some few to be read wholly, and with Diligence and Attention. Some Bookes also may be read by deputy, and ex-
tracts made of them by others: but that would be onely in the lesse
important arguments, and the meaner sort of Bookes, else distilled Bookes
are like common distilled waters, flashy things. Reading maketh a full
man; Conference a ready man; and Writing an exact man. And therefore, if a man Write little, he had need have a great memory; if he Con-
ferre little, he had need have a present wit; and if he Reade litle, he had
need have much cunning, to seeme to know that he doth not. Histories
make men wise; Poets witty; the Mathematicks subtill; Natural Philosophy deepe; Morall grave; Logick and Rhetorick able to contend. *Abeunt
studia in mores.* Nay there is no stond or impediment in the wit, but
may be wrought out by fit Studies; like as diseases of the body may have
appropriate exercises. Bowling is good for the stone and reines; Shooting
for the lungs and breast; gentle Walking for the stomacke; Riding for
the head; and the like. So if a man's wit be wandring, let him study the
Mathematicks; for in demonstrations, if his wit be called away never so
little, he must begin again: if his wit be not apt to distinguish or find
differences, let him study the schoole-men; for they are *cymini sectores.*
If he be not apt to beat over matters, and to call up one thing to prove
and illustrate another, let him study the Lawyer's Cases: so every defect
of the minde may have a speciall receit.

OF BUILDING

Houses are built to live in, and not to looke on: therefore let use bee
preferred before uniformitie; except where both may be had. Leave the
goodly fabrickes of Houses, for beautie only, to the enchanted pallaces of
the poets: who build them with small cost. Hee that builds a faire House
upon an ill Seat, committeth himselfe to prison. Neither doe I reckon it

an ill Seat, only, where the aire is unwholesome; but likewise where the aire is unequall; as you shall see many fine Seats set upon a knap of ground, environed with higher hilles round about it: whereby the heat of the Sunne is pent in, and the Wind gathereth as in troughes; so as you shall have, and that suddenly, as great diversitie of heat and cold as if you dwelt in severall places. Neither is it ill Aire onely that maketh an ill Seat, but ill Wayes, ill Markets; and, if you will consult with Momus, ill Neighbours. I speake not of many more: want of Water; want of Wood, Shade, and Shelter; want of Fruitfulnesse, and mixture of Grounds of severall natures; want to Prospect; want of Levell Grounds; want of Places at some neare distance for sports of Hunting, Hauking, and Races; too neare the Sea, too remote; having the commoditie of Navigable Rivers, or the discommoditie of their overflowing; too farre off from great Cities, which may hinder businesse; or too neare them, which lurcheth all provisions, and maketh every thing deare; where a man hath a great Living laid together, and where he is scanted: all which, as it is impossible perhaps to finde together, so it is good to know them, and thinke of them, that a man may take as many as he can: and if he have severall Dwellings, that he sort them so, that what hee wanteth in the one hee may finde in the other. Lucullus answered Pompey well; who, when hee saw his stately galleries, and roomes, so large and lightsome, in one of his Houses, said; *Surely an excellent place for Summer, but how doe you in Winter?* Lucullus answered; *Why doe you not think me as wise as some fowle are, that ever change their aboad towards the Winter?*

To passe from the Seat, to the House it selfe; we will doe as Cicero doth, in the oratour's art; who writes bookes *De Oratore,* and a booke he entitles *Orator:* whereof the former delivers the precepts of the art, and the latter the perfection. We will therefore describe a princely Pallace, making a briefe modell thereof. For it is strange to see, now in Europe, such huge buildings as the Vatican and Escuriall and some others be, and yet scarce a very faire roome in them.

First therefore, I say, you cannot have a perfect Pallace, except you have two severall sides; a side for the Banquet as is spoken of in the booke of Hester; and a side for the Houshold: the one for feasts and triumphs, and the other for dwelling. I understand both these sides to be not onely returnes but parts of the front; and to be uniforme without, though severally partitioned within; and to be on both sides of a great and stately Tower, in the middest of the front; that as it were, joyneth them together on either hand. I would have on the side of the Banquet, in front, one only goodly roome above staires, of some fortie foot high; and under it a roome for a dressing or preparing place at times of Triumphs. On the other side, which is the Household side, I wish it divided at the first into a Hall, and a Chappell (with a partition betweene); both of good state and bignesse: and those not to goe all the length, but to have at the further end, a Winter and a Summer Parler, both faire. And under these roomes, a faire and large Cellar sunke under ground: and likewise, some privie Kitchins, with Butteries and Pantries, and the like. As for the Tower, I would have it two stories, of eighteene foot high a peece, above the two wings; and a goodly Leads upon the top, railed with Statuas interposed; and the same Tower to bee divided into roomes, as shall be thought fit. The Staires likewise, to the upper roomes, let them bee upon a faire open Newell and finely raild in, with Images of wood, cast into a brasse colour: and a very faire Landing Place at the top. But this to be, if you doe not point any of the lower roomes for a dining place of servants. For otherwise you shall have the servants' dinner after your owne: for the steame of it will come up as in a tunnell. And so much for the Front. Only, I understand the height of the first staires to be sixteene foot, which is the height of the lower roome.

Beyond this Front is there to be a faire Court, but three sides of it of a farre lower building then the Front. And in all the foure corners of that Court, faire staire cases, cast into Turrets on the outside, and not within the row of Buildings themselves. But those Towers are not to be of the height of the Front; but rather proportionable to the lower building. Let the Court not be paved, for that striketh up a great heat in Summer and much cold in Winter. But onely some side alleys, with a crosse, and the quarters to graze, being kept shorne, but not too neare shorne. The row of Returne, on the Banquet side, let it be all stately Galleries; in which Galleries let there be three, or five, fine Cupolas in the length of it, placed at equall distance: and fine coloured Windowes of severall workes. On the household side, Chambers of Presence, & ordinary entertainments, with some Bedchambers; and let all three sides be a double House, without thorow lights on the sides, that you may have roomes from the Sunne, both for fore-noone and after-noone. Cast it also, that you may have roomes, both for Summer, and Winter: shadie for Summer and warme for Winter. You shall have sometimes faire Houses so full of glasse that one cannot tell where to become to be out of the Sunne or cold. For inbowed Windowes, I hold them of good use; (in cities indeed, upright doe better, in respect of the uniformitie towards the street); for

187

36. Villa Farnesina, Rome.

they bee prettie retiring places for conference; and besides, they keepe both the wind and sunne off: for that which would strike almost thorow the Roome, doth scarce passe the Window. But let them be but few, foure in the Court, on the sides onely.

Beyond this Court, let there be an inward Court of the same square and height; which is to be environed, with the Garden, on all sides: and in the inside, cloistered on all sides, upon decent and beautifull arches, as high as the first Story. On the under Story, towards the Garden, let it be turned to a Grotta, or place of shade, or estivation. And onely have opening and Windowes towards the Garden; and be levell upon the floare, no whit sunke under ground, to avoid all dampishnesse. And let there be a Fountaine, or some faire worke of Statuas, in the middest of this Court; and to be paved as the other Court was. These buildings to be for privie Lodgings, on both sides; and the end for privie Galleries. Whereof you must fore-see that one of them be for an Infirmary, if the Prince or any speciall person should be sicke, with Chambers, Bed-chamber, Anticamera, and Recamera, joyning to it. This upon the second story. Upon the ground story, a faire Gallery, open, upon pillars: and upon the third story likewise, an open Gallery upon pillars, to take the prospect and freshnesse of the Garden. At both corners of the further side, by way of returne, let there be two delicate or rich Cabinets, daintily paved, richly hanged, glased with crystalline glasse, and a rich Cupola in the middest; and all other elegancie that may be thought upon. In the upper Gallery too, I wish that there may be, if the place will yeeld it, some Fountaines running in divers places from the wall, with some fine avoidances. And thus much for the modell of the Pallace: save that you must have, before you come to the front, three Courts. A greene Court plain, with a wall about it: a second Court of the same, but more garnished, with little turrets, or rather embellishments, upon the wall: and a third Court, to make a square with the front, but not to be built nor yet enclosed with a naked wall, but enclosed with Tarrasses, leaded aloft, and fairely garnished on the three sides; and cloistered on the inside with pillars, and not with arches below. As for Offices, let them stand at distance, with some low Galleries, to passe from them to the Pallace it selfe.

BALDASSARE CASTIGLIONE

THE PERFECT COURTIER

Within myself I have long doubted, dearest messer Alfonso, which of two things were the harder for me: to deny you what you have often begged of me so urgently, or to do it. For while it seemed to me very hard to deny anything (and especially a thing in the highest degree laudable) to one whom I love most dearly and by whom I feel myself to be most dearly loved, yet to set about an enterprise that I am not sure of being able to finish, seemed to me ill befitting a man who esteems just censure as it ought to be esteemed. At last, after much thought, I am resolved to try in this matter how much aid my assiduity may gain from that affection and intense desire to please, which in other things are so wont to stimulate the industry of man.

You ask me then to write what is to my thinking the form of Courtiership most befitting a gentleman who lives at the court of princes, by which he may have the ability and knowledge perfectly to serve them in every reasonable thing, winning from them favour, and praise from other

189

men; in short, what manner of man he ought to be who may deserve to be called a perfect Courtier without flaw. Wherefore, considering your request, I say that had it not seemed to me more blameworthy to be reputed somewhat unamiable by you than too conceited by everyone else, I should have avoided this task, for fear of being held over bold by all who know how hard it is, from among such a variety of customs as are in use at the courts of Christendom, to choose the perfect form and as it were the flower of Courtiership. For custom often makes the same thing pleasing and displeasing to us; whence it sometimes follows that customs, habits, ceremonies and fashions that once were prized, become vulgar, and contrariwise the vulgar become prized. Thus it is clearly seen that use rather than reason has power to introduce new things among us, and to do away with the old; and he will often err who seeks to determine which are perfect. Therefore being conscious of this and many other difficulties in the subject set before me to write of, I am constrained to offer some apology, and to testify that this error (if error it may indeed be called) is common to us both, to the end that if I be blamed for it, the blame may be shared by you also; for your offence in setting me a task beyond my powers should not be deemed less than mine in having accepted it.

So now let us make a beginning of our subject, and if possible let us form such a Courtier that any prince worthy to be served by him, although of but small estate, might still be called a very great lord.

.   .   .

"I wish, then, that this Courtier of ours should be nobly born and of gentle race; because it is far less unseemly for one of ignoble birth to fail in worthy deeds, than for one of noble birth, who, if he strays from the path of his predecessors, stains his family name, and not only fails to achieve but loses what has been achieved already; for noble birth is like a bright lamp that manifests and makes visible good and evil deeds, and kindles and stimulates to virtue both by fear of shame and by hope of praise. And since this splendour of nobility does not illumine the deeds of the humbly born, they lack that stimulus and fear of shame, nor do they feel any obligation to advance beyond what their predecessors have done; while to the nobly born it seems a reproach not to reach at least the goal set them by their ancestors. And thus it nearly always happens that both in the profession of arms and in other worthy pursuits the most famous men have been of noble birth, because nature has implanted in everything that hidden seed which gives a certain force and quality of its own essence to all things that are derived from it, and makes them like itself: as we see not only in the breeds of horses and of other animals, but also in trees, the shoots of which nearly always resemble the trunk; and if they sometimes degenerate, it arises from poor cultivation. And so it is with men, who if rightly trained are nearly always like those from whom they spring, and often better; but if there be no one to give them proper care, they become like savages and never reach perfection.

"It is true that, by favour of the stars or of nature, some men are endowed at birth with such graces that they seem not to have been born, but rather as if some god had formed them with his very hands and adorned them with every excellence of mind and body. So too there are many men so foolish and rude that one cannot but think that nature brought them into the world out of contempt or mockery. Just as these can usually accomplish little even with constant diligence and good training, so with slight pains those others reach the highest summit of excellence. And to give you an instance: you see my lord Don Ippolite d' Este, Cardinal of Ferrara, who has enjoyed such fortune from his birth, that his person, his aspect, his words and all his movements are so disposed and imbued with this grace, that—although he is young—he exhibits among the most aged prelates such weight of character that he seems fitter to teach than to be taught; likewise in conversation with men and woman of every rank, in games, in pleasantry and in banter, he has certain sweetness and manners so gracious, that whoso speaks with him or even sees him, must needs remain attached to him forever.

"But to return to our subject: I say that there is a middle state between perfect grace on the one hand and senseless folly on the other; and those who are not thus perfectly endowed by nature, with study and toil can in great part polish and amend their natural defects. Besides his noble birth, then, I would have the Courtier favoured in this regard also, and endowed by nature not only with talent and beauty of person and feature, but with a certain grace and (as we say) air that shall make him at first sight pleasing and agreeable to all who see him; and I would have this an ornament that should dispose and unite all his actions, and in his outward aspect give promise of whatever is worthy the society and favour of every great lord."

. . .

"But to come to some details, I am of opinion that the principal and true profession of the Courtier ought to be that of arms; which I would have him follow actively above all else, and be known among others as bold and strong, and loyal to whomsoever he serves. And he will win a reputation for these good qualities by exercising them at all times and in all places, since one may never fail in this without severest censure. And just as among women, their fair fame once sullied never recovers its first lustre, so the reputation of a gentleman who bears arms, if once it be in the least tarnished with cowardice or other disgrace, remains forever infamous before the world and full of ignominy. Therefore the more our Courtier excels in this art, the more he will be worthy of praise; and yet I do not deem essential in him that perfect knowledge of things and those other qualities that befit a commander; since this would be too wide a sea, let us be content, as we have said, with perfect loyalty and unconquered courage, and that he be always seen to possess them. For the courageous are often recognized even more in small things than in great; and frequently in perils of importance and where there are many spectators, some men are to be found, who, although their hearts be dead within them, yet, moved by shame or by the presence of others, press forward almost with their eyes shut, and do their duty God knows how. While on occasions of little moment, when they think they can avoid putting themselves in danger without being detected, they are glad to keep safe. But those who, even when they do not expect to be observed or seen or recognized by anyone, show their ardour and neglect nothing, however paltry, that may be laid to their charge,—they have that strength of mind which we seek in our Courtier."

.   .   .

". . . And of such sort I would have our Courtier's aspect; not so soft and effeminate as is sought by many, who not only curl their hair and pluck their brows, but gloss their faces with all those arts employed by the most wanton and unchaste women in the world; and in their walk, posture and every act, they seem so limp and languid that their limbs are like to fall apart; and they pronounce their words so mournfully that they appear about to expire upon the spot: and the more they find themselves with men of rank, the more they affect such tricks. Since nature has not made them women, as they seem to wish to appear and be, they should be treated not as good women but as public harlots, and driven not merely from the courts of great lords but from the society of honest men.

"Then coming to the bodily frame, I say it is enough if this be neither extremely short nor tall, for both of these conditions excite a certain contemptuous surprise, and men of either sort are gazed upon in much the same way that we gaze on monsters. Yet if we must offend in one of the two extremes, it is preferable to fall a little short of the just measure of height than to exceed it, for besides often being dull of intellect, men thus huge of body are also unfit for every exercise of agility, which thing I should much wish in the Courtier. And so I would have him well built and shapely of limb, and would have him show strength and lightness and suppleness, and know all bodily exercises that befit a man of war; whereof I think the first should be to handle every sort of weapon well on foot and on horse, to understand the advantages of each, and especially to be familiar with those weapons that are ordinarily used among gentlemen; for besides the use of them in war, where such subtlety in contrivance is perhaps not needful, there frequently arise differences between one gentleman and another, which afterwards result in duels often fought with such weapons as happen at the moment to be within reach: thus knowledge of this kind is a very safe thing. Nor am I one of those who say that skill is forgotten in the hour of need; for he whose skill forsakes him at such a time, indeed gives token that he has already lost heart and head through fear.

"Moreover I deem it very important to know how to wrestle, for it is a great help in the use of all kinds of weapons on foot. Then, both for his own sake and for that of his friends, he must understand the quarrels and differences that may arise, and must be quick to seize an advantage, always showing courage and prudence in all things. Nor should he be too ready to fight except when honour demands it; for besides the great danger that the uncertainty of fate entails, he who rushes into such affairs recklessly and without urgent cause, merits the severest censure even though he be successful. But when he finds himself so far engaged that he cannot withdraw without reproach, he ought to be most deliberate, both in the preliminaries to the duel and in the duel itself, and always show readiness and daring. Nor must he act like some, who fritter the affair away in disputes and controversies, and who, having the choice of weapons, select those that neither cut nor pierce, and arm themselves as if they were expecting a cannonade; and thinking it enough not to be defeated, stand ever on the defensive and retreat,—showing therein their utter cowardice. . . ."

.   .   .

"But as Count Ludovico has explained very minutely the chief profession of the Courtier, and has insisted it be that of arms, methinks it is also fitting to tell what in my judgment is that of the Court Lady: and when I have done this, I shall think myself quit of the greater part of my duty.

"Laying aside, then, those faculties of the mind that she ought to have in common with the Courtier (such as prudence, magnanimity, continence, and many others), and likewise those qualities that befit all women (such as kindness, discretion, ability to manage her husband's property and her house and children if she be married, and all those capacities that are requisite in a good housewife), I say that in a lady who lives at court methinks above all else a certain pleasant affability is befitting, whereby she may be able to entertain politely every sort of man with agreeable and seemly converse, suited to the time and place, and to the rank of the person with whom she may speak, uniting with calm and modest manners, and with that seemliness which should ever dispose all her actions, a quick vivacity of spirit whereby she may show herself alien to all indelicacy; but with such a kindly manner as shall make us think of her no less chaste, prudent and benign, than agreeable, witty and discreet: and so she must preserve a certain mean (difficult and composed almost of contraries), and must barely touch certain limits but not pass them.

"Thus, in her wish to be thought good and pure, the Lady ought not to be so coy and seem so to abhor company and talk that are a little free, as to take her leave as soon as she finds herself therein; for it might easily be thought that she was pretending to be thus austere in order to hide something about herself which she feared others might come to know; and such prudish manners are always odious. Nor ought she, on the other hand, for the sake of showing herself free and agreeable, to utter unseemly words or practise a certain wild and unbridled familiarity and ways likely to make that believed of her which perhaps is not true; but when she is present at such talk, she ought to listen with a little blush and shame.

"Likewise she ought to avoid an error into which I have seen many women fall, which is that of saying and of willingly listening to evil about other women. For those women who, on hearing the unseemly ways of other women described, grow angry thereat and seem to disbelieve it and to regard it almost monstrous that a woman should be immodest,—they, by accounting the offence so heinous, give reason to think that they do not commit it. But those who go about continually prying into other women's intrigues, and narrate them so minutely and with such zest, seem to be envious of them and to wish that everyone may know it, to the end that like matters may not be reckoned as a fault in their own case; and thus they fall into certain laughs and ways that show they then feel greatest pleasure. And hence it comes that men, while seeming to listen gladly, usually hold such women in small respect and have very little regard for them, and think these ways of theirs are an invitation to advance farther, and thus often go such lengths with them as bring them deserved reproach, and finally esteem them so lightly as to despise their company and even find them tedious.

"And on the other hand, there is no man so shameless and insolent as not to have reverence for those women who are esteemed good and virtuous; because this gravity (tempered with wisdom and goodness) is as it were a shield against the insolence and coarseness of the presumptuous. Thus we see that a word or laugh or act of kindness (however small it be) from a virtuous woman is more prized by everyone, than all the endearments and caresses of those who show their lack of shame so openly; and if they are not immodest, by their unseemly laughter, their loquacity, insolence and like scurrile manners, they give sign of being so.

"And since words that carry no meaning of importance are vain and puerile, the Court Lady must have not only the good sense to discern the quality of him with whom she is speaking, but knowledge of many things, in order to entertain him graciously; and in her talk she should know how to choose those things that are adapted to the quality of him with whom she is speaking, and should be cautious lest occasionally, without intending it, she utter words that may offend him. Let her guard against wearying him by praising herself indiscreetly or by being too prolix. Let her not go about mingling serious matters with her playful or humorous discourse, or jests and jokes with her serious discourse. Let her not stupidly pretend to know that which she does not know, but modestly seek to do herself credit in that which she does know,—in all things avoiding affectation, as has been said. In this way she will be adorned with good manners, and will perform with perfect grace the bodily exercises proper to women; her discourse will be rich and full of prudence, virtue and pleasantness; and thus she will be not only loved but revered by everyone, and perhaps worthy to be placed side by side with this great Courtier as well in qualities of the mind as in those of the body."

.   .   .

37. *A Young Man Among Roses,*
Nicholas Hilliard.

". . . Hence I think that the perfect Courtier, such as Count Ludovico
and messer Federico have described, may be a truly good thing and
worthy of praise, not however simply, and in himself, but in respect
to the end to which he may be directed. For indeed if by being nobly
born, graceful, agreeable, and expert in so many exercises, the Courtier
brought forth no other fruit than merely being what he is, I should not
deem it right for a man to devote so much study and pains to acquiring
this perfection of Courtiership, as anyone must who wishes to attain it.
Nay, I should say that many of those accomplishments that have been
ascribed to him (like dancing, merry-making, singing and playing) were
follies and vanities, and in a man of rank worthy rather of censure than
of praise: for these elegances, devices, mottoes, and other like things that
pertain to discourse about women and love, although perhaps many other
men think the contrary, often serve only to effeminate the mind, to cor-

rupt youth, and to reduce it to great wantonness of living; whence then it comes to pass that the Italian name is brought into opprobrium, and but few are to be found who dare, I will not say to die, but even to run into danger.

"And surely there are countless other things, which, if industry and study were spent upon them, would be of much greater utility in both peace and war than this kind of Courtiership in itself merely; but if the Courtier's actions are directed to that good end to which they ought, and which I have in mind, methinks they are not only not harmful or vain, but very useful and deserving of infinite praise.

"I think then that the aim of the perfect Courtier, which has not been spoken of till now, is so to win for himself, by means of the accomplishments ascribed to him by these gentlemen, the favour and mind of the prince whom he serves, that he may be able to say, and always shall say, the truth about everything which it is fitting for the prince to know, without fear, or risk of giving offence thereby; and that when he sees his prince's mind inclined to do something wrong, he may be quick to oppose, and gently to make use of the favour acquired by his good accomplishments, so as to banish every bad intent and lead his prince into the path of virtue. And thus, possessing the goodness which these gentlemen have described, together with readiness of wit and pleasantness, and shrewdness and knowledge of letters and many other things,—the Courtier will in every case be able deftly to show the prince how much honour and profit accrue to him and his from justice, liberality, magnanimity, gentleness, and the other virtues that become a good prince; and on the other hand how much infamy and loss proceed from the vices opposed to them. Therefore I think that just as music, festivals, games, and the other pleasant accomplishments are as it were the flower, in like manner to lead or help one's prince towards right, and to frighten him from wrong, are the true fruit of Courtiership.

"And since the merit of well-doing lies chiefly in two things, one of which is the choice of an end for our intentions that shall be truly good, and the other ability to find means suitable and fitting to conduce to that good end marked out,—certain it is that man's mind tends to the best end, who purposes to see to it that his prince shall be deceived by no one, shall hearken not to flatterers or to slanderers and liars, and shall distinguish good and evil, and love the one and hate the other."

.   .   .

"Nor do I think that Aristotle and Plato would have scorned the name of perfect Courtier, for we clearly see that they performed the works of Courtiership and wrought to this end,—the one with Alexander the Great, the other with the kings of Sicily. And since the office of a good Courtier is to know the prince's character and inclinations, and thus to enter tactfully into his favour according to need and opportunity, as we have said, by those ways that afford safe access, and then to lead him towards virtue,—Aristotle so well knew the character of Alexander, and tactfully fostered it so well, that he was loved and honoured more than a father by Alexander. Thus, among many other tokens that Alexander gave him of good will, the king ordered the rebuilding of his native city, Stagira, which had been destroyed; and besides directing Alexander to that most glorious aim,—which was the desire to make the world as one single universal country, and all men as a single people to live in amity and mutual concord under a single government and a single law, which should shine equally on all like the light of the sun,—Aristotle so instructed him in the natural sciences and in the virtues of the mind as to make him most wise, brave, continent, and a true moral philosopher, not only in words but in deeds; for a nobler philosophy cannot be imagined than to bring into civilized living such savage people as those who inhabited Bactria and Caucasia, India, Scythia; and to teach them marriage, agriculture, honour to their fathers, abstention from rapine, murder and other evil ways; to build so many very noble cities in distant lands;—so that countless men were by his laws reduced from savage life to civilization. And of these achievements of Alexander the author was Aristotle, using the means of a good Courtier: which Callisthenes knew not how to do, although Aristotle showed him; for in his wish to be a pure philosopher and austere minister of naked truth, without mingling Courtiership therewith, he lost his life and brought not help but rather infamy to Alexander.

"By these same means of Courtiership, Plato schooled Dio of Syracuse; and having afterwards found the tyrant Dionysius like a book all full of faults and errors and in need of complete erasure rather than of any change or correction (since it was not possible to remove from him that tinge of tyranny wherewith he had so long been stained), Plato was unwilling to practise the ways of Courtiership upon him, thinking that they all would surely be in vain. Which our Courtier also ought to do, if by chance he finds himself in the service of a prince of so evil a disposition as to be inveterate in vice, like consumptives in their malady; for in such

case he ought to escape that bondage, in order not to receive blame for
his lord's evil deeds, and in order not to feel that distress which all good
men feel who serve the wicked."

(from *The Book of the Courtier*)

BENVENUTO CELLINI

THE LIFE OF AN ARTIST

All men of whatsoever quality they be, who have done anything
of excellence, or which may properly resemble excellence, ought, if they
are persons of truth and honesty, to describe their life with their own
hand; but they ought not to attempt so fine an enterprise till they have
passed the age of forty. This duty occurs to my own mind, now that I
am travelling beyond the term of fifty-eight years, and am in Florence,
the city of my birth. Many untoward things can I remember, such as
happen to all who live upon our earth; and from those adversities I am
now more free than at any previous period of my career—nay, it seems
to me that I enjoy greater content of soul and health of body than ever
I did in bygone years. I can also bring to mind some pleasant goods and
some inestimable evils, which, when I turn my thoughts backward, strike
terror in me, and astonishment that I should have reached this age of
fifty-eight, wherein, thanks be to God, I am still travelling prosperously
forward.

．　　．　　．

At Siena I waited for the mail to Rome which I afterwards joined;
and when we passed the Paglia, we met a courier carrying news of the
new Pope, Clement VII. Upon my arrival in Rome, I went to work in
the shop of the master-goldsmith Santi. He was dead; but a son of his
carried on the business. He did not work himself, but entrusted all his
commissions to a young man named Lucagnolo from Iesi, a country
fellow, who while yet a child had come into Santi's service. This man
was short but well proportioned, and was a more skilful craftsman than
any one whom I had met with up to that time; remarkable for facility
and excellent in design. He executed large plate only; that is to say, vases

of the utmost beauty, basons, and such pieces. Having put myself to work there, I began to make some candelabra for the Bishop of Salamanca, a Spaniard. They were richly chased, so far as that sort of work admits. A pupil of Raffaello da Urbino called Gian Francesco, and commonly known as Il Fattore, was a painter of great ability; and being on terms of friendship with the Bishop, he introduced me to his favour, so that I obtained many commissions from that prelate, and earned considerable sums of money.

During that time I went to draw, sometimes in Michel Agnolo's chapel, and sometimes in the house of Agostino Chigi of Siena, which contained many incomparable paintings by the hand of that great master Raffaello. This I did on feast-days, because the house was then inhabited by Messer Gismondo, Agostino's brother. They plumed themselves exceedingly when they saw young men of my sort coming to study in their palaces. Gismondo's wife, noticing my frequent presence in that house—she was a lady as courteous as could be, and of surpassing beauty—came up to me one day, looked at my drawings, and asked me if I was a sculptor or a painter; to whom I said I was a goldsmith. She remarked that I drew too well for a goldsmith; and having made one of her waiting-maids bring a lily of the finest diamonds set in gold, she showed it to me, and bade me value it. I valued it at eight hundred crowns.

Then she said that I had very nearly hit the mark, and asked me whether I felt capable of setting the stones really well. I said that I should much like to do so, and began before her eyes to make a little sketch for it, working all the better because of the pleasure I took in conversing with so lovely and agreeable a gentlewoman. When the sketch was finished, another Roman lady of great beauty joined us; she had been above, and now descending to the ground-floor, asked Madonna Porzia what she was doing there. She answered with a smile: 'I am amusing myself watching this worthy young man at his drawing; he is as good as he is handsome.' I had by this time acquired a trifle of assurance, mixed, however, with some honest bashfulness; so I blushed and said: 'Such as I am, lady, I shall ever be most ready to serve you.' The gentlewoman, also slightly blushing, said: 'You know well that I want you to serve me'; and reaching me the lily, told me to take it away; and gave me besides twenty golden crowns which she had in her bag, and added: 'Set me the jewel after the fashion you have sketched, and keep for me the old gold in which it is new set.' On this the Roman lady observed: 'If I were in that young man's body, I should go off without asking leave.'

Madonna Porzia replied that virtues rarely are at home with vices, and that if I did such a thing, I should strongly belie my good looks of an honest man. Then turning round, she took the Roman lady's hand, and with a pleasant smile said: 'Farewell, Benvenuto.' I stayed on a short while at the drawing I was making, which was a copy of a Jove by Raffaello. When I had finished it and left the house, I set myself to making a little model of wax, in order to show how the jewel would look when it was completed. This I took to Madonna Porzia, whom I found with the same Roman lady. Both of them were highly satisfied with my work, and treated me so kindly that, being somewhat emboldened, I promised the jewel should be twice as good as the model. Accordingly I set hand to it, and in twelve days I finished it in the form of a fleur-de-lys, as I have said above, ornamenting it with little masks, children, and animals, exquisitely enamelled, whereby the diamonds which formed the lily were more than doubled in effect.

While I was working at this piece, Lucagnolo, of whose ability I have before spoken, showed considerable discontent, telling me over and over again that I might acquire far more profit and honour by helping him to execute large plate, as I had done at first. I made him answer that, whenever I chose, I should always be capable of working at great silver pieces; but that things like that on which I was now engaged were not commissioned every day; and beside their bringing no less honour than large silver plate, there was also more profit to be made by them. He laughed me in the face, and said: 'Wait and see, Benvenuto; for by the time you have finished that work of yours, I will make haste to have finished this vase, which I took in hand when you did the jewel; and then experience shall teach you what profit I shall get from my vase, and what you will get from your ornament.' I answered that I was very glad indeed to enter into such a competition with so good a craftsman as he was, because the end would show which of us was mistaken. Accordingly both the one and the other of us, with a scornful smile upon our lips, bent our heads in grim earnest to the work, which both were now desirous of accomplishing; so that after about ten days, each had finished his undertaking with great delicacy and artistic skill.

Lucagnolo's was a huge silver piece, used at the table of Pope Clement, into which he flung away bits of bone and the rind of divers fruits, while eating; an object of ostentation rather than necessity. The vase was adorned with two fine handles, together with many masks, both small and great, and masses of lovely foliage, in as exquisite a style of elegance as could be imagined; on seeing which I said it was the most beautiful vase that ever I set eyes on. Thinking he had convinced me, Lucagnolo replied: 'Your work seems to me no less beautiful, but we shall soon perceive the difference between the two.' So he took his vase and carried it to the Pope, who was very well pleased with it, and ordered at once that he should be paid at the ordinary rate of such large plate. Meanwhile I carried mine to Madonna Porzia, who looked at it with astonishment, and told me I had far surpassed my promise. Then she bade me ask for my reward whatever I liked; for it seemed to her my desert was so great that if I craved a castle she could hardly recompense me; but since that was not in her hands to bestow, she added laughing that I must beg what lay within her power. I answered that the greatest reward I could desire for my labour was to have satisfied her ladyship. Then, smiling in my turn, and bowing to her, I took my leave, saying I wanted no reward but that. She turned to the Roman lady and said: 'You see that the qualities we discerned in him are companied by virtues, and not vices.' They both expressed their admiration and then Madonna Porzia continued: 'Friend Benvenuto, have you never heard it said that when the poor give to the rich, the devil laughs?' I replied: 'Quite true! and yet, in the midst of all his troubles, I should like this time to see him laugh'; and as I took my leave, she said that this time she had no will to bestow on him that favour.

When I came back to the shop, Lucagnolo had the money for his vase in a paper packet; and on my arrival he cried out: 'Come and compare the price of your jewel with the price of my plate.' I said that he must leave things as they were till the next day, because I hoped that even as my work in its kind was not less excellent than his, so I should be able to show him quite an equal price for it.

On the day following, Madonna Porzia sent a major-domo of hers to my shop, who called me out, and putting into my hands a paper packet full of money from his lady, told me that she did not choose the devil should have his whole laugh out: by which she hinted that the money sent me was not the entire payment merited by my industry, and other messages were added worthy of so courteous a lady. Lucagnolo, who was burning to compare his packet with mine, burst into the shop; then in the presence of twelve journeymen and some neighbours, eager to behold the result of this competition, he seized his packet, scornfully exclaiming 'Ou! ou!' three or four times, while he poured his money on the counter with a great noise. They were twenty-five crowns in giulios; and he fancied that mine would be four or five crowns *di moneta*. I for my part, stunned and stifled by his cries, and by the looks and smiles of the bystanders, first peeped into my packet; then, after seeing that it contained nothing but gold, I retired to one end of the counter, and, keeping my eyes lowered and making no noise at all, I lifted it with both hands suddenly above my head, and emptied it like a mill hopper. My coin was twice as much as his; which caused the onlookers, who had fixed their eyes on me with some derision, to turn round suddenly to him and say: 'Lucagnolo, Benvenuto's pieces, being all of gold and twice as many as yours, make a far finer effect.' I thought for certain that, what with jealousy and what with shame, Lucagnolo would have fallen dead upon the spot; and though he took the third part of my gain, since I was a journeyman (for such is the custom of the trade, two-thirds fall to the workman and one-third to the masters of the shop), yet inconsiderate envy had more power in him than avarice: it ought indeed to have worked quite the other way, he being a peasant's son from Iesi. He cursed his art and those who taught it him, vowing that thenceforth he would never work at large plate, but give his whole attention to those whoreson gewgaws, since they were so well paid. Equally enraged on my side, I answered that every bird sang its own note; that he talked after the fashion of the hovels he came from; but that I dared swear that I should succeed with ease in making his lubberly lumber, while he would never be successful in my whoreson gewgaws. Thus I flung off in a passion, telling him that I would soon show him that I spoke truth. The bystanders openly declared against him, holding him for a lout, as indeed he was, and me for a man, as I had proved myself.

.   .   .

The Duke of Florence at this time, which was the month of August 1545, had retired to Poggio a Caiano, ten miles distant from Florence. Thither then I went to pay him my respects, with the sole object of acting as duty required, first because I was a Florentine, and next because my forefathers had always been adherents of the Medicean party, and I yielded to none of them in affection for this Duke Cosimo. As I have said, then, I rode to Poggio with the sole object of paying my respects, and with no intention of accepting service under him, as God, who does all things well, did then appoint for me.

When I was introduced, the Duke received me very kindly; then he and the Duchess put questions concerning the works which I had executed for the King. I answered willingly and in detail. After listening to my story, he answered that he had heard as much, and that I spoke the truth. Then he assumed a tone of sympathy, and added: 'How small a recompense for such great and noble masterpieces! Friend Benvenuto, if you feel inclined to execute something for me too, I am ready to pay you far better than that King of yours has done, for whom your excellent nature prompts you to speak so gratefully.' When I understood his drift, I described the deep obligations under which I lay to his Majesty, who first obtained my liberation from that iniquitous prison, and afterwards supplied me with the means of carrying out more admirable works than any artist of my quality had ever had the chance to do. While I was thus speaking, my lord the Duke writhed on his chair, and seemed as though he could not bear to hear me to the end. Then, when I had concluded, he rejoined: 'If you are disposed to work for me, I will treat you in a way that will astonish you, provided the fruits of your labours give me satisfaction, of which I have no doubt.' I, poor unhappy mortal, burning with desire to show the noble school of Florence that, after leaving her in youth, I had practised other branches of the art than she imagined, gave answer to the Duke that I would willingly erect for him in marble or in bronze a mighty statue on his fine piazza. He replied that, for a first essay, he should like me to produce a Perseus; he had long set his heart on having such a monument, and he begged me to begin a model for the same. I very gladly set myself to the task, and in a few weeks I finished my model, which was about a cubit high, in yellow wax and very delicately finished in all its details. I had made it with the most thorough study and art.

The Duke returned to Florence, but several days passed before I had an opportunity of showing my model. It seemed indeed as though he had never set eyes on me or spoken with me, and this caused me to augur ill of my future dealings with his Excellency. Later on, however, one day after dinner, I took it to his wardrobe, where he came to inspect it with the Duchess and a few gentlemen of the court. No sooner had he seen it than he expressed much pleasure, and extolled it to the skies; wherefrom I gathered some hope that he might really be a connoisseur of art. After having well considered it for some time, always with greater satisfaction, he began as follows: 'If you could only execute this little model, Benvenuto, with the same perfection on a large scale, it would be the finest piece in the piazza.' I replied: 'Most excellent my lord, upon the piazza are now standing works by the great Donatello and the incomparable Michel Angelo, the two greatest men who have ever lived since the days of the ancients. But since your Excellency encourages my model with such praise, I feel the heart to execute it at least thrice as well in bronze.' No slight dispute arose upon this declaration; the Duke protesting that he understood these matters perfectly, and was quite aware what could be done. I rejoined that my achievements would resolve his dubitations and debates; I was absolutely sure of being able to perform far more than I had promised for his Excellency, but that he must give me means for carrying my work out, else I could not fulfil my undertaking. In return for this his Excellency bade me formulate my demands in a petition, detailing all my requirements; he would see them liberally attended to.

It is certain that if I had been cunning enough to secure by contract all I wanted for my work, I should not have incurred the great troubles which came upon me through my own fault. But he showed the strongest desire to have the work done, and the most perfect willingness to arrange preliminaries. I therefore, not discerning that he was more a merchant than a duke, dealt very frankly with his Excellency, just as if I had to do with a prince, and not with a commercial man. I sent in my petition, to which he replied in large and ample terms. The memorandum ran as follows: 'Most rare and excellent my patron, petitions of any validity and compacts between us of any value do not rest upon words or writings; the whole point is that I should succeed in my work according to my promise; and if I so succeed, I feel convinced that your most illustrious Excellency will very well remember what you have engaged to do for me.' This language so charmed the Duke both with my ways of acting and of speaking that he and the Duchess began to treat me with extraordinary marks of favour.

.   .

While the workshop for executing my Perseus was in building, I used to work in a ground-floor room. Here I modelled the statue in plaster, giving it the same dimensions as the bronze was meant to have, and intending to cast it from this mould. But finding that it would take rather long to carry it out in this way, I resolved upon another expedient, especially as now a wretched little studio had been erected, brick on brick, so miserably built that the mere recollection of it gives me pain. So then I began the figure of Medusa, and constructed the skeleton in iron. Afterwards I put on the clay, and when that was modelled, baked it.

.   .   .

Meanwhile I was advancing with my great statue of Medusa. I had covered the iron skeleton with clay, which I modelled like an anatomical subject, and about half an inch thinner than the bronze would be. This I baked well, and then began to spread on the wax surface, in order to complete the figure to my liking. The Duke, who often came to inspect it, was so anxious lest I should not succeed with the bronze, that he wanted me to call in some master to cast it for me.

.   .   .

The first piece I cast in bronze was that great bust, the portrait of his Excellency, which I had modelled in the goldsmith's workroom while suffering from those pains in my back. It gave much pleasure when it was completed, though my sole object in making it was to obtain experience of clays suitable for bronze-casting. I was of course aware that the admirable sculptor Donatello had cast his bronzes with the clay of Florence; yet it seemed to me that he had met with enormous difficulties in their execution. As I thought that this was due to some fault in the earth, I wanted to make these first experiments before I undertook my Perseus. From them I learned that the clay was good enough, but had not been well understood by Donatello, inasmuch as I could see that his pieces had been cast with the very greatest trouble. Accordingly, as I have described above, I prepared the earth by artificial methods, and found it serve me well, and with it I cast the bust; but since I had not yet constructed my own furnace, I employed that of Maestro Zanobi di Pagno, a bell-founder.

When I saw that this bust came out sharp and clean, I set at once to construct a little furnace in the workshop erected for me by the Duke, after my own plans and design, in the house which the Duke had given me. No sooner was the furnace ready than I went to work with all diligence upon the casting of Medusa, that is, the woman twisted in a heap beneath the feet of Perseus. It was an extremely difficult task, and I was anxious to observe all the niceties of art which I had learned, so as not to lapse into some error. The first cast I took in my furnace succeeded in the superlative degree, and was so clean that my friends thought I should not need to retouch it. It is true that certain Germans and Frenchmen, who vaunt the possession of marvellous secrets, pretend that they can cast bronzes without retouching them; but this is really nonsense, because the bronze, when it has first been cast, ought to be worked over and beaten in with hammers and chisels, according to the manner of the ancients and also to that of the moderns—I mean such moderns as have known how to work in bronze.

.   .   .

Having succeeded so well with the cast of the Medusa, I had great hope of bringing my Perseus through; for I had laid the wax on, and felt confident that it would come out in bronze as perfectly as the Medusa. The waxen model produced so fine an effect, that when the Duke saw it and was struck with its beauty—whether somebody had persuaded him it could not be carried out with the same finish in metal, or whether he thought so for himself—he came to visit me more frequently than usual, and on one occasion said: 'Benvenuto, this figure cannot succeed in bronze; the laws of art do not admit of it.' These words of his Excellency stung me so sharply that I answered: 'My lord, I know how very little confidence you have in me; and I believe the reason of this is that your most illustrious Excellency lends too ready an ear to my calumniators, or else indeed that you do not understand my art.' He hardly let me close the sentence when he broke in: 'I profess myself a connoisseur, and understand it very well indeed.' I replied: 'Yes, like a prince, not like an artist; for if your Excellency understood my trade as well as you imagine, you would trust me on the proofs I have already given. These are, first, the colossal bronze bust of your Excellency, which is now in Elba; secondly, the restoration of the Ganymede in marble, which offered so many difficulties and cost me so much trouble, that I would rather have made the whole statue new from the beginning; thirdly, the Medusa, cast by me in bronze, here now before your Excellency's eyes, the execution of which was a greater triumph of strength and skill than any of my predecessors in this fiendish art have yet achieved. Look you, my lord! I constructed that furnace anew on principles quite different from those of other founders; in addition to many technical improvements and ingenious devices, I supplied it with two issues for the metal, because this difficult and twisted figure could not otherwise have come out perfect.

It is only owing to my intelligent insight into means and appliances that the statue turned out as it did; a triumph judged impossible by all the practitioners of this art. I should like you furthermore to be aware, my lord, for certain, that the sole reason why I succeeded with all those great and arduous works in France under his most admirable Majesty King Francis, was the high courage which that good monarch put into my heart by the liberal allowances he made me, and the multitude of work-people he left at my disposal. I could have as many as I asked for, and employed at times above forty, all chosen by myself. These were the causes of my having there produced so many masterpieces in so short a space of time. Now then, my lord, put trust in me; supply me with the aid I need. I am confident of being able to complete a work which will delight your soul. But if your Excellency goes on disheartening me, and does not advance me the assistance which is absolutely required, neither I nor any man alive upon this earth can hope to achieve the slightest thing of value.'

It was as much as the Duke could do to stand by and listen to my pleadings. He kept turning first this way and then that; while I, in despair, poor wretched I, was calling up remembrance of the noble state I held in France, to the great sorrow of my soul. All at once he cried: 'Come, tell me, Benvenuto, how is it possible that yonder splendid head of Medusa, so high up there in the grasp of Perseus, should ever come out perfect?' I replied upon the instant: 'Look you now, my lord! If your Excellency possessed that knowledge of the craft which you affirm you have, you would not fear one moment for the splendid head you speak of. There is good reason, on the other hand, to feel uneasy about this right foot, so far below and at a distance from the rest.' When he heard these words, the Duke turned, half in anger, to some gentlemen in waiting, and exclaimed: 'I verily believe that this Benvenuto prides himself on contradicting everything one says.' Then he faced round to me with a touch of mockery, upon which his attendants did the like, and began to speak as follows: 'I will listen patiently to any argument you can possibly produce in explanation of your statement, which may convince me of its probability.' I said in answer: 'I will adduce so sound an argument that your Excellency shall perceive the full force of it.' So I began: 'You must know, my lord, that the nature of fire is to ascend, and therefore I promise you that Medusa's head will come out famously; but since it is not in the nature of fire to descend, and I must force it downwards six cubits by artificial means, I assure your Excellency upon this most convincing ground of proof that the foot cannot possibly come out. It will, however, be quite easy for me to restore it.' 'Why, then,' said the Duke, 'did you not devise it so that the foot should come out as well as you affirm the head will?' I answered: 'I must have made a much larger furnace, with a conduit as thick as my leg; and so I might have forced the molten metal by its own weight to descend so far. Now, my pipe, which runs six cubits to the statue's foot, as I have said, is not thicker than two fingers. However, it was not worth the trouble and expense to make a larger; for I shall easily be able to mend what is lacking. But when my mould is more than half full, as I expect, from this middle point upwards, the fire ascending by its natural property, then the heads of Perseus and Medusa will come out admirably; you may be quite sure of it.' After I had thus expounded these convincing arguments, together with many more of the same kind, which it would be tedious to set down here, the Duke shook his head and departed without further ceremony.

Abandoned thus to my own resources, I took new courage, and banished the sad thoughts which kept recurring to my mind, making me often weep bitter tears of repentance for having left France; for though I did so only to revisit Florence, my sweet birthplace, in order that I might charitably succour my six nieces, this good action, as I well perceived, had been the beginning of my great misfortune. Nevertheless, I felt convinced that when my Perseus was accomplished, all these trials would be turned to high felicity and glorious well-being.

Accordingly I strengthened my heart, and with all the forces of my body and my purse, I set to work. First I provided myself with several loads of pinewood from the forests of Serristori, in the neighbourhood of Montelupo. While these were on their way, I clothed my Perseus with the clay which I had prepared many months beforehand, in order that it might be duly seasoned. After making its clay tunic (for that is the term used in this art) and properly arming it and fencing it with iron girders, I began to draw the wax out by means of a slow fire. This melted and issued through numerous air-vents I had made; for the more there are of these, the better will the mould fill. When I had finished drawing off the wax, I constructed a funnel-shaped furnace all around the model of my Perseus. It was built of bricks, so interlaced, the one above the other, that numerous apertures were left for the fire to exhale at. Then I began to lay on wood by degrees, and kept it burning two whole days and nights. At length, when all the wax was gone, and the mould was well baked, I set to work at digging the pit in which to sink it. This I performed with scrupulous regard to all the rules of art. When I had finished that part of my work, I raised the mould by windlasses and stout ropes to a perpendicular position, and suspending it with the greatest care one cubit above the level of the furnace, so that it hung exactly above the middle of the pit, I next lowered it gently down into the very bottom of the furnace, and had it firmly placed with every possible precaution for its safety. When this delicate operation was accomplished, I began to bank it up with the earth I had excavated; and, ever as the earth grew higher, I introduced its proper air-vents, which were little tubes of earthenware, such as folk use for drains and such-like purposes. At length, I felt sure that it was admirably fixed, and that the filling-in of the pit and the placing of the air-vents had been properly performed. I also could see that my work-people understood my method, which differed very considerably from that of all the other masters in the trade. Feeling confident, then, that I could rely upon them, I next turned to my furnace, which I had filled with numerous pigs of copper and other bronze stuff. The pieces were piled according to the laws of art, that is to say, so resting one upon the other that the flames could play freely through them, in order that the metal might heat and liquefy the sooner. At last I called out heartily to set the furnace going. The logs of pine were heaped in, and, what with the unctuous resin of the wood and the good draught I had given, my furnace worked so well that I was obliged to rush from side to side to keep it going. The labour was more than I could stand; yet I forced myself to strain every nerve and muscle. To increase my anxieties, the workshop took fire, and we were afraid lest the roof should fall upon our heads; while, from the garden, such a storm of wind and rain kept blowing in, that it perceptibly cooled the furnace.

Battling thus with all these untoward circumstances for several hours, and exerting myself beyond even the measure of my powerful constitution, I could at last bear up no longer, and a sudden fever, of the utmost possible intensity, attacked me. I felt absolutely obliged to go and fling myself upon my bed. Sorely against my will having to drag myself away from the spot, I turned to my assistants, about ten or more in all, what with master-founders, hand-workers, country-fellows, and my own special journeymen, among whom was Bernardino Mannellini of Mugello, my apprentice through several years. To him in particular I spoke: 'Look, my dear Bernardino, that you observe the rules which I have taught you;

do your best with all despatch, for the metal will soon be fused. You cannot go wrong; these honest men will get the channels ready; you will easily be able to drive back the two plugs with this pair of iron crooks; and I am sure that my mould will fill miraculously. I feel more ill than I ever did in all my life, and verily believe that it will kill me before a few hours are over.' Thus, with despair at heart, I left them, and betook myself to bed.

No sooner had I got to bed, than I ordered my serving-maids to carry food and wine for all the men into the workshop; at the same time I cried; 'I shall not be alive to-morrow.' They tried to encourage me, arguing that my illness would pass over, since it came from excessive fatigue. In this way I spent two hours battling with the fever, which steadily increased, and calling out continually; 'I feel that I am dying.' My housekeeper, who was named Mona Fiore da Castel del Rio, a very notable manager and no less warm-hearted, kept chiding me for my discouragement; but, on the other hand, she paid me every kind attention which was possible. However, the sight of my physical pain and moral dejection so affected her, that, in spite of that brave heart of hers, she could not refrain from shedding tears; and yet, so far as she was able, she took good care I should not see them. While I was thus terribly afflicted, I beheld the figure of a man enter my chamber, twisted in his body into the form of a capital S. He raised a lamentable, doleful voice, like one who announces their last hour to men condemned to die upon the scaffold, and spoke these words: 'O Benvenuto! your statue is spoiled, and there is no hope whatever of saving it.' No sooner had I heard the shriek of that wretch than I gave a howl which might have been heard from the sphere of flame. Jumping from my bed, I seized my clothes and began to dress. The maids, and my lad, and every one who came around to help me, got kicks or blows of the fist, while I kept crying out in lamentation: 'Ah! traitors! enviers! This is an act of treason, done by malice prepense! But I swear by God that I will sift it to the bottom, and before I die will leave such witness to the world of what I can do as shall make a score of mortals marvel.'

When I had got my clothes on, I strode with soul bent on mischief toward the workshop; there I beheld the men, whom I had left erewhile in such high spirits, standing stupefied and downcast. I began at once and spoke: 'Up with you! Attend to me! Since you have not been able or willing to obey the directions I gave you, obey me now that I am with you to conduct my work in person. Let no one contradict me, for in cases like this we need the aid of hand and hearing, not of advice.' When I had uttered these words, a certain Maestro Alessandro Lastricati broke silence and said: 'Look you, Benvenuto, you are going to attempt an enterprise which the laws of art do not sanction, and which cannot succeed.' I turned upon him with such fury and so full of mischief, that he and all the rest of them exclaimed with one voice: 'On then! Give orders! We will obey your least commands, so long as life is left in us.' I believe they spoke thus feelingly because they thought I must fall shortly dead upon the ground. I went immediately to inspect the furnace, and found that the metal was all curdled; an accident which we express by 'being caked.' I told two of the hands to cross the road, and fetch from the house of the butcher Capretta a load of young oak-wood, which had lain dry for about a year; this wood had been previously offered me by Madame Ginevra, wife of the said Capretta. So soon as the first armfuls arrived, I began to fill the grate beneath the furnace. Now oak-wood of that kind heats more powerfully than any other sort of tree; and for this reason, where a slow fire is wanted, as in the case of gun-foundry, alder or pine is preferred. Accordingly, when the logs took fire, oh! how the cake began to stir beneath that awful heat, to glow and sparkle in a blaze! At the same time I kept stirring up the channels, and sent men upon the roof to stop the conflagration, which had gathered force from the increased combustion in the furnace; also I caused boards, carpets and other hangings to be set up against the garden, in order to protect us from the violence of the rain.

When I had thus provided against these several disasters, I roared out first to one man and then to another: 'Bring this thing here! Take that thing there!' At this crisis, when the whole gang saw the cake was on the point of melting, they did my bidding, each fellow working with the strength of three. I then ordered half a pig of pewter to be brought, which weighed about sixty pounds, and flung it into the middle of the cake inside the furnace. By this means, and by piling on wood and stirring now with pokers and now with iron rods, the curdled mass rapidly began to liquefy. Then, knowing I had brought the dead to life again, against the firm opinion of those ignoramuses, I felt such vigour fill my veins, that all those pains of fever, all those fears of death, were quite forgotten.

All of a sudden an explosion took place, attended by a tremendous flash of flame, as though a thunderbolt had formed and been discharged amongst us. Unwonted and appalling terror astonied every one, and me more even than the rest. When the din was over and the dazzling light extinguished, we began to look each other in the face. Then I discovered that the cap of the furnace had blown up, and the bronze was bubbling over from its source beneath. So I had the mouths of my mould immediately opened, and at the same time drove in the two plugs which kept back the molten metal. But I noticed that it did not flow as rapidly as usual, the reason being probably that the fierce heat of the fire we kindled had consumed its base alloy. Accordingly I sent for all my pewter platters, porringers, and dishes, to the number of some two hundred pieces, and had a portion of them cast, one by one, into the channels, the rest into the furnace. This expedient succeeded, and every one could now perceive that my bronze was in most perfect liquefaction, and my mould was filling; whereupon they all with heartiness and happy cheer assisted and obeyed my bidding, while I, now here, now there, gave orders, helped with my own hands, and cried aloud: 'O God! Thou that by Thy immeasurable power didst rise from the dead, and in Thy glory didst ascend to heaven!' . . . even thus in a moment my mould was filled; and seeing my work finished, I fell upon my knees, and with all my heart gave thanks to God.

After all was over, I turned to a plate of salad on a bench there, and ate with hearty appetite, and drank together with the whole crew. Afterwards I retired to bed, healthy and happy, for it was now two hours before morning, and slept as sweetly as though I had never felt a touch of illness. My good housekeeper, without my giving any orders, had prepared a fat capon for my repast. So that, when I rose, about the hour for breaking fast, she presented herself with a smiling countenance, and said: 'Oh! is that the man who felt that he was dying? Upon my word, I think the blows and kicks you dealt us last night, when you were so enraged, and had that demon in your body as it seemed, must have frightened away your mortal fever! The fever feared that it might catch it too, as we did!' All my poor household, relieved in like measure from anxiety and overwhelming labour, went at once to buy earthen vessels in order to replace the pewter I had cast away. Then we dined together joyfully; nay, I cannot remember a day in my whole life when I dined with greater gladness or a better appetite.

After our meal I received visits from the several men who had assisted me. They exchanged congratulations, and thanked God for our success, saying they had learned and seen things done which other masters judged impossible. I too grew somewhat glorious; and deeming I had shown myself a man of talent, indulged a boastful humour. So I thrust my hand

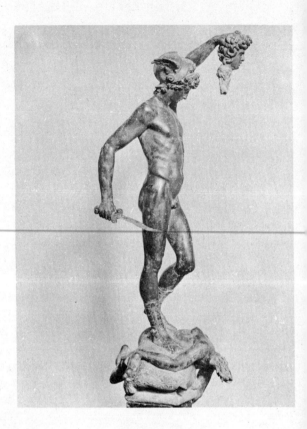

38. *Perseus,* Benvenuto
Cellini.

into my purse, and paid them all to their full satisfaction.

That evil fellow, my mortal foe, Messer Pier Francesco Riccio, major-domo of the Duke, took great pains to find out how the affair had gone. In answer to his questions, the two men whom I suspected of having caked my metal for me, said I was no man, but of a certainty some powerful devil, since I had accomplished what no craft of the art could do; indeed they did not believe a mere ordinary fiend could work such miracles as I in other ways had shown. They exaggerated the whole affair so much, possibly in order to excuse their own part in it, that the major-domo wrote an account to the Duke, who was then in Pisa, far more marvellous and full of thrilling incidents than what they had narrated.

After I had let my statue cool for two whole days, I began to uncover it by slow degrees. The first thing I found was that the head of Medusa had come out most admirably, thanks to the air-vents; for, as I had told the Duke, it is the nature of fire to ascend. Upon advancing farther, I discovered that the other head, that, namely, of Perseus, had succeeded no less admirably; and this astonished me far more, because it is at a considerably lower level than that of the Medusa. Now the mouths of the mould were placed above the head of Perseus and behind his shoulders; and I found that all the bronze my furnace contained had been exhausted in the head of this figure. It was a miracle to observe that not one fragment remained in the orifice of the channel, and that nothing was wanting to the statue. In my great astonishment I seemed to see in this the hand of God arranged and controlling all.

I went on uncovering the statue with success, and ascertained that everything had come out in perfect order, until I reached the foot of the right leg on which the statue rests. There the heel itself was formed, and going farther, I found the foot apparently complete. This gave me great joy on the one side, but was half unwelcome to me on the other, merely because I had told the Duke that it could not come out. However, when I reached the end, it appeared that the toes and a little piece above them were unfinished, so that about half the foot was wanting. Although I knew that this would add a trifle to my labour, I was very well pleased, because I could now prove to the Duke how well I understood my business. It is true that far more of the foot than I expected had been perfectly formed; the reason of this was that, from causes I have recently described, the bronze was hotter than our rules of art prescribe; also that I had been obliged to supplement the alloy with my pewter cups and platters, which no one else, I think, had ever done before.

Having now ascertained how successfully my work had been accomplished, I lost no time in hurrying to Pisa, where I found the Duke. He gave me a most gracious reception, as did also the Duchess; and although the major-domo had informed them of the whole proceedings, their Excellencies deemed my performance far more stupendous and astonishing when they heard the tale from my own mouth. When I arrived at the foot of Perseus, and said it had not come out perfect, just as I previously warned his Excellency, I saw an expression of wonder pass over his face, while he related to the Duchess how I had predicted this beforehand. Observing the princes to be so well disposed towards me, I begged leave from the Duke to go to Rome. He granted it in most obliging terms, and bade me return as soon as possible to complete his Perseus; giving me letters of recommendation meanwhile to his ambassador, Averardo Serristori. We were then in the first years of Pope Giulio de' Monti.

(from *The Life of Benvenuto Cellini*)

Sir Philip Sidney
from AN APOLOGIE FOR POETRIE

When the right vertuous *Edward Wotton* and I were at the Emperors Court together, wee gaue our selues to learne horsemanship of *Iohn Pietro Pugliano,* one that with great commendation had the place of an Esquire in his stable. And hee, according to the fertilnes of the Italian wit, did not onely afoord vs the demonstration of his practise, but sought to enrich our mindes with the contemplations therein which hee thought most precious. But with none I remember mine eares were at any time more loden, then when (either angred with slowe paiment, or mooued with our learner-like admiration) he exercised his speech in the prayse of his facultie. Hee sayd, Souldiours were the noblest estate of mankinde, and horsemen the noblest of Souldiours. Hee sayde they were the Maisters of warre, and ornaments of peace; speedy goers, and strong abiders; triumphers both in Camps and Courts. Nay, to so vnbeleeued a poynt hee proceeded, as that no earthly thing bred such wonder to a Prince as to be a good horseman. Skill of gouernment was but a Pedanteria in comparison. Then would hee adde certaine prayses, by telling what a peerlesse beast a horse was; the onely seruiceable Courtier without flattery, the beast of most beutie, faithfulnes, courage, and such more, that if I had not beene a peece of a Logician before I came to him, I think he would haue perswaded mee to haue wished my selfe a horse. But thus much at least with his no fewe words hee draue into me, that selfe-loue is better then any guilding to make that seeme gorgious wherein our selues are parties. Wherein, if *Pugliano* his strong affection and weake arguments will not satisfie you, I wil giue you a neerer example of my selfe, who (I knowe not by what mischance) in these my not old yeres and idelest times, hauing slipt into the title of a Poet, am prouoked to say somthing vnto you in the defence of that my vnelected vocation, which if I handle with more good will then good reasons, beare with me, sith the scholler is to be pardoned that foloweth the steppes of his Maister. And yet I must say that as I haue iust cause to make a pittifull defence of poore Poetry, which from almost the highest estimation of learning is fallen to be the laughing-stocke of children; so haue I need to bring some more auaileable proofes: sith the former is by no man barred of his deserued credite, the silly latter hath had euen the names of Philosophers vsed to the defacing of it, with great danger of ciuill war among the Muses.

. . .

Poesie therefore is an arte of imitation, for so *Aristotle* termeth it in his word *Mimesis,* that is to say, a representing, counterfetting, or figuring foorth: to speake metaphorically, a speaking picture: with this end, to teach and delight. Of this haue beene three seuerall kindes.

The chiefe both in antiquitie and excellencie were they that did imitate the inconceiuable excellencies of GOD. Such were *Dauid* in his Psalmes, *Salomon* in his song of Songs, in his Ecclesiastes, and Prouerbs, *Moses* and *Debora* in theyr Hymnes, and the writer of *Job;* which, beside other, the learned *Emanuell Tremelius* and *Franciscus Iunius* doe entitle the poeticall part of the Scripture. Against these none will speake that hath the holie Ghost in due holy reuerence. In this kinde, though in a full wrong diuinitie, were *Orpheus, Amphion, Homer* in his hymnes, and many other, both Greekes and Romaines: and this Poesie must be vsed, by whosoeuer will follow S. *Iames* his counsell, in singing Psalmes when they are merry: and I knowe is vsed with the fruite of comfort by some, when, in sorrowfull pangs of their death-bringing sinnes, they find the consolation of the neuer-leauing goodnesse.

The second kinde is of them that deale with matters Philosophicall; eyther morrall, as *Tirteus, Phocilides,* and *Cato;* or naturall, as *Lucretius* and *Virgils Georgicks;* or Astronomicall, as *Manilius* and *Pontanus;* or historical, as *Lucan;* which who mislike, the faulte is in their iudgements quite out of taste, and not in the sweet foode of sweetly vttered knowledge.

But because thys second sorte is wrapped within the folde of the proposed subiect, and takes not the course of his owne inuention, whether they properly be Poets or no let Gramarians dispute: and goe to the thyrd, indeed right Poets, of whom chiefly this question ariseth; betwixt whom and these second is such a kinde of difference as betwixt the meaner sort of Painters (who counterfet onely such faces as are sette before them) and the more excellent, who, hauing no law but wit, bestow that in collours vpon you which is fittest for the eye to see: as the constant though lamenting looke of *Lucrecia,* when she punished in her selfe an others fault; wherein he painteth not *Lucrecia* whom he neuer sawe, but painteth the outward beauty of such a vertue. For these third be they which most properly do imitate to teach and delight, and to imitate borrow nothing of what is, hath been, or shall be: but range, onely rayned with learned discretion, into the diuine consideration of what may be, and should be. These bee they that, as the first and most noble sorte, may iustly bee termed *Vates,* so these are waited on in the excellen[te]st languages and best vnderstandings, with the fore described name of

Poets: for these indeede doo meerely make to imitate, and imitate both to delight and teach, and delight to moue men to take that goodnes in hande, which without delight they would flye as from a stranger, and teach, to make them know that goodnes whereunto they are mooued, which being the noblest scope to which euer any learning was directed, yet want there not idle tongues to barke at them.

.   .   .

The Philosopher therfore and the Historian are they which would win the gole, the one by precept, the other by example. But both not hauing both, doe both halte. For the Philosopher, setting down with thorny argument the bare rule, is so hard of vtterance, and so mistic to bee conceiued, that one that hath no other guide but him shall wade in him till hee be olde before he shall finde sufficient cause to bee honest: for his knowledge standeth so vpon the abstract and generall, that happie is that man who may vnderstande him, and more happie that can applye what hee dooth vnderstand. On the other side, the Historian, wanting the precept, is so tyed, not to what shoulde bee but to what is, to the particular truth of things and not to the general reason of things, that hys example draweth no necessary consequence, and therefore a lesse fruitfull doctrine.

Nowe dooth the peerelesse Poet performe both: for whatsoeuer the Philosopher sayth shoulde be doone, hee giueth a perfect picture of it in some one, by whom hee presupposeth it was doone. So as hee coupleth the generall notion with the particuler example. A perfect picture I say, for hee yeeldeth to the powers of the minde an image of that whereof the Philosopher bestoweth but a woordish description: which dooth neyther strike, pierce, nor possesse the sight of the soule so much as that other dooth.

For as in outward things, to a man that had neuer seene an Elephant or a Rinoceros, who should tell him more exquisitely all theyr shapes, cullour, bignesse, and perticular markes, or of a gorgeous Pallace the Architecture, with declaring the full beauties, might well make the hearer able to repeate, as it were by rote, all hee had heard, yet should neuer satisfie his inward conceits with being witnes to it selfe of a true liuely knowledge: but the same man, as soone as hee might see those beasts well painted, or the house wel in moddel, should straightwaies grow, without need of any description, to iudicial comprehending of them: so no doubt the Philosopher with his learned definition, bee it of vertue, vices, matters of publick policie or priuat gouernment, replenisheth the memory with many infallible grounds of wisdom, which, notwithstanding, lye darke before the imaginatiue and iudging powre, if they bee not illuminated or figured foorth by the speaking picture of Poesie.

.   .   .

Nowe therein of all Sciences (I speak still of humane, and according to the humaine conceits) is our Poet the Monarch. For he dooth not only show the way, but giueth so sweete a prospect into the way, as will intice any man to enter into it. Nay, he dooth, as if your iourney should lye through a fayre Vineyard, at the first giue you a cluster of Grapes, that, full of that taste, you may long to passe further. He beginneth not with obscure definitions, which must blur the margent with interpretations, and load the memory with doubtfulnesse; but hee commeth to you with words sent in delightfull proportion, either accompanied with, or prepared for, the well inchaunting skill of Musicke; and with a tale forsooth he commeth vnto you, with a tale which holdeth children from play, and old men from the chimney corner. And, pretending no more, doth intende the winning of the mind from wickednesse to vertue: euen as the childe is often brought to take most wholsom things by hiding them in such other as haue a pleasant tast: which, if one should beginne to tell them the nature of *Aloes* or *Rubarb* they shoulde receiue, woulde sooner take their Phisicke at their eares then at their mouth. So is it in men (most of which are childish in the best things, till they bee cradled in their graues): glad they will be to heare the tales of *Hercules, Achilles, Cyrus,* and *Aeneas;* and, hearing them, must needs heare the right description of wisdom, valure, and iustice; which, if they had been barely, that is to say Philosophically, set out, they would sweare they bee brought to schoole againe.

.   .   .

Sith then Poetrie is of all humane learning the most auncient and of most fatherly antiquitie, as from whence other learnings haue taken theyr beginnings; sith it is so vniuersall that no learned Nation dooth

39. *Parnassus,* Andrea Mantegna

despise it, nor no barbarous Nation is without it; sith both Roman and Greek gaue diuine names vnto it, the one of prophecying, the other of making; and that indeede that name of making is fit for him, considering that where as other Arts retaine themselues within their subiect, and receiue, as it were, their beeing from it, the Poet onely bringeth his owne stuffe, and dooth not learne a conceite out of a matter, but maketh matter for a conceite; Sith neither his description nor his ende contayneth any euill, the thing described cannot be euill; Sith his effects be so good as to teach goodnes and to delight the learners; Sith therein (namely in morrall doctrine, the chiefe of all knowledges) hee dooth not onely farre passe the Historian, but, for instructing, is well nigh comparable to the Philosopher, and, for mouing, leaues him behind him; Sith the holy scripture (wherein there is no vncleannes) hath whole parts in it poeticall, and that euen our Sauiour Christ vouchsafed to vse the flowers of it; Sith all his kindes are not onlie in their vnited formes but in their seuered dissections fully commendable: I think (and think I thinke rightly) the Lawrell· crowne appointed for tryumphing Captaines does worthilie (of al other learnings) honor the Poets tryumph.

.   .   .

But sith I haue runne so long a careere in this matter, me thinks, before I giue my penne a fulle stop, it shalbe but a little more lost time to inquire why England (the Mother of excellent mindes) should bee growne so hard a step-mother to Poets, who certainly in wit ought to passe all other; sith all onely proceedeth from their wit, being indeede makers of themselues, not takers of others. How can I but exclaime,

Musa mihi causas memora, quo numine laeso.

Sweete Poesie, that hath aunciently had Kings, Emperors, Senators, great Captaines, such as, besides a thousand others, *Dauid, Adrian, Sophocles, Germanicus,* not onely to favour Poets, but to be Poets. And of our neerer times can present for her Patrons a *Robert,* king of Sicil, the great king *Francis* of France, King *Iames* of Scotland. Such Cardinals as *Bembus* and *Bibiena.* Such famous Preachers and Teachers as *Beza* and *Melancthon.* So learned Philosophers as *Fracastorius* and *Scaliger.* So great Orators as *Pontanus* and *Muretus.* So piercing wits as *George Buchanan.* So graue Counsellors as, besides many, but before all, that *Hospitall* of Fraunce, then whom (I thinke) that Realme neuer brought forth a more accomplished iudgement, more firmely builded vpon vertue. I say these, with numbers of others, not onely to read others Poesies, but to Poetise for others reading. That Poesie, thus embraced in all other places, should onely finde in our time a hard welcome in England, I think the very earth lamenteth it, and therfore decketh our Soyle with fewer Laurels then it was accustomed. For heertofore Poets haue in England also flourished; and, which is to be noted, euen in those times when the trumpet of *Mars* did sounde loudest. And now that an ouer-faint quietnes should seeme to strew the house for Poets, they are almost in as good reputation as the *Mountibancks* at *Venice.*

.   .   .

Chaucer, vndoubtedly, did excellently in hys *Troylus* and *Cresseid;* of whom, truly, I know not whether to meruaile more, either that he in

that mistie time could see so clearely, or that wee in this cleare age walke
so stumblingly after him. Yet had he great wants, fitte to be forgiuen in
so reuerent antiquity. I account the *Mirrour of Magistrates* meetely fur
nished of beautiful parts; and in the Earle of Surries *Liricks* many things
tasting of a noble birth, and worthy of a noble minde. The *Sheapheards*
Kalender hath much Poetrie in his Eglogues: indeede worthy the reading
if I be not deceiued. That same framing of his stile to an old rustick
language I dare not alowe, sith neyther *Theocritus* in Greeke, *Virgill* in
Latine, nor *Sanazar* in Italian did affect it. Besides these, doe I not re
member to haue seene but fewe (to speake boldely) printed, that haue
poeticall sinnewes in them: for proofe whereof, let but most of the verses
bee put in Prose, and then aske the meaning; and it will be found that
one verse did but beget another, without ordering at the first what should
be at the last; which becomes a confused masse of words, with a tingling
sound of ryme, barely accompanied with reason.

Our Tragedies and Comedies (not without cause cried out against)
obseruing rules neyther of honest ciuilitie nor of skilfull Poetrie, ex
cepting *Gorboduck* (againe, I say, of those that I haue seene), which not
withstanding, as it is full of stately speeches and well sounding Phrases,
clyming to the height of *Seneca* his stile, and as full of notable moralitie
which it doth most delightfully teach, and so obtayne the very end o
Poesie, yet in troth it is very defectious in the circumstaunces, which
greeueth mee, because it might not remaine as an exact model of al
Tragedies. For it is faulty both in place and time, the two necessary com
panions of all corporall actions. For where the stage should alwaie
represent but one place, and the vttermost time presupposed in it should
be, both by *Aristotles* precept and common reason, but one day, there i
both many dayes, and many places, inartificially imagined. But if it be
so in *Gorboduck*, how much more in al the rest? where you shal haue
Asia of the one side, and *Affrick* of the other, and so many other vnder
kingdoms, that the Player, when he commeth in, must euer begin with
telling where he is, or els the tale wil not be conceiued. Now ye sha
haue three Ladies walke to gather flowers, and then we must beleeue the
stage to be a Garden. By and by, we heare newes of shipwracke in the
same place, and then wee are to blame if we accept it not for a Rock
Vpon the backe of that, comes out a hidious Monster, with fire and smoke
and then the miserable beholders are bounde to take it for a Caue
While in the meantime two Armies flye in, represented with foure sword
and bucklers, and then what harde heart will not receiue it for a pitche

fielde? Now, of time they are much more liberall, for ordinary it is that two young Princes fall in loue. After many trauerces, she is got with childe, deliuered of a faire boy; he is lost, groweth a man, falls in loue, and is ready to get another child; and all this in two hours space: which how absurd it is in sence euen sence may imagine, and Arte hath taught, and all auncient examples iustified, and, at this day, the ordinary Players in Italie wil not erre in. Yet wil some bring in an example of *Eunuchus* in *Terence,* that containeth matter of two dayes, yet far short of twenty yeeres. True it is, and so was it to be played in two daies, and so fitted to the time it set forth. And though *Plautus* hath in one place done amisse, let vs hit with him, and not misse with him. But they wil say, how then shal we set forth a story, which containeth both many places and many times? And doe they not knowe that a Tragedie is tied to the lawes of Poesie, and not of Historie? not bound to follow the story, but, hauing liberty, either to faine a quite newe matter, or to frame the history to the most tragicall conueniencie. Againe, many things may be told which cannot be shewed, if they knowe the difference betwixt reporting and representing. As, for example, I may speake (though I am heere) of *Peru,* and in speech digresse from that to the description of *Calicut;* but in action I cannot represent it without *Pacolets* horse: and so was the manner the Auncients tooke, by some *Nuncius,* to recount thinges done in former time or other place. Lastly, if they wil represent an history, they must not (as *Horace* saith) beginne *Ab ouo,* but they must come to the principall poynt of that one action which they wil represent. By example this wil be best expressed. I haue a story of young *Polidorus,* deliuered for safe- ties sake, with great riches, by his Father *Priamus* to *Polimnestor,* king of *Thrace,* in the Troyan war time. Hee after some yeeres, hearing the ouer- throwe of *Priamus,* for to make the treasure his owne, murthereth the child; the body of the child is taken vp by *Hecuba;* shee the same day findeth a slight to bee reuenged most cruelly of the Tyrant: where nowe would one of our Tragedy writers begin, but with the deliuery of the childe? Then should he sayle ouer into *Thrace,* and so spend I know not how many yeeres, and trauaile numbers of places. But where dooth *Euripides?* Euen with the finding of the body, leauing the rest to be tolde by the spirit of *Polidorus.* This need no further to be inlarged; the dull- est wit may conceiue it.

But besides these grosse absurdities, how all theyr Playes be neither right Tragedies, nor right Comedies; mingling Kings and Clownes, not because the matter so carrieth it, but thrust in Clownes by head and shoulders, to play a part in maiesticall matters, with neither decencie nor discretion: So as neither the admiration and commiseration, nor the right sportfulnes, is by their mungrell Tragy-comedie obtained. I know *Apuleius* did some-what so, but that is a thing recounted with space of time, not represented in one moment: and I knowe the Auncients haue one or two examples of Tragy-comedies, as *Plautus* hath *Amphitrio*. But, if we marke them well, we shall find, that they neuer, or very daintily, match Horn-pypes and Funeralls. So falleth it out that, hauing indeed no right Comedy, in that comicall part of our Tragedy we haue nothing but scurrility, vnwoorthy of any chast eares, or some extreame shew of doltishness, indeed fit to lift vp a loude laughter, and nothing els: where the whole tract of a Comedy shoulde be full of delight, as the Tragedy shoulde be still maintained in a well raised admiration. But our Comedians thinke there is no delight without laughter; which is very wrong, for though laughter may come with delight, yet commeth if not of delight, as though delight should be the cause of laughter; but well may one thing breed both together: nay, rather in themselues they haue, as it were, a kind of contrarietie: for delight we scarcely doe but in things that haue a conueniencie to our selues or to the generall nature: laughter almost euer commeth of things most disproportioned to our selues and nature. Delight hath a ioy in it, either permanent or present. Laughter hath onely a scornful tickling. For example, we are rauished with delight to see a faire woman, and yet are far from being moued to laughter. We laugh at deformed creatures, wherein certainely we cannot delight. We delight in good chaunces, we laught at mischaunches; we delight to heare the happines of our friends, or Country, at which he were worthy to be laughed at that would laugh; wee shall, contrarily, laugh sometimes to finde a matter quite mistaken and goe downe the hill agaynst the byas, in the mouth of some such men, as for the respect of them one shalbe hartely sorry, yet he cannot chuse but laugh; and so is rather pained then delighted with laughter. Yet deny I not but that they may goe well together; for as in *Alexanders* picture well set out wee delight without laughter, and in twenty mad Anticks we laugh without delight, so in *Hercules,* painted with his great beard and furious countenance, in womans attire, spinning at *Omphales* commaundment, it breedeth both delight and laughter. For the representing of so strange a power in loue procureth delight: and the scornefulnes of the action stirreth laughter. But I speake to this purpose, that all the end of the comicall part bee not vpon such scornefull matters as stirreth laughter onely, but, mixt with it, that delightful teaching which is the end of Poesie. And the great fault euen in that point of laughter, and forbidden plainely by *Aristotle,* is that they styrre laughter in sinfull things, which are rather execrable then ridiculous: or in miserable, which are rather to be pittied then scorned. For what is it to make folkes gape at a wretched Begger, or a beggerly Clowne? or, against lawe of hospitality, to iest at straungers, because they speake not English so well as we doe? what do we learne? sith it is certaine

> *Nil habet infelix paupertas durias in se,*
> *Quam quod ridiculos homines facet.**

But rather a busy louing Courtier, a hartles threatening *Thraso,* a selfe-wise-seeming schoolemaster, a awry-transformed Traueller: These if wee sawe walke in stage names, which wee play naturally, therein were de-lightfull laughter, and teaching delightfulnes: as in the other, the Trage-dies of *Buchanan* doe iustly bring forth a diuine admiration. But I haue lauished out too many wordes of this play matter. I doe it because as they are excelling parts of Poesie, so is there none so much vsed in England, and none can be more pittifully abused. Which like an vnmannerly Daughter, shewing a bad education, causeth her mother Poesies honesty to bee called in question.

Other sorts of Poetry almost haue we none, but that Lyricall kinds of Songs and Sonnets: which, Lord, if he gaue vs so good mindes, how well it might be imployed, and with howe heauenly fruite, both priuate and publique, in singing the prayses of the immortall beauty, the immortall goodnes of that God who gyueth vs hands to write and wits to conceiue; of which we might well want words, but neuer matter; of which we could turne our eies to nothing, but we should euer haue new budding oc-casions. But truely many of such writings as come vnder the banner of vnresistable loue, if I were a Mistres, would neuer perswade mee they were in loue; so coldely they apply fiery speeches, as men that had rather red Louers writings, and so caught vp certaine swelling phrases, which hang together like a man which once tolde mee the winde was at North West, and by South, because he would be sure to name windes enowe,— then that in truth they feele those passions, which easily (as I think) may be bewrayed by that same forciblenes, or *Energia* (as the Greekes cal it), of the writer. But let this bee a sufficient though short note, that wee misse the right vse of the materiall point of Poesie.

.　　.　　.

---

* "Harsh poverty has nothing worse than this—that it makes men ridiculous." uvenal, *Satires,* III, 152-3.

So that sith the euer-praise-worthy Poesie is full of vertue-breeding delightfulnes, and voyde of no gyfte that ought to be in the noble name of
learning: sith the blames laid against it are either false or feeble; sith
the cause why it is not esteemed in Englande is the fault of Poet-apes, not
Poets; sith, lastly, our tongue is most fit to honor Poesie, and to bee honored by Poesie; I coniure you all that haue had the euill lucke to reade
this incke-wasting toy of mine, euen in the name of nyne Muses, no more
to scorne the sacred misteries of Poesie, no more to laugh at the name of
Poets, as though they were next inheritours to Fooles, no more to iest at
the reuerent title of a Rymer; but to beleeue, with *Aristotle,* that they
were the auncient Treasurers of the Graecians Diuinity. To beleeue, with
Bembus, that they were first bringers in of all ciuilitie. To beleeue, with
Scaliger, that no Philosophers precepts can sooner make you an honest
man then the reading of *Virgill.* To beleeue, with *Clauserus,* the Transla-
tor of *Cornutus,* that it pleased the heauenly Deitie, by *Hesiod* and
Homer, vnder the vayle of fables, to giue vs all knowledge, Logick,
Rethorick, Philosophy, naturall and morall; and *Quid non?* To beleeue,
with me, that there are many misteries contained in Poetrie, which of
purpose were written darkely, least by prophane wits it should bee abused.
To beleeue, with *Landin,* that they are so beloued of the Gods that what
soeuer they write proceeds of a diuine fury. Lastly, to beleeue themselues
when they tell you they will make you immortall by their verses.

Thus doing, your name shal florish in the Printers shoppes; thus doing, you shall bee of kinne to many a poeticall Preface; thus doing, you
shall be most fayre, most ritch, most wise, most all; you shall dwell vpon
Superlatiues. Thus dooing, though you be *Libertino patre natus,* you shall
suddenly grow *Herculea proles,**

*Si quid mea carmina possunt.** *

Thus doing, your soule shal be placed with *Dantes Beatrix,* or *Virgil*
Anchises. But if (fie of such a but) you be borne so neere the dull making
Cataphract of *Nilus* that you cannot heare the Plannet-like Musick of
Poetrie, if you haue so earth-creeping a mind that it cannot lift it selfe
vp to looke to the sky of Poetry, or rather, by a certaine rusticall dis-
daine, will become such a Mome as to be a *Momus* of Poetry; then

* ". . . though you be the son of a freedman, you shall suddenly grow [i.e.
become] a child of Hercules."

** "If my songs are of any avail." Virgil, *Aeneid,* IX, 446.

though I will not wish vnto you the Asses eares of *Midas,* nor to bee driuen by a Poets verses (as *Bubonax* was) to hang himselfe, nor to be rimed to death, as is sayd to be doone in Ireland; yet thus much curse I must send you, in the behalfe of all Poets, that while you liue, you liue in loue, and neuer get fauor for lacking skill of a *Sonnet;* and when you die, your memory die from the earth for want of an *Epitaph.*

LOPE DE VEGA

THE NEW ART OF WRITING PLAYS

An Address to the Academy at Madrid

You command me, noble spirits, flower of Spain—who in this congress and renowned academy will in short space of time surpass not only the assemblies of Italy which Cicero, envious of Greece, made famous with his own name, hard by the Lake of Avernus, but also Athens where in the Lyceum of Plato was seen high conclave of philosophers—to write you an art of the play which is today acceptable to the taste of the crowd.

Easy seems this subject, and easy it would be for anyone of you who had written very few comedies, and who knows more about the art of writing them and of all these things; for what condemns me in this task is that I have written them without art.

Not because I was ignorant of the precepts; thank God, even while I was a tyro in grammar, I went through the books which treated the subject, before I had seen the sun run its course ten times from the Ram to the Fishes:

But because, in fine, I found that comedies were not at that time, in Spain, as their first devisers in the world thought that they should be written; but rather as many rude fellows managed them, who confirmed the crowd in its own crudeness; and so they were introduced in such wise that he who now writes them artistically dies without fame and guerdon; for custom can do more among those who lack light of art than reason and force.

True it is that I have sometimes written in accordance with the art which few know; but, no sooner do I see coming from some other source the monstrosities full of painted scenes where the crowd congregates and the women who canonize this sad business, than I return to that same barbarous habit, and when I have to write a comedy I lock in the precepts with six keys, I banish Terence and Plautus from my study that they may not cry out at me; for truth, even in dumb books, is wont to call aloud; and I write in accordance with that art which they devised who aspired to the applause of the crowd; for, since the crowd pays for the comedies it is fitting to talk foolishly to it to satisfy its taste.

Yet true comedy has its end established like every kind of poem or poetic art, and that has always been to imitate the actions of men and to paint the customs of their age. Furthermore, all poetic imitation whatsoever is composed of three things, which are discourse, agreeable verse harmony, that is to say music, which so far was common also to tragedy comedy being different from tragedy in that it treats of lowly and plebeian actions, and tragedy of royal and great ones. Look whether there be in our comedies few failings.

Auto was the name given to them, for they imitate the actions and the doings of the crowd. Lope de Rueda was an example in Spain of these principles, and today are to be seen in print prose comedies of his so lowly that he introduces into them the doings of mechanics and the love of the daughter of a smith; whence there has remained the custom of calling the old comedies *entremeses,* where the art persists in all its force there being one action and that between plebeian people; for an *entremé* with a king has never been seen. And thus it is shown how the art, for very lowness of style, came to be held in great disrepute, and the king in the comedy to be introduced for the ignorant.

Aristotle depicts in his *Poetics*—although obscurely—the beginning of comedy; the strife between Athens and Megara as to which of them was the first inventor; they of Megara say that it was Epicarmus, while Athens would have it that Magnetes was the man. Elias Donatus says it had its origin in ancient sacrifices. He names Thespis as the author of tragedy—following Horace, who affirms the same—as of comedies, Aristophanes Homer composed the *Odyssey* in imitation of comedy, but the *Iliad* was a famous example of tragedy, in imitation of which I called my *Jerusalem* an epic, and added the term *tragic;* and in the same manner all people commonly term the *Inferno,* the *Purgatorio,* and the *Paradiso* of the celebrated poet Dante Alighieri a comedy, and this Manetti recognizes in his prologue.

Now everybody knows that comedy, as if under suspicion, was silenced for a certain time, and that hence also satire was born, which, being more cruel, more quickly came to an end, and gave place to the New Comedy. The choruses were the first things; then the fixed number of the characters was introduced; but Menander, whom Terence followed, held the choruses in despite, as offensive. Terence was more circumspect as to the principles; since he never elevated the style of comedy to the greatness of tragedy, which many have condemned as vicious in Plautus; for in this respect Terence was more wary.

Tragedy has as its argument history, and comedy fiction; for this reason it was called flat-footed, of humble argument, since the actor performed without buskin or stage. There were comedies with the *pallium,* mimes, comedies with the toga, *fabulae atellanae,* and comedies of the tavern, which were also, as now, of various sorts.

With Attic elegance the men of Athens chided vice and evil custom in their comedies, and they gave their prizes both to the writers of verse and to the devisers of action. For this Tully called comedies "the mirror of custom and a living image of the truth"—a very high tribute, in that comedy ran even with history. Look whether it be worthy of this crown and glory!

But now I perceive that you are saying that this is merely translating books and wearying you with painting this mixed-up affair. Believe me, there has been a reason why you should be reminded of some of these things; for you see that you ask me to describe the art of writing plays in Spain, where whatever is written is in defiance of art; and to tell how they are now written contrary to the ancient rule and to what is founded on reason, is to ask me to draw on my experience, not on art, for art speaks truth which the ignorant crowd gainsays.

If, then, you desire art, I beseech you, men of genius, to read the very learned Robortello of Udine and you will see in what he says concerning Aristotle, and especially in what he writes about comedy, as much as is scattered among many books; for everything of today is in a state of confusion.

If you wish to have my opinion of the comedies which now have the upper hand and to know why it is necessary that the crowd with its laws should maintain the vile chimera of this comic monster, I will tell you what I hold, and do you pardon me, since I must obey whoever has power to command me—that, gilding the error of the crowd, I desire to tell you of what sort I would have them; for there is no recourse but to follow art observing a mean between the two extremes.

Let the subject be chosen and do not be amused—may you excuse these precepts!—if it happens to deal with kings; though, for that matter, I understand that Philip the Prudent, King of Spain and our lord, was offended at seeing a king in them; either because the matter was hostile to art or because the royal authority ought not to be represented among the lowly and the vulgar.

This is merely turning back to the Old Comedy, where we see that Plautus introduced gods, as in his *Amphitryon* he represents Jupiter. God knows that I have difficulty in giving this my approbation, since Plutarch, speaking of Menander, does not highly esteem Old Comedy. But since we are so far away from art and in Spain do it a thousand wrongs, let the learned this once close their lips.

Tragedy mixed with comedy and Terence with Seneca, though it be like another minotaur of Pasiphaë, will render one part grave, the other ridiculous; for this variety causes much delight. Nature gives us good example, for through such variety it is beautiful.

Bear in mind that this subject should contain one action only, seeing to it that the story in no manner be episodic; I mean the introduction of other things which are beside the main purpose; nor that any member be omitted which might ruin the whole of the context. There is no use in advising that it should take place in the period of one sun, though this is the view of Aristotle, but we lose our respect for him when we mingle tragic style with the humbleness of mean comedy. Let it take place in as little time as possible, except when the poet is writing history in which some years have to pass; these he can relegate to the space between the acts, wherein, if necessary, he can have a character go on some journey; a thing that greatly offends whoever perceives it. But let not him who is offended go to see them.

Oh! how lost in admiration are many at this very time at seeing that years are passed in an affair to which an artificial day sets a limit; though for this they would not allow the mathematical day! But, considering that the wrath of a seated Spaniard is immoderate, when in two hours there is not presented to him everything from Genesis to the Last Judgment, I deem it most fitting, if it be for us here to please him, for us to adjust everything so that it succeeds.

The subject once chosen, write in prose, and divide the matter into three acts of time, seeing to it, if possible, that in each one the space of the day be not broken. Captain Verués, a worthy wit, divided comedy into three acts, which before had gone on all fours, as on baby's feet, for comedies were then infants. I wrote them myself, when eleven or twelve years of age, of four acts and of four sheets of paper, for a sheet contained each act; and then it was the fashion that for the three intermissions were made three little *entremeses,* but today scarce one, and then a dance, for the dancing is so important in comedy that Aristotle approves of it, and Athenaeus, Plato, and Xenophon treat of it, though this last disapproves of indecorous dancing; and for this reason he is vexed at Callipides, wherein he pretends to ape the ancient chorus. The matter divided into two parts, see to the connection from the beginning until the action runs down· but do not permit the untying of the plot until reaching the last scene; for the crowd, knowing what the end is, will turn its face to the door and its shoulder to what it has awaited three hours face to face; for in what appears nothing more is to be known.

Very seldom should the stage remain without someone speaking, because the crowd becomes restless in these intervals and the story spins itself out at great length; for, besides its being a great defect, the avoidance of it increases grace and artifice.

Begin then, and, with simple language, do not spend sententious thoughts and witty sayings on family trifles, which is all that the familiar talk of two or three people is representing. But when the character who is introduced persuades, counsels, or dissuades, then there should be gravity and wit; for then doubtless is truth observed, since a man speaks in a different style from what is common when he gives counsel, or persuades, or argues against anything. Aristides, the rhetorician, gave us warrant for this; for he wishes the language of comedy to be pure, clear, and flexible, and he adds also that it should be taken from the usage of the people, this being different from that of polite society; for in the latter case the diction will be elegant, sonorous, and adorned. Do not drag in quotations, nor let your language offend because of exquisite words; for, if one is to imitate those who speak, it should not be by the language of Panchaia, of the Metaurus, of hippogriffs, demigods, and centaurs.

If the king should speak, imitate as much as possible the gravity of a king; if the sage speak, observe a sententious modesty; describe lovers with those passions which greatly move whoever listens to them; manage soliloquies in such a manner that the recitant is quite transformed, and in changing himself, changes the listener. Let him ask questions and reply to himself, and if he shall make plaints, let him observe the respect due to women. Let not ladies disregard their character, and if they change costumes, let it be in such wise that it may be excused; for male disguise usually is very pleasing. Let him be on his guard against impossible things, for it is of the chiefest importance that only the likeness of truth should be represented. The lackey should not discourse of lofty affairs, nor express the conceits which we have seen in certain foreign plays; and in no wise let the character contradict himself in what he has said; I mean to say, forget—as in Sophocles one blames Oedipus for not remembering that he has killed Laius with his own hand. Let the scenes end with epigram, with wit, and with elegant verse, in such wise that, at his exit, he who spouts leave not the audience disgusted. In the first act set forth the case. In the second weave together the events, in such wise that until the middle of the third act one may hardly guess the outcome. Always trick expectancy; and hence it may come to pass that something quite far from what is promised may be left to the understanding. Tactfully suit your verse to the subjects being treated. *Décimas* are good for complainings; the sonnet is good for those who are waiting in expectation; recitals of events ask for *romances*, though they shine brilliantly in octavas. *Tercets* are for grave affairs and *redondillos* for affairs of love. Let rhetorical figures be brought in, as repetition or anadiplosis, and in the beginning of these same verses the various forms of anaphora; and also irony, questions, apostrophes, and exclamations.

To deceive the audience with the truth is a thing that has seemed well as Miguel Sánchez, worthy of this memorial for the invention, was wont to do in all his comedies. Equivoque and the uncertainty arising from ambiguity have always held a large place among the crowd, for it thinks that it alone understands what the other one is saying. Better still are the subjects in which honor has a part, since they deeply stir everybody, along with them go virtuous deeds, for virtue is everywhere loved; hence we see, if an actor chance to represent a traitor, he is so hateful to every one that what he wishes to buy is not sold him, and the crowd flees when it meets him; but if he is loyal, they lend to him and invite him, and even the chief men honor him, love him, seek him out, entertain him, and acclaim him.

Let each act have but four sheets, for twelve are well suited to the time and the patience of him who is listening. In satirical parts, be not clear or open, since it is known that for this very reason comedies were forbidden by law in Greece and Italy; wound without hate, for if, perchance, slander be done, expect not applause, nor aspire to fame.

These things you may regard as aphorisms which you get not from the ancient art, which the present occasion allows no further space for treating; since whatever has to do with the three kinds of stage properties which Vitruvius speaks of concerns the impresario; just as Valerius Maximus, Petrus Crinitus, Horace in his epistles, and others describe these properties, with their drops, trees, cabins, houses, and simulated marbles.

Of costume Julius Pollux would tell us if it were necessary, for in Spain it is the case that the comedy of today is replete with barbarous things; a Turk wearing the neck-gear of a Christian and a Roman in tight breeches.

But of all, nobody can I call more barbarous than myself, since in defiance of art I dare to lay down precepts, and I allow myself to be borne along in the vulgar current, wherefore Italy and France call me ignorant. But what can I do if I have written four hundred and eighty-three comedies, along with one which I finished this week? For all of these, except six, gravely sin against art. Yet, in fine, I defend what I have written, and I know that, though they might have been better in another manner, they would not have had the vogue which they have had; for sometimes that which is contrary to what is just, for that very reason, pleases the taste.

> How Comedy reflects this life of man,
>   How true her portraiture of young and old;
> How subtle wit, polished in narrow span,
>   And purest speech, and more too you behold;
> What grave consideration mixed with smiles,
>   What seriousness, along with pleasant jest;
> Deceit of slaves; how woman oft beguiles
>   How full of slyness is her treacherous breast;
> How silly, awkward swains to sadness run,
>   How rare success, though all seems well begun,

Let one hear with attention, and dispute not of the art; for in comedy everything will be found of such a sort that in listening to it everything becomes evident.

COMMEDIA DELL' ARTE SCENARIO
THE THREE CUCKOLDS

A Comedy

Dramatis Personae

Pantalone.
Flaminia, his wife.   *Lucinda.*
Coviello.   *Ubaldo.*
Cintia, his wife.   *Ardelia.*
~~Zanni.~~   ~~*Cola.*~~
Franceschina, his wife.   *Columbina*
Leandro, a young man.   *Ottavio.*
    Valerio.
    Stoppino, servant.

Properties. A washing basket with sheets; chest for lemons; cask; tow; fire; candle; broth; dress for a rogue.

Act I

Coviello, Cintia have their scene of reciprocal jealousy. Cintia goes in and leaves Coviello to disclose his passion for Flaminia, the wife of Pantalone; he knocks at her door:

Flaminia appears. They have their love scene and in the end she tells him about the chest of lemons. Coviello goes in, Flaminia stays; at this:

Pantalone is asked to provide her with lemons; he promises to send them in a chest. Flaminia goes in. Pantalone is left to disclose his love for Franceschina, Zanni's wife; he knocks at her door:

Franceschina hears everything and declares that she favours Pantalone; he departs, she remains; at this:

Zanni tells his wife to go to work; they have many antics. Franceschina goes in and he stays saying what a nuisance she is; at this:

Coviello asks Zanni to carry him in a chest and explains everything. They go off down the street.

Leandro declares his love for Cintia and knocks at her door:

Cintia hears everything and instructs him to come dressed as a rogue, dumb and disguised. She goes in and he departs to dress up.

Pantalone can wait no longer and says that at last it is time; he knocks for Franceschina.

Franceschina leads him into the house and they have their antics over the entrance.

Zanni, with the chest, exhorts Coviello not to speak or move; he puts him inside; at this:

Leandro as a dumb beggar is forced to shoulder the chest by Zanni who does not recognize him; at this:

Flaminia receives the chest. Zanni enters. Leandro is left and knocks for Cintia.

Cintia receives him into the house, they have their scene and the act ends.

Act II

Zanni blames Flaminia for the trick played on her husband and congratulates himself on the honesty of his wife Franceschina; meanwhile she is heard within singing and slapping up and down with the washing; then she comes out.

Franceschina appears with the cask which she puts over her husband's head, playing the trick of the tart; at this:

Pantalone comes out of Franceschina's house grinning, he goes to knock at his own home. Zanni and Franceschina go in. Pantalone is left calling his wife.

Flaminia with much circumstance recounts the dream of the eye and makes him hide his eyes from Flaminia; at this:

Coviello comes out of Flaminia's house laughing at the trick. He goes to knock at his own. Pantalone and Flaminia go in; Coviello knocks.

Cintia makes much of Coviello and caresses him, and then tells him of the poor beggar she has in the house; at this:

Leandro disguised comes in with some soup. Coviello scolds and goes into the house with Cintia. Leandro laughs at the hoax and seeing Zanni approaching pretends to be dumb again.

Zanni after several jokes recognizes Leandro and tells him what has been going on in Pantalone's house. Leandro tells him what has happened at Coviello's and goes in laughing. Zanni stays; at this:

Pantalone learns from Zanni the jest of the rogue. Pantalone tells him the jest of the cask and Zanni in the end tells about the lemon-chest and goes in. Pantalone is left; at this:

Coviello is told of the hoax of the rogue; they have their scene together shouting 'Cuckold' at each other.

40. A typical *Scene of Horseplay in Commedia dell' Arte*.

Act III

Franceschina to borrow a buck-basket knocks for

Cintia who promises to give it her with the washing and takes her into the house.

Pantalone wishes to return to Franceschina who had pleased him; at this:

Franceschina comes with the basket and the clothes. Pantalone explains his intentions and she makes him get into the basket and covers him with clothes; at this:

Zanni aware of all that is going on and knowing there is someone in the basket has many antics about throwing the clothes into the copper and boiling them. He carries in the basket and coming out again tells Franceschina that he is going into the country. She is delighted and goes into the house. Zanni goes down the street.

Coviello after his former success wishes to try again, he knocks for

Flaminia who hears his wish and receives him once more and leads him into the house.

Leandro, Cintia do the same; Cintia embraces him and takes him into the house again.

Zanni comes to make sure about his wife; he draws near to the door and hears caresses going on; he knocks in a fury.

Franceschina hearing that Zanni wants to burn down the house makes him carry out the basket of clothes, before he sets fire to the place. With an uproar

Pantalone comes out among the clothes in the basket; at this

All the couples arm in arm rush to the alarm of fire in the room. Leandro explains what each has done to the other and delivers over to each his proper wife with whom he is at last content. They go in and the comedy ends.

THOMAS DEKKER

FROM THE SHOEMAKERS' HOLIDAY

Dramatis Personae

THE KING	(Henry V?)
EARL OF LINCOLN	(Sir Hugh Lacy)
EARL OF CORNWALL	
ROWLAND LACY,	LINCOLN's nephew
ASKEW,	another relative
LOVELL,	a courtier
DODGER,	servant to LINCOLN
SIR ROGER OTLEY,	Lord Mayor of London
MASTER HAMMON,	
MASTER WARNER,	Citizens of London
MASTER SCOTT,	
SIMON EYRE,	the Shoemaker
ROGER (known as HODGE),	
FIRK,	EYRE's workmen
RAFE DAMPORT,	
ROSE,	daughter of OTLEY
SYBIL,	her maid
MARGERY,	wife of EYRE
JANE,	wife of RAFE

A Dutch Skipper, a Boy, Officers,
Soldiers, Shoemakers, and Apprentices.

Scene: The City of London and the adjacent village of Old Ford.

The Prologue

As it was pronounced before the Queen's Majesty

As wretches in a storm, expecting day,
With trembling hands and eyes cast up to heaven,
Make prayers the anchor of their conquer'd hopes,
So we, dear goddess, wonder of all eyes,
Your meanest vassals, through mistrust and fear
To sink into the bottom of disgrace
By our imperfect pastimes, prostrate thus
On bended knees, our sails of hope do strike,
Dreading the bitter storms of your dislike.
Since then, unhappy men, our hap is such
That to ourselves ourselves no help can bring,
But needs must perish, if your saint-like ears,
Locking the temple where all mercy sits,
Refuse the tribute of our begging tongues;
Oh, grant, bright mirror of true chastity,
From those life-breathing stars, your sun-like eyes,
One gracious smile; for your celestial breath
Must send us life, or sentence us to death.

Act I

Scene I.—A London Street.

Enter LORD MAYOR, [*and the* EARL OF] LINCOLN.

LINCOLN. My lord mayor, you have sundry times
　　Feasted myself and many courtiers more;
　　Seldom or never can we be so kind
　　To make requital of your courtesy.
　　But, leaving this, I hear my cousin Lacy
　　Is much affected to your daughter Rose.

LORD MAYOR. True, my good lord, and she loves him so well
　　That I mislike her boldness in the chase.

LINCOLN. Why, my lord mayor, think you it then a shame,
　　To join a Lacy with an Otley's name?

LORD MAYOR. Too mean is my poor girl for his high birth;
    Poor citizens must not with courtiers wed,
    Who will in silks and gay apparel spend
    More in one year than I am worth, by far:
    Therefore your honour need not doubt my girl.

LINCOLN. Take heed, my lord; advise you what you do!
    A verier unthrift lives not in the world,
    Than is my cousin; for I'll tell you what:
    'T is now almost a year since he requested
    To travel countries for experience.
    I furnish'd him with coin, bills of exchange,
    Letters of credit, men to wait on him,
    Solicited my friends in Italy
    Well to respect him. But, to see the end!
    Scant had he journey'd through half Germany,
    But all his coin was spent, his men cast off,
    His bills embezzl'd, and my jolly coz,
    Asham'd to show his bankrupt presence here,
    Became a shoemaker in Wittenberg.
    A goodly science for a gentleman
    Of such descent! Now judge the rest by this.
    Suppose your daughter have a thousand pound,
    He did consume me more in one half year:
    And make him heir to all the wealth you have,
    One twelvemonth's rioting will waste it all.
    Then seek, my lord, some honest citizen
    To wed your daughter to.

LORD MAYOR.   I thank your lordship.
    [Aside.] Well, fox, I understand your subtlety.—
    As for your nephew, let your lordship's eye
    But watch his actions, and you need not fear,
    For I have sent my daughter far enough.
    And yet your cousin Rowland might do well,
    Now he hath learn'd an occupation:
    And yet I scorn to call him son-in-law.

LINCOLN. Ay, but I have a better trade for him.
    I thank his grace, he hath appointed him
    Chief colonel of all those companies

Must'red in London and the shires about,
To serve his highness in those wars of France.
See where he comes!—

Enter LOVELL, LACY, *and* ASKEW.

Lovell, what news with you?

LOVELL. My lord of Lincoln, 't is his highness' will,
That presently your cousin ship for France
With all his powers; he would not for a million,
But they should land at Dieppe within four days.

LINCOLN. Go certify his grace, it shall be done.

Exit LOVELL.

Now, cousin Lacy in what forwardness
Are all your companies?

LACY.   All well prepar'd.
The men of Hertfordshire lie at Mile-end;
Suffolk and Essex train in Tothill-fields;
The Londoners and those of Middlesex,
All gallantly prepar'd in Finsbury,
With frolic spirits long for their parting hour.

LORD MAYOR. They have their imprest, coats, and furniture;
And, if it please your cousin Lacy come
To the Guildhall, he shall receive his pay;
And twenty pounds besides my brethren
Will freely give him, to approve our loves
We bear unto my lord, your uncle here.

LACY. I thank your honour.

LINCOLN. Thanks, my good lord mayor.

LORD MAYOR. At the Guildhall we will expect your coming.   *Exit.*

LINCOLN. To approve your loves to me! No subtlety!
Nephew, that twenty pound he doth bestow
For joy to rid you from his daughter Rose.
But, cousins both, now here are none but friends.
I would not have you cast an amorous eye
Upon so mean a project as the love
Of a gay, wanton, painted citizen.
I know, this churl even in the height of scorn

Doth hate the mixture of his blood with thine.
I pray thee, do thou so! Remember, coz,
What honourable fortunes wait on thee.
Increase the king's love, which so brightly shines,
And gilds thy hopes. I have no heir but thee,—
And yet not thee, if with a wayward spirit
Thou start from the true bias of my love.

LACY. My lord, I will for honour, not desire
Of land or livings, or to be your heir,
So guide my actions in pursuit of France,
As shall add glory to the Lacies' name.

LINCOLN. Coz, for those words here's thirty portagues,
And, nephew Askew, there's a few for you.
Fair Honour, in her loftiest eminence,
Stays in France for you, till you fetch her thence.
Then, nephews, clap swift wings on your designs.
Begone, begone, make haste to the Guildhall;
There presently I'll meet you. Do not stay;
Where honour beckons, shame attends delay.   *Exit.*

ASKEW. How gladly would your uncle have you gone!

LACY. True, coz, but I'll o'erreach his policies.
I have some serious business for three days,
Which nothing but my presence can dispatch.
You, therefore, cousin, with the companies,
Shall haste to Dover; there I'll meet with you:
Or, if I stay past my prefixed time,
Away for France; we'll meet in Normandy.
The twenty pounds my lord mayor gives to me
You shall receive, and these ten portagues,
Part of mine uncle's thirty. Gentle coz,
Have care to our great charge; I know your wisdom
Hath tried itself in higher consequence.

ASKEW. Coz, all myself am yours: yet have this care,
To lodge in London with all secrecy.
Our uncle Lincoln hath, besides his own,
Many a jealous eye, that in your face
Stares only to watch means for your disgrace.

LACY. Stay, cousin, who be these?

Enter SIMON EYRE, [MARGERY] *his wife,* HODGE, FIRK, JANE, *and* RAFE *with a piece.*

EYRE. Leave whining, leave whining! Away with this whimp'ring, this puling, these blubb'ring tears, and these wet eyes! I'll get thy husband discharg'd, I warrant thee, sweet Jane. Go to!

HODGE. Master, here be the captains.

EYRE. Peace, Hodge; husht, ye knave, husht!

FIRK. Here be the cavaliers and the coronels, master.

EYRE. Peace, Firk; peace, my fine Firk! Stand by with your pishery-pashery; away! I am a man of the best presence; I'll speak to them, and they were Popes.—Gentlemen, captains, colonels, commanders! Brave men, brave leaders, may it please you to give me audience. I am Simon Eyre, the mad shoemaker of Tower Street; this wench, with the mealy mouth that will never tire, is my wife, I can tell you; here's Hodge, my man and my foreman; here's Firk, my fine firking journeyman, and this is blubbered Jane. All we come to be suitors for this honest Rafe. Keep him at home, and as I am a true shoemaker and a gentleman of the gentle craft, buy spurs yourself, and I'll find ye boots these seven years.

WIFE. Seven years, husband?

EYRE. Peace, midriff, peace! I know what I do. Peace!

FIRK. Truly, master cormorant, you shall do God good service to let Rafe and his wife stay together. She's a young new-married woman; if you take her husband away from her a-night, you undo her. She may beg in the daytime, for he's as good a workman at a prick and an awl as any is in our trade.

JANE. O let him stay, else I shall be undone.

FIRK. Ay, truly, she shall be laid at one side like a pair of old shoes else, and be occupied for no use.

LACY. Truly, my friends, it lies not in my power:
  The Londoners are press'd, paid, and set forth
  By the lord mayor; I cannot change a man.

HODGE. Why, then you were as good be a corporal as a colonel, if you cannot discharge one good fellow; and I tell you true, I think you do more than you can answer, to press a man within a year and a day of his marriage.

41. *A Tailor,* Giambattista Moroni. Reproduced by courtesy of the Trustees, The National Gallery, London.

EYRE. Well said, melancholy Hodge; gramercy, my fine foreman.

WIFE. Truly, gentlemen, it were ill done for such as you, to stand so stiffly against a poor young wife, considering her case, she is new-married; but let that pass. I pray, deal not roughly with her; her husband is a young man, and but newly ent'red; but let that pass.

EYRE. Away with your pishery-pashery, your pols and your edipols! Peace, midriff; silence, Cicely Bumtrinket! Let your head speak.

FIRK. Yea, and the horns too, master.

EYRE. Too soon, my fine Firk, too soon! Peace, scoundrels! See you this man? Captains, you will not release him? Well, let him go; he's a proper shot; let him vanish! Peace, Jane, dry up thy tears, they'll make his powder dankish. Take him, brave men! Hector

243

of Troy was an hackney to him, Hercules and Termagant scoundrels, Prince Arthur's Round-table—by the Lord of Ludgate—
ne'er fed such a tall, such a dapper swordman; by the life of
Pharaoh, a brave resolute swordman! Peace, Jane! I say no more,
mad knaves.

FIRK. See, see, Hodge, how my master raves in commendation of Rafe!

HODGE. Rafe, th' art a gull, by this hand, and thou goest not.

ASKEW. I am glad, good Master Eyre, it is my hap
　　To meet so resolute a soldier.
　　Trust me, for your report and love to him,
　　A common slight regard shall not respect him.

LACY. Is thy name Rafe?

RAFE. 　　　　　　　　Yes, sir.

LACY. 　　　　　　　　　　Give me thy hand;
　　Thou shalt not want, as I am a gentleman.
　　Woman, be patient. God, no doubt, will send
　　Thy husband safe again; but he must go,
　　His country's quarrel says it shall be so.

HODGE. Th' art a gull, by my stirrup, if thou dost not go. I will not
　　have thee strike thy gimlet into these weak vessels; prick thine
　　enemies, Rafe.

Enter DODGER.

DODGER. My lord, your uncle on the Towerhill
　　Stays with the lord mayor and the aldermen,
　　And doth request you, with all speed you may,
　　To hasten thither.

ASKEW. 　　　　　　Cousin, let's go.

LACY. Dodger, run you before, tell them we come.—　　*Exit* DODGER.
　　This Dodger is mine uncle's parasite,
　　The arrant'st varlet that e'er breath'd on earth.
　　He sets more discord in a noble house
　　By one day's broaching of his pickthank tales,
　　Than can be salv'd again in twenty years;
　　And he, I fear, shall go with us to France,
　　To pry into our actions.

ASKEW.   Therefore, coz,
    It shall behoove you to be circumspect.

LACY. Fear not, good cousin.—Rafe, hie to your colours.

Exit LACY *and* ASKEW.

RAFE. I must, because there's no remedy;
    But, gentle master and my loving dame,
    As you have always been a friend to me,
    So in mine absence think upon my wife.

JANE. Alas, my Rafe!

WIFE. She cannot speak for weeping.

EYRE. Peace, you crack'd groats, you mustard tokens, disquiet not the
    brave soldier. Go thy ways, Rafe!

JANE. Ay, ay, you bid him go! what shall I do
    When he is gone?

FIRK. Why, be doing with me or my fellow Hodge; be not idle.

EYRE. Let me see thy hand, Jane. This fine hand, this white hand,
    these pretty fingers must spin, must card, must work; work, you
    bombast cotton-candle-quean; work for your living, with a pox to
    you.—Hold thee, Rafe, here's five sixpences for thee; fight for
    the honour of the gentle craft, for the gentlemen shoemakers, the
    courageous cordwainers, the flower of St. Martin's, the mad knaves
    of Bedlam, Fleet Street, Tower Street and Whitechapel; crack me
    the crowns of the French knaves; a pox on them, crack them; fight,
    by the Lord of Ludgate; fight, my fine boy!

FIRK. Here, Rafe, here's three twopences; two carry into France, the
    third shall wash our souls at parting, for sorrow is dry. For my
    sake, firk the *Basa mon cues.*

HODGE. Rafe, I am heavy at parting; but here's a shilling for thee.
    God send thee to cram thy slops with French crowns, and thy
    enemies' bellies with bullets.

RAFE. I thank you, master, and I thank you all.
    Now, gentle wife, my loving lovely Jane,
    Rich men, at parting, give their wives rich gifts,
    Jewels and rings, to grace their lily hands.
    Thou know'st our trade makes rings for women's heels:
    Here take this pair of shoes, cut out by Hodge,

Stitch'd by my fellow Firk, seam'd by myself,
Made up and pink'd with letters for thy name.
Wear them, my dear Jane, for thy husband's sake,
And every morning when thou pull'st them on,
Remember me, and pray for my return.
Make much of them; for I have made them so
That I can know them from a thousand mo.

Sound drum. Enter LORD MAYOR, LINCOLN, LACY, ASKEW, DODGER, *and* SOLDIERS. *They pass over the stage;* RAFE *falls in amongst them;* FIRK *and the rest cry "Farewell," etc., and so exeunt.*

PART III

The Here and Now:

New Ordering of the Sciences

The Renaissance's primary concern with the world of here and now stimulated experimentation rather than logic, observation rather than inherited precepts. The exploration of man and his environment helped to provide the basic orientation for modern science.

For Leonardo da Vinci, science, manual by nature, was inferior to painting, which he judged largely intellectual: the artist used all the techniques of science as the steps before creation. The scientific techniques, still crude in Leonardo's time, soon gave way to a more fruitful approach—both Vesalius and William Harvey, working from experiment rather than precept, showed something of the structure of the human body and helped establish modern scientific method. The Renaissance saw exploration not only in the laboratory but also on the high seas. Columbus found, not an ancient civilization, as he expected, but a brave new world, and he recounts some of its wonders here. Hakluyt, even though motivated by pride in country rather than pride in exploration per se, nonetheless recorded England's glories on the sea. Galileo explored not the earth but the heavens, and through his work man's traditional picture of himself at the center of the cosmos was destroyed. But superstition still prevailed, and alchemy and astrology remained powerful forces influencing men's minds. Shakespeare, though, knew the difference between the charlatan and the scientist, as even his villains make clear.

LEONARDO DA VINCI

PAINTING AND SCIENCE

Painting and Science. Which Science is Mechanical and Which is Not? They say knowledge born of experience is mechanical, but that knowledge born and consummated in the mind is scientific, while knowledge

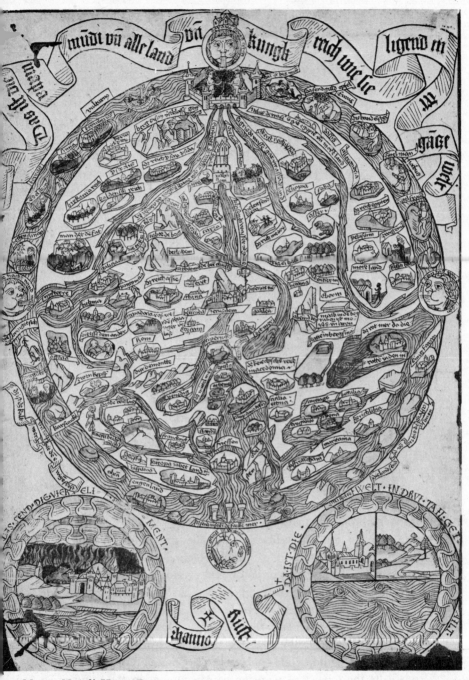

42. *Mappa Mundi*, Hanns Rust.

born of science and culminating in manual work is semimechanical. But to me it seems that all sciences are vain and full ·of errors that are not born of experience, mother of all certainty, and that are not tested by experience, that is to say, that do not at their origin, middle, or end pass through any of the five senses. (For if we are doubtful about the certainty of things that pass through the senses, how much more should we question the many things against which these senses rebel, such as the nature of God and the soul and the like, about which there are endless disputes and controversies. And truly it so happens that where reason is not, its place is taken by clamour. This never occurs when things are certain. Therefore, where there are quarrels, there true science is not; because truth can only end one way—wherever it is known, controversy is silenced for all time, and should controversy nevertheless again arise, then our conclusions must have been uncertain and confused and not truth which is reborn.) All true sciences are the result of experience which has passed through our senses, thus silencing the tongues of litigants. Experience does not feed investigators on dreams, but always proceeds from accurately determined first principles, step by step in true sequences, to the end; as can be seen in the elements of mathematics founded on numbers and measures called arithmetic and geometry, which deal with discontinuous and continuous quantities with absolute truth. Here no one argues as to whether twice three is more or less than six or whether the angles of a triangle are less than two right angles. Here all argument is destroyed by eternal silence and these sciences can be enjoyed by their devotees in peace. This the deceptive purely speculative sciences cannot achieve. If you say that these true sciences that are founded on observation must be classed as mechanical because they do not accomplish their end, without manual work, I reply that all arts that pass through the hands of scribes are in the same position, for they are a kind of drawing which is a branch of painting.

Astronomy and the other sciences also entail manual operations although they have their beginning in the mind, like painting, which arises in the mind of the contemplator but cannot be accomplished without manual operation. The scientific and true principles of painting first determine what is a shaded object, what is direct shadow, what is cast shadow, and what is light, that is to say, darkness, light, colour, body, figure, position, distance, nearness, motion, and rest. These are understood by the mind alone and entail no manual operation; and they constitute the science of painting which remains in the mind of its contemplators; and from it is then born the actual creation, which is far superior in dignity to the contemplation or science which precedes it.

(from *Paragone* or, *First Part of the Book on Painting*)

ANDREAS VESALIUS

FROM THE FABRICA

The Preface of Andreas Vesalius to his books De humani corporis fabrica *addressed to the divine Charles, great and invincible emperor.*

Various things, most gracious Emperor Charles, very seriously hinder those investigating the scientific arts so that they are not accurately or fully learned, and I believe furthermore that no little loss occurs through the too-great separation that has taken place between those disciplines that complement one another for the fullest comprehension of a single art; even much more the very capricious division by practitioners of an art into separate specialties so that those who set the limits of the art for themselves tenaciously grasp one part of it while other things which are in fact very closely related are cast aside. Consequently they never demonstrate excellence and never attain their proposed end but constantly fall away from the true foundation of that art.

Passing over the other arts in silence, I shall speak briefly of that which concerns the health of mankind; indeed, of all the arts the genius of man has discovered it is by far the most beneficial and of prime necessity, although difficult and laborious. Nothing was able to plague it more than when at one time, and especially after the Gothic invasions and the reign of Mansor, King of Persia—under whom the Arabs lived, as was proper, on terms of familiarity with the Greeks—medicine began to be maimed by the neglect of that primary instrument, the hand, so that [the manual aspects of medicine] were relegated to ordinary persons wholly untrained in the disciplines subserving the art of medicine. Once there were three medical sects, that is, Dogmatic, Empirical, and Methodical, but their members consulted the whole art as the means of preserving health and driving away sicknesses. All the thoughts of each sect were directed toward this goal and three methods were employed: The first was a regimen of diet, the second the use of drugs, and the third the use of the hands. Except for this last, the other methods clearly indicate that medicine is the addition of things lacking and the withdrawal of superfluities; as often as we resort to medicine it displays its usefulness in the treatment of sickness, as time and experience teach, and its great benefit to mankind. This triple method of treatment was equally familiar to the physicians of each sect, and those using their own hands according to the nature of the sickness used no less effort in training them than in establishing a theory of diet or in understanding and compounding drugs.

In addition to the other books so perfectly composed by the divine Hippocrates, this is very clearly demonstrated in those *On the function of the physician, On fractures of bones,* and *On dislocations of joints and similar ailments.* Furthermore, Galen, after Hippocrates the prince of medicine, in addition to his occasional boast that the care of the gladiators of Pergamum was entrusted solely to him, and that although age was already weighing him down it did not please him that the monkeys he was to dissect should be skinned by slaves, frequently assures us of his pleasure in the employment of his hands, and how zealously, like other Asiatic physicians, he used them. Indeed, none of the other ancients was so concerned that the treatment made with the hands, as well as that performed by diet and drugs, be handed down to posterity.

Especially after the devastation of the Goths when all the sciences, formerly so flourishing and fittingly practised, had decayed, the more fashionable physicians, first in Italy in imitation of the old Romans, despising the use of the hands, began to relegate to their slaves those things which had to be done manually for their patients and to stand over them like architects. Then when, by degrees, others who practised true medicine also declined those unpleasant duties—not, however, reducing their fees or dignity—they promptly degenerated from the earlier physicians, leaving the method of cooking and all the preparation of the patients' diet to nurses, the composition of drugs to apothecaries, and the use of the hands to barbers. And so in the course of time the art of treatment has been so miserably distorted that certain doctors assuming the name of physicians have arrogated to themselves the prescription of drugs and diet for obscure diseases, and have relegated the rest of medicine to those whom they call surgeons but consider scarcely as slaves. They have shamefully rid themselves of what is the chief and most venerable branch of medicine, that which based itself principally upon the investigation of nature—as if there were any other; even today [this branch of medicine] is exercised among the Indians, especially by the kings, and in Persia by law of inheritance it is handed down to the children as once the whole art was by the Asclepiads. The Thracians, with many other nations, cultivate and honor it very highly almost to the neglect of that other part of the art, the prescription of drugs. This the Romans once proscribed from the state considering it delusive and destructive of mankind, and of no benefit to nature since, although seeking to aid nature while it is wholly concerned in an attempt to throw off the sickness, drugs frequently make matters worse and distract nature from its proper function.

Hence it is that so many jibes are frequently cast at physicians and this very holy art is mocked, although part of it, which those trained in the liberal arts shamefully permit to be torn away from them, could readily adorn it forever with special lustre. When Homer, that source of genius, declared that a physician is more distinguished than a host of other men, and, with all the poets of Greece, celebrated Podalirius and Machaon, those divine sons of Aesculapius were praised not so much because they dispelled a little fever or something else of slight consequences, which nature alone could cure more readily without the aid of a physician than with it, nor because they yielded to the summons of men in obscure and desperate affections, but because they devoted themselves especially to the treatment of luxations, fractures, wounds, and other solutions of continuity and fluxions of blood, and because they freed Agamemnon's noble warriors of javelins, darts, and other evils of that sort which are the peculiar accompaniment of wars, and which always require the careful attention of the physician.

However, most august Emperor Charles, I certainly do not propose to give preference to one instrument of medicine over the others, since the aforesaid triple method of treatment can in no way be disunited and the whole of it belongs to the one practitioner; and that he may employ it properly all parts of medicine have been equally established so that the successful use of a single part depends upon the degree to which they are all combined, for how rare is the sickness that does not immediately require the three instruments of treatment. Hence a proper scheme of diet must be determined, and something must be done with drugs, and finally with the hands, so that the tyros of this art ought—if it please the gods —to be urged in every way, like the Greeks, to scorn the whisperings of those physicians and, as nature teaches, to employ their hands in treatment, lest they convert the mangled rationale of treatment into a calamity for the life of mankind. They ought to be urged the more strongly to this since we see learned physicians abstain from the use of the hands as from a plague lest the rabbins of medicine decry them before the ignorant mass as barbers and they acquire less wealth and honor than those [who are] scarcely half-physicians, and stand in less estimation before the uncomprehending mass of the people. Indeed, it is especially this detestable, vulgar opinion that prevents us, even in our age, from taking up the art of treatment as a whole, limiting us to the treatment of only internal diseases, to the great harm of mankind, and—if I may speak frankly—we strive to be physicians only in part.

When first the whole composition of drugs was relegated to the apothecaries, then the physicians promptly lost the necessary knowledge of simple medicines, and they were responsible for the apothecaries' shops becoming filled with barbarous names, and even false remedies, and for so many admirable compositions of the ancients being lost to us, several of which are still missing. Furthermore, they prepared an unending labor for learned men not only of our age but also for those who preceded it by some years, who have devoted themselves untiringly to the study of simple medicines and are seen to have contributed much through their effort to restore that knowledge to its former brilliance; Gerard van Veltwyck, secretary to your Majesty and rare example of this age, is representative of the many celebrated men engaged in this matter. Endowed with wide erudition in many disciplines and tongues he is the most skilled of our people in the knowledge of plants.

Furthermore, this very perverse distribution of the instruments of treatment among a variety of practitioners caused a very baleful disaster and a far more cruel blow to that chief branch of natural philosophy which, since it includes the description of man, ought rightfully to be considered the very beginning and solid foundation of the whole art of medicine. Hippocrates and Plato attributed so much to it that they did not hesitate to award it first place among the parts of medicine, and although at first it was especially cultivated by physicians, who strained every nerve to acquire it, finally it began miserably to collapse when they, resigning manual operations to others, destroyed anatomy. For when the physicians assumed that only the treatment of internal complaints concerned them, believing furthermore that knowledge of only the viscera was sufficient, they neglected the structure of the bones, muscles, nerves, and of the veins and arteries which creep through those bones and muscles, as of no concern to them. In addition, when the use of the hands was wholly entrusted to the barbers, not only was true knowledge of the viscera lost to the physicians, but also the practice of dissection soon died away, because they did not undertake it, and those to whom the manual skills had been entrusted were so unlearned that they did not understand the writings of the professors of dissection.

Thus it was impossible that so very difficult and abstruse an art, acquired mechanically by this latter type of men, could be preserved for us, for the deplorable division of the art of treatment introduced into the schools that detestable procedure by which usually some conduct the dissection of the human body and others present the account of its parts, the latter like jackdaws aloft in their high chair, with egregious arrogance croaking things they have never investigated but merely committed to memory from the books of others, or reading what has already been described. The former are so ignorant of languages that they are unable to explain their dissections to the spectators and muddle what ought to be displayed according to the instructions of the physician who, since he has never applied his hand to the dissection of the body, haughtily governs the ship from a manual. Thus everything is wrongly taught in the schools, and days are wasted in ridiculous questions so that in such confusion less is presented to the spectators than a butcher in his stall could teach a physician. I omit mention of several schools where scarcely ever is even consideration given to the presentation of human anatomy, so far has ancient medicine declined from its former glory.

In the great felicity of this age—which the gods desire to be controlled by your sagacious Majesty—with all studies greatly revitalized, anatomy has begun to raise its head from profound gloom, so that it may be said without contradiction that it seems almost to have recovered its ancient brilliance in some universities; and with nothing more urgently desired than that knowledge of the parts of the human body be recovered, I, aroused by the example of so many distinguished men, decided to give what assistance I could and by those means at my command. And lest all others should successfully accomplish something for the sake of our common studies while I alone remain idle, and lest I achieve less than my ancestors, I decided that this branch of natural philosophy ought to be recalled from the region of the dead. If it does not attain a fuller development among us than ever before or elsewhere among the early professors of dissection, at least it may reach such a point that one can assert

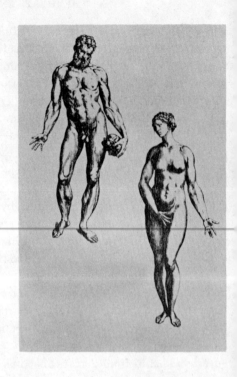

43. Adam and Eve, illustrations from *The Fabrica*, Andreas Vesalius.

without shame that the present science of anatomy is comparable to that of the ancients and that in our age nothing has been so degraded and then wholly restored as anatomy.

My intention could by no means have been fulfilled if, when I was studying medicine in Paris, I had not put my own hand to the matter but had accepted without question the several casual and superficial demonstrations of a few organs presented to me and to my fellow students in one or two public dissections by unskilled barbers. So perfunctory was the presentation of anatomy there where we first saw medicine reborn that I, experienced by several dissections of brutes under the direction of the never-to-be-sufficiently-praised Jacobus Sylvius, at the third dissection at which I was ever present and at the urging of my fellow students and the teachers, conducted it publicly and more completely than was usually the case. When I conducted it a second time—the barbers having been waved aside—I attempted to display the muscles of the arms as well as to make a more accurate dissection of the viscera, for, except for eight abdominal muscles shamefully mangled and in the wrong order, no other muscle or any bone, and much less an accurate series of nerves, veins, or arteries was ever demonstrated to me by anyone. Later at Louvain, whither I had to return because of the outbreak of war, and where for eighteen years the physicians had not even dreamed of anatomy, in order to assist the students of that university and to acquire greater skill in a subject still obscure but of the first importance for medicine, I dissected with somewhat greater accuracy than at Paris and lectured on the entire structure of the human body. As a result, the younger professors of that university now seem to be seriously engaged in gaining a knowledge of the parts of man, fully appreciating what valuable philosophical material is to be acquired from this knowledge. At Padua, in that most famous university of the whole world, in order not to dissociate myself from the rest of medicine and induced by the salary offered by the very illustrious Venetian Senate, by far the most liberal to professional studies, I gave the lectures on surgical medicine, and because anatomy is related to this, I devoted myself to the investigation of man's structure. Thus I have already conducted anatomy very often here and in Bologna, and, discarding the ridiculous fashion of the schools, I demonstrated and taught in such a way that there was nothing in my procedure that varied from the tradition of the ancients, and the construction of no part met with remained unstudied.

.   .   .

'Now I must recall the judgment of certain men who strongly condemn the presentation of anatomy to students, not merely by words but also, no matter how exquisitely executed, by pictorial delineation of the parts of the human body, maintaining that it is necessary for these things to be learned by careful dissection and observation of the parts themselves, as if I had inserted illustrations—very correct ones, and would that the illustrations of the parts were never spoiled by the printer—in the text so that the student relying on them might refrain from dissection of cadavers; whereas, on the contrary, I, with Galen, have encouraged the candidates of medicine in every way to undertake dissection with their own hands. If the practice of the ancients had lasted down to our times, the practice by which they trained the boys at home in the conduct of dissection just as in writing and reading, I, like the ancients, would readily agree to discard not only illustrations but also all commentaries. However, when for the sake of renown they decided to write about the practice of dissection, they communicated the art not only to the boys but also to foreigners out of respect for their virtues; but as soon as the boys were no longer given the usual training in dissection, as it was no longer accustomed to begin in boyhood, naturally they learned anatomy less well, so much so that the art deserted the family of the Asclepiads, and, by reason of its decline through many centuries, books became necessary to preserve a complete account of it.

Nevertheless, how greatly pictures assist the understanding of these matters and place them more exactly before the eyes than even the most precise language, no student of geometry and other mathematical disciplines can fail to understand. Furthermore, the illustrations of the human parts will greatly delight those for whom there is not always a supply of human bodies for dissection; or, if there is, those who have such a fastidious nature, little worthy of a physician, that, even if they are enthusiastic about that most pleasant knowledge of man attesting the wisdom of the Great Creator—if anything does—yet they cannot bring themselves even occasionally to be present at dissection. Whatever the case may be, I have done my best to this single end, to aid as many as possible in a very recondite as well as laborious matter, and truly and completely to describe the structure of the human body which is formed not of ten or twelve parts—as it may seem to the spectator—but of some thousands of different parts, and, among other monuments to that divine man Galen, to bring to posterity an understanding of those books of his requiring the help of a teacher. I bear to the candidates of medicine fruit not to be scorned.

I am aware that by reason of my age—I am at present twenty-eight years old—my efforts will have little authority, and that, because of my frequent indication of the falsity of Galen's teachings, they will find little shelter from the attacks of those who were not present at my anatomical demonstrations or have not themselves studied the subject sedulously; various schemes in defense of Galen will be boldly invented unless these books appear with the auspicious commendation and great patronage of some divine power. Because they cannot be more safely sheltered or more splendidly adorned than by the imperishable name of the great and invincible emperor, the divine Charles, I beseech your imperial Majesty with all reverence again and again, to permit this youthful work of mine to come into the hands of men—to whom for many reasons it is obnoxious—for a short time, under your splendid patronage, until through the experience, judgment, and erudition that come with age I may render it more worthy of so great a prince or I may offer another

ANDREAE VESALII
BRVXELLENSIS, SCHOLAE
medicorum Patauinæ profeſſoris, de
Humani corporis fabrica
Libri ſeptem.

44. Anatomy lesson, illustration from *The Fabrica*, Andreas Vesalius.

acceptable gift on some other subject taken from our art.

It is my opinion that out of the whole Apolline discipline, and so the whole of natural philosophy, nothing could be produced more pleasing or acceptable to your Majesty than an account from which we may learn about the body and mind and, furthermore, about a certain divine power arising from a harmony of both—indeed, about ourselves, that which in truth is the study of man. I came to this conclusion for many reasons, but I first conjectured it because among the large number of books dedicated to your grandfather of happy memory, the great Emperor of the Romans Maximilian, none was ever more pleasing than a little book on the present subject. Nor shall I ever forget with what pleasure you examined my *Tabulae anatomicae*, once presented for inspection by my father Andreas, chief and most faithful apothecary of your Majesty, and how carefully you inquired about each thing. I shall not mention your incredible love for all disciplines but chiefly for mathematics, and especially for that part of it that deals with the science of the universe and the stars and of the remarkable comprehension of it by so great and heroic a man. So great, that by no means can it be that you are interested solely in the science of the universe, but also perhaps you sometimes delight in consideration of the most perfectly constructed of all creatures, and take delight in considering the temporary lodging and instrument of the immortal soul, a dwelling that in many respects corresponds admirably to the universe and for that reason was called the little universe by the ancients.

Nevertheless I decided that your notable knowledge of the structure of man's body ought not be extolled here, that knowledge in itself by far the most commendable of things to which even in Rome men of the greatest attainment and especially those of philosophical learning applied themselves, since, keeping in mind that desire of Alexander the Great to be painted by none except Apelles, cast in bronze only by Lysippus, and sculpt only by Pyrgateles, I considered that it would not be fitting for me to recount your glories lest by a base and unskilled discourse I cover them with shadow instead of light. Furthermore, too great formalism of prefaces ought to be condemned, such as that in which, like some stereotyped formula and for the sake of some cheap reward, learning, singular prudence, astonishing clemency, keen judgment, unending liberality, wonderful love for men of letters and for learning, the greatest celerity in the management of affairs, and the whole chorus of virtues are customarily ascribed without discrimination and almost beyond merit.

Nonetheless, your Majesty surpasses all mortals in these virtues as well as in dignity, felicity, and success in your affairs. Such is clear to everyone, even though not mentioned here by me, and even while living you are venerated like some high divinity. I pray that the gods may not grudge this to the learned and to the whole world, but long preserve you unharmed for mankind and maintain and guard you in continued felicity.

Padua, 1 August 1542

WILLIAM HARVEY

OF THE MOTION, ACTION, AND OFFICE OF THE HEART

From these and other observations of the like kind, I am persuaded it will be found that the motion of the heart is as follows:

First of all, the auricle contracts, and in the course of its contraction throws the blood, (which it contains in ample quantity as the head of the veins, the storehouse, and cistern of the blood,) into the ventricle, which, being filled, the heart raises itself straightway, makes all its fibres tense, contracts the ventricles, and performs a beat, by which beat it immediately sends the blood supplied to it by the auricle into the arteries; the right ventricle sending its charge into the lungs by the vessel which is called vena arteriosa, but which, in structure and function, and all things else, is an artery; the left ventricle sending its charge into the aorta, and through this by the arteries to the body at large.

These two motions, one of the ventricles, another of the auricles, take place consecutively, but in such a manner that there is a kind of harmony or rhythm preserved between them, the two concurring in such wise that but one motion is apparent, especially in the warmer blooded animals, in which the movements in question are rapid. Nor is this for any other reason than it is in a piece of machinery, in which, though one wheel gives motion to another, yet all the wheels seem to move simultaneously; or in that mechanical contrivance which is adapted to firearms, where the trigger being touched, down comes the flint, strikes against the steel, elicts a spark, which falling among the powder, it is ignited, upon which the flame extends, enters the barrel, causes the explosion, propels the ball, and the mark is attained—all of which incidents, by reason of the celerity with which they happen, seem to take place in the twinkling of an eye. So also in deglutition: by the elevation of the root of the tongue, and the compression of the mouth, the food or drink is pushed into the fauces, the larynx is closed by its own muscles, and the epiglottis, whilst the pharynx, raised and opened by its muscles no otherwise than is a sac that is to be filled, is lifted up, and its mouth dilated; upon which, the mouthful being received, it is forced downwards by the transverse muscles, and then carried farther by the longitudinal ones. Yet are all these motions, though executed by different and distinct organs, performed harmoniously, and in such order, that they seem to constitute but a single motion and act, which we call deglutition.

Even so does it come to pass with the motions and action of the heart, which constitute a kind of deglutition, a transfusion of the blood from the veins to the arteries. And if any one, bearing these things in mind, will carefully watch the motions of the heart in the body of a living animal, he will perceive not only all the particulars I have mentioned, viz. the heart becoming erect, and making one continuous motion with its auricles; but farther, a certain obscure undulation and lateral inclination in the direction of the axis of the right ventricle, [the organ] twisting itself slightly in performing its work. And indeed every one may see, when a horse drinks, that the water is drawn in and transmitted to the stomach at each movement of the throat, the motion being accompanied with a sound, and yielding a pulse both to the ear and the touch; in the same way it is with each motion of the heart, when there is the delivery of a quantity of blood from the veins to the arteries, that a pulse takes place, and can be heard within the chest.

The motion of the heart, then, is entirely of this description, and the one action of the heart is the transmission of the blood and its distribution, by means of the arteries, to the very extremities of the body; so that the pulse which we feel in the arteries is nothing more than the impulse of the blood derived from the heart.

Whether or not the heart, besides propelling the blood, giving it motion locally, and distributing it to the body, adds anything else to it,—heat, spirit, perfection,—must be inquired into by and by, and decided upon other grounds. So much may suffice at this time, when it is shown that by the action of the heart the blood is transfused through the ventricles from the veins to the arteries, and distributed by them to all parts of the body.

So much, indeed, is admitted by all [physiologists], both from the structure of the heart and the arrangement and action of its valves. But still they are like persons purblind or groping about in the dark; and then they give utterence to diverse, contradictory, and incoherent sentiments, delivering many things upon conjecture, as we have already had occasion to remark.

The grand cause of hesitation and error in this subject appears to me to have been the intimate connection between the heart and the lungs. When men saw both the vena arteriosa [or pulmonary artery] and the arteriae venosae [or pulmonary veins] losing themselves in the lungs, of course it became a puzzle to them to know how or by what means the right ventricle should distribute the blood to the body, or the left draw it from the venae cavae. This fact is bore witness to by Galen, whose words, when writing against Erasistratus in regard to the origin and use of the veins and the coction of the blood, are the following: "You will reply," he says, "that the effect is so; that the blood is prepared in the liver, and is thence transferred to the heart to receive its proper form and last perfection; a statement which does not appear devoid of reason; for no great and perfect work is ever accomplished at a single effort, or receives its final polish from one instrument. But if this be actually so, then show us another vessel which draws the absolutely perfect blood from the heart, and distributes it as the arteries do the spirits over the whole body." Here then is a reasonable opinion not allowed, because, forsooth, besides not seeing the true means of transit, he could not discover the vessel which should transmit the blood from the heart to the body at large!

But had any one been there in behalf of Erasistratus, and of that opinion which we now espouse, and which Galen himself acknowledges in other respects consonant with reason, to have pointed to the aorta as the vessel which distributes the blood from the heart to the rest of the body, I wonder what would have been the answer of the most ingenious and learned man? Had he said that the artery transmits spirits and not blood, he would indeed sufficiently have answered Erasistratus, who imagined that the arteries contained nothing but spirits; but then he would have contradicted himself, and given a foul denial to that for which he had keenly contended in his writings against this very Erasistratus, to wit, that blood in substance is contained in the arteries, and not spirits; a fact which he demonstrated not only by many powerful arguments, but by experiments.

But if the divine Galen will here allow, as in other places he does, "that all the arteries of the body arise from the great artery, and that this takes its origin from the heart; that all these vessels naturally contain and carry blood; that the three semilunar valves situated at the orifice of the aorta prevent the return of the blood into the heart, and that nature never connected them with this, the most noble viscus of the body, unless for some most important end;" if, I say, this father of physic admits all these things,—and I quote his own words,—I do not see how he can deny that the great artery is the very vessel to carry the blood, when it has attained its highest term of perfection, from the heart for distribution to all parts of the body. Or would he perchance still hesitate, like all who have come after him, even to the present hour, because he did not perceive the route by which the blood was transferred from the veins to the arteries, in consequence, as I have already said, of the intimate connexion between the heart and the lungs? And that this difficulty puzzled anatomists not a little, when in their dissections they found the pulmonary artery and left ventricle full of thick, black, and clotted blood, plainly appears, when they felt themselves compelled to affirm that the blood made its way from the right to the left ventricle by sweating through the septum of the heart. But this I fancy I have already refuted. A new pathway for the blood must therefore be prepared and thrown open, and being once exposed, no further difficulty will, I believe, be experienced by any one in admitting what I have already proposed in regard to the pulse of the heart and arteries, viz. the passage of the blood from the veins to the arteries, and its distribution to the whole of the body by means of these vessels.

.   .   .

It will not be foreign to the subject if I here show further, from certain familiar reasonings, that the circulation is matter both of convenience and necessity. In the first place, since death is a corruption which takes place through deficiency of heat, and since all living things are warm, all dying things cold, there must be a particular seat and fountain, a kind of home and hearth, where the cherisher of nature, the original of the native fire, is stored and preserved; whence heat and life are dispensed to all parts as from a fountain head; whence sustenance may be derived; and upon which concoction and nutrition, and all vegetative energy may depend. Now, that the heart is this place, that the heart is the principle of life, and that all passes in the manner just mentioned, I trust no one will deny.

The blood, therefore, required to have motion, and indeed such a motion that it should return again to the heart; for sent to the external parts of the body far from its fountain, as Aristotle says, and without motion, it would become congealed. For we see motion generating and keeping up heat and spirits under all circumstances, and rest allowing them to escape and be dissipated. The blood, therefore, become thick or congealed by the cold of the extreme and outward parts, and robbed of its spirits, just as it is in the dead, it was imperative that from its fount and origin, it should again receive heat and spirits, and all else requisite to its preservation—that, by returning, it should be renovated and restored.

We frequently see how the extremities are chilled by the external cold, how the nose and cheeks and hands look blue, and how the blood, stagnating in them as in the pendent or lower parts of a corpse, becomes of a dusky hue; the limbs at the same time getting torpid, so that they can scarcely be moved, and seem almost to have lost their vitality. Now they can by no means be so effectually, and especially so speedily restored to heat and colour and life, as by a new afflux and appulsion of heat from its source. But how can parts attract in which the heat and life are almost extinct? Or how should they whose passages are filled with condensed and frigid blood, admit fresh aliment—renovated blood—unless they had first got rid of their old contents? Unless the heart were truly that fountain where life and heat are restored to the refrigerated fluid, and whence new blood, warm, imbued with spirits, being sent out by the arteries, that which has become cooled and effete is forced on, and all the particles recover their heat which was failing, and their vital stimulus well-nigh exhausted.

Hence it is that if the heart be unaffected, life and health may be restored to almost all the other parts of the body; but the heart being chilled, or smitten with any serious disease, it seems matter of necessity that the whole animal fabric should suffer and fall into decay. When the source is corrupted, there is nothing, as Aristotle says, which can be of service either to it or aught that depends on it. And hence, by the way, it may perchance be wherefore grief, and love, and envy, and anxiety, and all affections of the mind of a similar kind are accompanied with emaciation and decay, or with cacochemy and crudity, which engender all manner of diseases and consume the body of man. For every affection of the mind that is attended with either pain or pleasure, hope or fear, is the cause of an agitation whose influence extends to the heart, and there induces change from the natural constitution, in the temperature, the pulse and the rest, which impairing all nutrition in its source and abating the powers at large, it is no wonder that various forms of incurable disease in the extremities and in the trunk are the consequence, inasmuch as in such circumstances the whole body labours under the effects of vitiated nutrition and a want of native heat.

Moreover, when we see that all animals live through food concocted in their interior, it is imperative that the digestion and distribution be perfect; and, as a consequence, that there be a place and receptacle where the aliment is perfected and whence it is distributed to the several members. Now this place is the heart, for it is the only organ in the body which contains blood for the general use; all the others receive it merely for their peculiar or private advantage, just as the heart also has a supply for its own especial behoof in its coronary veins and arteries; but it is of the store which the heart contains in its auricles and ventricles that I here speak; and then the heart is the only organ which is so situated and constituted that it can distribute the blood in due proportion to the several parts of the body, the quantity sent to each being according to the dimensions of the artery which supplies it, the heart serving as a magazine or fountain ready to meet its demands.

Further, a certain impulse or force, as well as an impeller or forcer, such as the heart, was required to effect this distribution and motion of the blood; both because the blood is disposed from slight causes, such as cold, alarm, horror, and the like, to collect in its source, to concentrate like parts to a whole, or the drops of water spilt upon a table to the mass of liquid; and then because it is forced from the capillary veins into the smaller ramifications, and from these into the larger trunks by the motion of the extremities and the compression of the muscles generally. The blood is thus more disposed to move from the circumference to the centre than in the opposite direction, were there even no valves to oppose its motion; whence that it may leave its source and enter more confined and colder channels, and flow against the direction to which it spontaneously inclines, the blood requires both force and an impelling power. Now such is the heart and the heart alone, and that in the way and manner already explained.

> (from *An Anatomical Disquisition on the Motion of the Heart and Blood in Animals*)

ANATOMICAL EXAMINATION
OF THE BODY OF THOMAS PARR

Thomas Parr, a poor countryman, born near Winnington, in the county of Salop, died on the 14th of November, in the year of grace 1635, after having lived one hundred and fifty-two years and nine months, and survived nine princes. This poor man, having been visited by the illustrious Earl of Arundel when he chanced to have business in these parts, (his lordship being moved to the visit by the fame of a thing so incredible,) was brought by him from the country to London; and, having been most kindly treated by the earl both on the journey and during a residence in his own house, was presented as a remarkable sight to his Majesty the King.

Having made an examination of the body of this aged individual, by command of his Majesty, several of whose principal physicians were present, the following particulars were noted:

The body was muscular, the chest hairy, and the hair on the forearms still black; the legs, however, were without hair, and smooth.

The organs of generation were healthy, the penis neither retracted nor extenuated, nor the scrotum filled with any serous infiltration, as happens so commonly among the decrepid; the testes, too, were sound and large; so that it seemed not improbable that the common report was true, viz. that he did public penance under a conviction for incontinence, after he had passed his hundredth year; and his wife, whom he had married as a widow in his hundred-and-twentieth year, did not deny that he had intercourse with her after the manner of other husbands with their wives, nor until about twelve years back had he ceased to embrace her frequently.

The chest was broad and ample; the lungs, nowise fungous, adhered, especially on the right side, by fibrous bands to the ribs. They were much loaded with blood, as we find them in cases of peripneumony, so that until the blood was squeezed out they looked rather blackish. Shortly before his death I had observed that the face was livid, and he suffered from difficult breathing and orthopnoea. This was the reason why the axillae and chest continued to retain their heat long after his death: this and other signs that present themselves in cases of death from suffocation were observed in the body.

We judged, indeed, that he had died suffocated, through inability to breathe, and this view was confirmed by all the physicians present, and

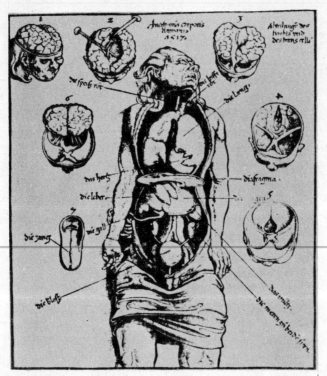

45. Woman anatomized, illustration from *The Fabrica*,
Andreas Vesalius.

46. Man anatomized, illustration from
The Fabrica, Andreas Vesalius.

reported to the King. When the blood was expressed, and the lungs were wiped, their substance was beheld of a white and almost milky hue.

The heart was large, and thick, and fibrous, and contained a considerable quantity of adhering fat, both in its circumference and over its septum. The blood in the heart, of a black colour, was dilute, and scarcely coagulated; in the right ventricle alone some small clots were discovered.

In raising the sternum, the cartilages of the ribs were not found harder or converted into bone in any greater degree than they are in ordinary men; on the contrary, they were soft and flexible.

The intestines were perfectly sound, fleshy, and strong, and so was the stomach: the small intestines presented several constrictions, like rings, and were muscular. Whence it came that, by day or night, observing no rules or regular times for eating, he was ready to discuss any kind of eatable that was at hand; his ordinary diet consisting of sub-rancid cheese, and milk in every form, coarse and hard bread, and small drink, generally sour whey. On this sorry fare, but living in his home, free from care, did this poor man attain to such length of days. He even ate something about midnight shortly before his death.

The kidneys were bedded in fat, and in themselves sufficiently healthy; on their anterior aspects, however, they contained several small watery abscesses or serous collections, one of which, the size of a hen's egg, containing a yellow fluid in a proper cyst, had made a rounded depression in the substance of the kidney. To this some were disposed to ascribe the suppression of urine under which the old man had laboured shortly before his death; whilst others, and with greater show of likelihood, ascribed it to the great regurgitation of serum upon the lungs.

There was no appearance of stone either in the kidneys or bladder.

The mesentery was loaded with fat, and the colon, with the omentum, which was likewise fat, was attached to the liver, near the fundus of the gall-bladder; in like manner the colon was adherent from this point posteriorly with the peritoneum.

The viscera were healthy; they only looked somewhat white externally, as they would have done had they been parboiled; internally they were (like the blood) of the colour of dark gore.

The spleen was very small, scarcely equalling one of the kidneys in size.

All the internal parts, in a word, appeared so healthy, that had nothing happened to interfere with the old man's habits of life, he might perhaps have escaped paying the debt due to nature for some little time longer.

The cause of death seemed fairly referrible to a sudden change in the non-naturals, the chief mischief being connected with the change of air, which through the whole course of life had been inhaled of perfect purity,—light, cool, and mobile, whereby the praecordia and lungs were more freely ventilated and cooled; but in this great advantage, in this grand cherisher of life this city is especially destitute; a city whose grand characteristic is an immense concourse of men and animals, and where ditches abound, and filth and offal lie scattered about, to say nothing of the smoke engendered by the general use of sulphureous coal as fuel, whereby the air is at all times rendered heavy, but much more so in the autumn than at any other season. Such an atmosphere could not have been found otherwise than insalubrious to one coming from the open, sunny, and healthy region of Salop; it must have been especially so to one already aged and infirm.

And then for one hitherto used to live on food unvaried in kind, and very simple in its nature, to be set at a table loaded with variety of viands, and tempted not only to eat more than wont, but to partake of strong drink, it must needs fall out that the functions of all the natural organs would become deranged. Whence the stomach at length failing, and the excretions long retained, the work of concoction proceeding languidly, the liver getting loaded, the blood stagnating in the veins, the spirits frozen, the heart, the source of life, oppressed, the lungs infarcted, and made impervious to the ambient air, the general habit rendered more compact, so that it could no longer exhale or perspire—no wonder that the soul, little content with such a prison, took its flight.

The brain was healthy, very firm and hard to the touch; hence, shortly before his death, although he had been blind for twenty years, he heard extremely well, understood all that was said to him, answered immediately to questions, and had perfect apprehension of any matter in hand; he was also accustomed to walk about, slightly supported between two persons. His memory, however, was greatly impaired, so that he scarcely recollected anything of what had happened to him when he was a young man, nothing of public incidents, or of the kings or nobles who had made a figure, or of the wars or troubles of his earlier life, or of the manners of society, or of the prices of things—in a word, of any of the ordinary incidents which men are wont to retain in their memories. He only recollected the events of the last few years. Nevertheless, he was accustomed, even in his hundred and thirtieth year, to engage lustily in every kind of agricultural labour, whereby he earned his bread, and he had even then the strength required to thrash the corn.

Christopher Columbus

LETTER TO THE KEEPER
OF THE PRIVY PURSE

Sir, forasmuch as I know that you will take pleasure in the great triumph with which Our Lord has crowned my voyage, I write this to you, from which you will learn how, in twenty days I reached the Indies with the fleet which the most illustrious King and Queen, our lords, gave to me. And there I found very many islands filled with people without number, and of them all have I taken possession for Their Highnesses, by proclamation and with the royal standard displayed, and nobody objected. To the first island which I found I gave the name *Sant Salvador,* in recognition of His Heavenly Majesty, who marvelously hath given all this; the Indians call it *Guanahani.* To the second I gave the name *Isla de Santa María de Concepción;* to the third, *Ferrandina;* to the fourth, *La Isla Bella;* to the fifth *La Isla Juana;* and so to each one I gave a new name.

When I reached Juana, I followed its coast to the westward, and I found it to be so long that I thought it must be the mainland, the province of Catayo. And since I found neither towns nor cities along the coast, but only small villages, with the people of which I could not have speech because they all fled forthwith, I went forward on the same course, thinking that I should not fail to find great cities and towns. And, at the end of many leagues, seeing that there was no change and that the coast was bearing me northwards, which was contrary to my desire since winter was already beginning and I proposed to go thence to the south, and as moreover the wind was favorable, I determined not to wait for a change of weather and backtracked to a certain harbor already noted, and thence I sent two men upcountry to learn if there were a king or great cities. They traveled for three days and found an infinite number of small villages and people without number, but nothing of importance; hence they returned.

I understood sufficiently from other Indians, whom I had already taken, that continually this land was an island, and so I followed its coast eastward 107 leagues up to where it ended. And from that cape I saw toward the east another island, distant 18 leagues from the former, to which I at once gave the name *La Spañola.* And I went there and followed its northern part, as I had in the case of Juana, to the eastward for 178 great leagues in a straight line. As Juana, so all the others are very fertile to an excessive degree, and this one especially. In it there are many harbors on the sea coast, beyond comparison with others which I know in Christendom, and numerous rivers, good and large, which is marvelous. Its lands are lofty and in it there are many sierras and very high mountains, to which the island *Centrefrei* is not comparable. All are most beautiful, of a thousand shapes, and all accessible, and filled with trees of a thousand kinds and tall, and they seem to touch the sky; and I am told that they never lose their foliage, which I can believe, for I saw them as green and beautiful as they are in Spain in May, and some of them were flowering, some with fruit, and some in another condition, according to their quality. And there were singing the nightingale and other little birds of a thousand kinds in the month of November, there where I went. There are palm trees of six or eight kinds, which are a wonder to behold because of their beautiful variety, and so are the other trees and fruits and plants; therein are marvelous pine groves, and extensive meadow country; and there is honey, and there are many kinds of birds and a great variety of fruits. Upcountry there are many mines of metals, and the population is innumerable. *La Spañola* is marvelous, the sierras and the mountains and the plains and the meadows and the lands are so beautiful and rich for planting and sowing, and for livestock of every sort, and for building towns and villages. The harbors of the sea here are such as you could not believe it without seeing them; and so the rivers, many and great, and good streams, the most of which bear gold. And the trees and fruits and plants have great differences from those of La Juana; in this [island] there are many spices and great mines of gold and of other metals.

The people of this island and of all the other islands which I have found and seen, or have not seen, all go naked, men and women, as their mothers bore them, except that some women cover one place only with the leaf of a plant or with a net of cotton which they make for that purpose. They have no iron or steel or weapons, nor are they capable of using them, although they are well-built people of handsome stature, because they are wondrous timid. They have no other arms than arms of canes, [cut] when they are in seed time, to the ends of which they fix a sharp little stick; and they dare not make use of these, for oftentimes it has happened that I have sent ashore two or three men to some town to have speech, and people without number have come out to them, and as soon as they saw them coming, they fled; even a father would not stay for his son; and this not because wrong has been done to anyone; on the contrary, at every point where I have been and have been able to have speech, I have given them of all that I had, such as cloth and many other things, without receiving anything for it; but they are like that, timid beyond cure. It is true that after they have been reassured and have lost this fear, they are so artless and so free with all they possess, that no one would believe it without having seen it. Of anything they have, if you ask them for it, they never say no; rather they invite the person to share it, and show as much love as if they were giving their hearts; and whether the thing be of value or of small price, at once they are content with whatever little thing of whatever kind may be given to them. I forbade that they should be given things so worthless as pieces of broken crockery and broken glass, and lace points, although when they were able to get them, they thought they had the best jewel in the world; thus it was learned that a sailor for a lace point received gold to the weight of two and a half *castellanos,* and others much more for other things which were worth much less; yea, for new *blancas,* for them they would give all that they had, although it might be two or three *castellanos'* weight of gold or an arroba or two of spun cotton; they even took pieces of the broken hoops of the wine casks and, like animals, gave what they had, so that it seemed to me to be wrong and I forbade it, and I gave them a thousand good, pleasing things which I had brought, in order that they might be fond of us, and furthermore might become Christians and be inclined to the love and service of Their Highnesses and of the whole Castilian nation, and try to help us and to give us of the things which they have in abundance and which are necessary to us. And they know neither sect nor idolatry, with the exception that all believe that the source of all power and goodness is in the sky, and they believe very firmly that I, with these ships and people, came from the sky, and in this belief they everywhere received me, after they had overcome their fear. And this does not result from their being ignorant (for they are of a very keen intelligence and men who navigate all those seas, so that it is wondrous the good account they give of everything), but because they have never seen people clothed or ships like ours.

And as soon as I arrived in the Indies, in the first island which I found, I took by force some of them in order that they might learn [Castilian] and give me information of what they had in those parts; it so worked out that they soon understood us, and we them, either by speech or signs, and they have been very serviceable. I still have them with me, and they are still of the opinion that I come from the sky, in spite of all the intercourse which they have had with me, and they were the first to announce

47. *St. Mark Stilling the Storm,* Paris Bordone.

this wherever I went, and the others went running from house to house and to the neighboring towns with loud cries of, "Come! Come! See the people from the sky!" They all came, men and women alike, as soon as they had confidence in us, so that not one, big or little, remained behind, and all brought something to eat and drink, which they gave with marvelous love. In all the islands they have very many *canoas* like rowing *fustes,* some bigger and some smaller, and some are bigger than a *fusta* of eighteen benches. They are not so beamy, because they are made of a single log, but a *fusta* could not keep up with them by rowing, since they make incredible speed, and in these they navigate all those islands, which are innumerable, and carry their merchandise. Some of these canoes I have seen with 70 and 80 men on board, each with his oar.

In all these islands, I saw no great diversity in the appearance of the people or in their manners and language, but they all understand one another, which is a very singular thing, on account of which I hope that

Their Highnesses will determine upon their conversion to our holy faith, towards which they are much inclined.

I have already said how I went 107 leagues in a straight line from west to east along the coast of the island Juana, and as a result of that voyage I can say that this island is larger than England and Scotland together; for, beyond these 107 leagues, there remain to the westward two provinces where I have not been, one of which they call Avan, and there the people are born with tails. Those provinces cannot have a length of less than 50 or 60 leagues, as I could understand from those Indians whom I retain and who know all the islands. The other, *Española,* in circuit is greater than all Spain, from *Colonya* by the coast to *Fuenterauia* in Vizcaya, since I went along one side 188 great leagues in a straight line from west to east. It is a desirable land and, once seen, is never to be relinquished; and in it, although of all I have taken possession for their Highnesses and all are more richly supplied than I know or could tell, I hold them all for their Highnesses, which they may dispose of as absolutely as of the realms of Castile. In this *Española,* in the most convenient place and in the best district for the gold mines and for all trade both with this continent and with that over there belong to the Grand Khan, where there will be great trade and profit, I have taken possession of a large town to which I gave the name *La Villa de Nauidad,* and in it I have built a fort and defenses, which already, at this moment, will be all complete, and I have left in it enough people for such a purpose, with arms and artillery and provisions for more than a year, and a *fusta,* and a master of the sea in all [maritime] arts to build others; and great friendship with the king of that land, to such an extent that he took pride in calling me and treating me as brother; and even if he were to change his mind and offer insult to these people, neither he nor his people know the use of arms and they go naked, as I have already said, and are the most timid people in the world, so that merely the people whom I have left there could destroy all that land; and the island is without danger for their persons, if they know how to behave themselves.

In all these islands, it appears, all the men are content with one woman, but to their *Maioral,* or king, they give up to twenty. It appears to me that the women work more than the men. I have been unable to learn whether they hold private property, but it appeared true to me that all took a share in anything that one had, especially in victuals.

In these islands I have so far found no human monstrosities, as many expected, on the contrary, among all these people good looks are esteemed; nor are they Negroes, as in Guinea, but with flowing hair, and they are not born where there is excessive force in the solar rays; it is true that the sun there has great strength, although it is distant from the Equator 26 degrees. In these islands, where there are high mountains, the cold this winter was severe, but they endure it through habit and with the help of food which they eat with many and excessively hot spices. Thus I have neither found monsters nor had report of any, except in an island which is the second at the entrance to the Indies, which is inhabited by a people who are regarded in all the islands as very ferocious and who eat human flesh; they have many canoes with which they range all the islands of India and pillage and take as much as they can; they are no more malformed than the others, except that they have the custom of wearing their hair long like women, and they use bows and arrows of the same stems of cane with a little piece of wood at the tip for want of iron, which they have not. They are ferocious toward these other people, who are exceedingly great cowards, but I make no more account of them than of the rest. These are those who have intercourse with the women of *Matremomio,* which is the first island met on the way from Spain to the Indies, in which there is not one man. These women use no feminine exercises, but bows and arrows of cane, like the abovesaid; and they arm and cover themselves with plates of copper, of which they have plenty. In another island which they assure me is larger than *Española,* the people have no hair. In this there is countless gold, and from it and from the other islands I bring with me *Indios* as evidence.

In conclusion, to speak only of that which has been accomplished on this voyage, which was so hasty, Their Highnesses can see that I shall give them as much gold as they want if Their Highnesses will render me a little help; besides spice and cotton, as much as Their Highnesses shall command; and gum mastic, as much as they shall order shipped, and which, up to now, has been found only in Greece, in the island of Chios, and the Seignory sell it for what it pleases; and aloe wood, as much as they shall order shipped, and slaves, as many as they shall order, who will be idolaters. And I believe that I have found rhubarb and cinnamon, and I shall find a thousand other things of value, which the people whom I have left there will have discovered, for I tarried nowhere, provided the wind allowed me to sail, except in the town of Navidad, where I stayed [to have it] secured and well seated. And the truth is I should have done much more if the vessels had served me as the occasion required.

This is enough. And the Eternal God, Our Lord, Who gives to all those who walk in His way victory over things which appear impossible; and this was notably one. For, although men have talked or have written of these lands, all was conjecture, without getting a look at it, but amounted only to this; that those who heard for the most part listened and judged it more a fable than that there was anything in it, however, small.

So since our Redeemer has given this triumph to our most illustrious King and Queen, and to their renowned realms, in so great a matter, for this all Christendom ought to feel joyful and make great celebrations and give solemn thanks to the Holy Trinity with many solemn prayers for the great exaltation which it will have, in the turning of so many peoples to our holy faith, and afterwards for material benefits, since not only Spain but all Christians will hence have refreshment and profit. This is exactly what has been done, though in brief.

Done on board the caravel off the Canary Islands, on the fifteenth of February, year 1493.

At your service.

The Admiral.

RICHARD HAKLUYT

THE VOYAGES OF SIR FRANCIS DRAKE

The West Indian Voyage

·　　·　　·

From hence putting off to the West Indies, wee were not many dayes at Sea, but there beganne among our people such mortalitie, as in fewe dayes there were dead above two or three hundred men. And until some seven or eight dayes after our comming from S. Iago, there had not died any one man of sicknesse in all the fleete: the sicknesse shewed not his infection wherewith so many were stroken, until we were departed thence, and then seazed our people with extreme hot burning and continuall agues, whereof very fewe escaped with life, and yet those for the most part not without great alteration and decay of their wittes and strength for a long time after. In some that died were plainely shewed the small spots, which are often found upon those that be infected with the plague:

48. Probably *Drake's Flag-
ship,* from the Egerton
manuscript.

wee were not above eighteene dayes in passage betweene the sight of
Saint Iago aforesaid, and the Island of Dominica, being the first Island
of the West Indies that we fell withall, the same being inhabited with
savage people, which goe all naked, their skinne coloured with some
painting of a reddish tawney, very personable and handsome strong
men, who doe admit litle conversation with the Spanyards: for as some
of our people might understand them, they had a Spaniard or twaine
prisoners with them, neither doe I thinke that there is any safetie for
any of our nation, or any other to be within the limits of their commande-
ment, albeit they used us very kindly for those few houres of time which
wee spent with them, helping our folkes to fill and carry on their bare
shoulders fresh water from the river to our ship boates, and fetching
from their houses great store of Tabacco, as also a kind of bread which
they fed on, called Cassavi, very white and savourie, made of the rootes
of Cassavi. In recompence whereof, we bestowed liberall rewards of
glasse, coloured beades, and other things, which we had found at Saint
Iago, wherewith (as it seemed) they rested very greatly satisfied, and

278

shewed some sorowfull countenance when they perceived that we would depart.

From hence wee went to another Island Westward of it, called Saint Christophers Island, wherein we spent some dayes of Christmas, to refresh our sicke people, and to cleanse and ayre our ships. In which Island were not any people at all that we could heare of.

In which time by the General it was advised and resolved, with the consent of the Lieutenant generall, the Vice-admiral, and all the rest of the Captaines to proceede to the great Islande of Hispaniola, aswell for that we knewe our selves then to bee in our best strength, as also the rather allured thereunto, by the glorious fame of the citie of S. Domingo, being the ancientest and chiefe inhabited place in all the tract of Countrey thereabouts. And so proceeding in this determination, by the way we mette a small Frigat, bound for the same place, the which the Vice-admirall tooke: and having duely examined the men that were in her, there was one found, by whom wee were advertised, the Haven to be a barren Haven, and the shore or land thereof to bee well fortified having a Castle thereupon furnished with great store of Artillerie, without the danger whereof was no convenient landing place within ten English miles of the Citie, to which the sayd Pilot tooke upon him to conduct us.

All things being thus considered on, the whole forces were commaunded in the Evening to embarke themselves in Pinnesses, boats, and other small barkes appoynted for this service. Our souldiers being thus imbarked, the Generall put himselfe into the barke Francis as Admirall, and all this night we lay on the sea, bearing small saile untill our arrivall to the landing place, which was about the breaking of the day, and so we landed, being Newyeeres day, nine or ten miles to the Westwards of that brave Citie of S. Domingo: for at that time nor yet is knowen to us any landing place, where the sea-surge doth not threaten to overset a Pinnesse or boate. Our Generall having seene us all landed in safetie, returned to his Fleete, bequeathing us to God, and the good conduct of Master Carliell our Lieutenant Generall: at which time, being about eight of the clocke, we began to march, and about noone time, or towards one of the clocke, we approched the towne, where the Gentlemen and those of the better sort, being some hundred and fiftie brave horses or rather more, began to present themselves; but our small shot played upon them, which were so susteined with good proportion of pikes in all parts, as they finding no part of our troope unprepared to receive them (for you must understand they viewed all round about) they were thus driven to give us leave to proceed towards the two gates of the towne, which were the next to the seaward. They had manned them both, and planted their ordinance for that present, and sudden alarme without the gate, and also some troopes of small shot in Ambuscado upon the hie way side. We divided our whole force, being some thousand or twelve hundred men into two partes, to enterprise both the gates at one instant, the Lieutenant Generall having openly vowed to Captaine Powel (who led the troope that entered the other gate) that with Gods good favour he would not rest untill our meeting in the market place.

Their ordinance had no sooner discharged upon our neere approch, and made some execution amongst us, though not much, but the Lieutenant generall began forthwith to advance both his voice of encouragement, and pace of marching: the first man that was slaine with the ordinance being very neere unto himselfe: and thereupon hasted all that hee might, to keepe them from the recharging of the ordinance. And notwithstanding their Ambuscados, we marched or rather ran so roundly in to them, as pell mell wee entered the gates, and gave them more care every man to save himselfe by flight, then reason to stand any longer to their broken fight. Wee forthwith repayred to the market place: but to be more truely understood, a place of very faire spacious square ground, whither also came as had bene agreed Captaine Powel with the other troope: which place with some part next unto it, we strengthened with Barricados, and there as the most convenient place assured our selves, the Citie being farre too spacious for so small and weary a troope to undertake to guarde. Somewhat after midnight, they who had the guard of the Castle, hearing us busie about the gates of the said Castle, abandoned the same: some being taken prisoners, and some fleeing away by the helpe of boates to the othei side of the Haven, and so into the countrey.

The next day we quartered a litle more at large, but not into the halfe part of the towne, and so making substantiall trenches, and planting all the ordinance, that ech part was correspondent to other, we held this towne the space of one moneth.

In the which time happened some accidents, more then are well remembred for the present, but amongst other things, it chanced that the Generall sent on his message to the Spanyards a Negro boy with a flagge of white, signifying truce, as is the Spanyards ordinarie maner to doe there, when they approch to speake to us: which boy unhappily was first mette withall by some of those, who had bene belonging as officers for the King in the Spanish Galley, which with the Towne was lately fallen into our hands, who without all order or reason, & contrary to that good usage wherewith wee had intertained their messengers, furiously strooke the poore boy thorow the body with one of their horsemens staves: with which wound the boy returned to the General, and after hee had declared the maner of this wrongfull crueltie, died foorthwith in his presence, wherewith the Generall being greatly passioned, commaunded the Provost Martiall, to cause a couple of Friers then prisoners, to be caried to the same place where the boy was stroken, accompanied with sufficient guard of our souldiers, and there presently to be hanged, dispatching at the same instant another poore prisoner, with this reason wherefore this execution was done, & with this message further, that until the party who had thus murdered the Generals messenger were delivered into our hands, to receive condigne punishment, there should no day passe, wherein there should not two prisoners be hanged, until they were all consumed which were in our hands.

Whereupon the day following, hee that had bene Captaine of the kings Galley, brought the offender to the townes end, offring to deliver him into our hands; but it was thought to be a more honourable revenge to make them there in our sight, to performe the execution themselves: which was done accordingly.

During our being in this towne, as formerly also at S. Iago there had passed justice upon the life of one of our owne company for an odious matter, so heere likewise was there an Irishman hanged, for the murthering of his Corporall.

In this time also passed many treaties betweene their Commissioners and us, for ransome of their Citie; but upon disagreements we still spent the early mornings in fiering the outmost houses: but they being built very magnificently of stone, with high loftes, gave us no small travell to ruine them. And albeit for divers dayes together we ordeined ech morning by day breake, until the heat began at nine of the clocke, that two hundred Mariners did nought els but labour to fire and burne the said houses without our trenches, whilst the souldiers in a like proportion stood forth for their guard: yet did wee not, or could not in this time consume so much as one third part of the towne: which towne is plainely described and set forth in a certaine Map. And so in the end, what wearied with firing, and what hastened by some other respects, wee were contented to accept of five and twentie thousand Ducats of five shillings sixe pence the peece, for the ransome of the rest of the towne.

Amongst other things which happened and were found at S. Domingo, I may not omit to let the world know one very notable marke & token of the unsatiable ambition of the Spanish king and his nation, which was found in the kings house, wherein the chiefe governour of that Citie and Countrey is appoynted alwayes to lodge, which was this: In the comming to the Hall or other roomes of this house, you must first ascend up by a faire large paire of staires; at the head of which staires is a handsome spacious place to walke in, somewhat like unto a gallery: wherein upon one of the wals, right over against you as you enter the said place, so as your eye cannot escape the sight of it, there is described & painted in a very large Scutchion the armes of the king of Spaine, and in the lower part of the said Scutchion, there is likewise described a Globe, conteining in it the whole circuit of the sea and the earth wherupon is a horse standing on his hinder part within the globe, and the other fore-part without the globe, lifted up as it were to leape, with a scroll painted in his mouth, wherein was written these words in Latin, Non sufficit orbis: which is as much to say, as the world sufficeth not. Whereof the meaning was required to be knowen of some of those of the better sort, that came in commission to treate upon the ransome of the towne, who would shake their heads, and turne aside their countenance in some smyling sort, without answering any thing, as greatly ashamed thereof. For by some of our company it was tolde them, that if the Queene of England would resolutely prosecute the warres against the king of Spaine, hee should be forced to lay aside that proude and unreasonable reaching vaine of his: for hee should finde more then inough to doe to keepe that which hee had alreadie, as by the present example of their lost towne they might for a beginning perceive well inough.

Now to the satisfying of some men, who marvell greatly that such a famous and goodly builded Citie so well inhabited of gallant people, very brave in their apparell (whereof our souldiers found good store for their reliefe) should afoord no greater riches then was found there: herein it is to be understood that the Indian people, which were the naturals of this whole Island of Hispaniola (the same being neere hand as great as England) were many yeeres since cleane consumed by the tyrannie of the Spanyards, which was ye cause, that for lacke of people to worke in the Mines, the golde and silver Mines of this Island are wholy given over, and thereby they are faine in this Island to use Copper money, whereof was found very great quantitie. The chiefe trade of this place consisteth of Sugar and Ginger, which groweth in the Island, and of Hides of oxen and kine, which in this waste countrey of the Island are bredde in infinite numbers, the soyle being very fertile: and the sayd beasts are fedde up to a very large grouth, and so killed for nothing so much, as for their Hides aforesayd. Wee found heere great store of strong wine, sweete oyle, vinegar, olives, and other such like provisions, as excellent Wheate-meale packed up in wine-pipes and other caske, and other commodities likewise, as Woollen and Linnen cloth, and some Silkes: all which provisions are brought out of Spaine, and served us for great reliefe. There was but a little Plate or vessell of Silver, in comparison of the great pride in other things of this towne, because in these hotte Countreys they use much of those earthen dishes finely painted or varnished, which they call Porcellana, which is had out of the East India: & for their drinking, they use glasses altogether, whereof they make excellent good and faire in the same place. But yet some plate we found, and many other good things, as their houshold garniture very gallant and rich, which had cost them deare, although unto us they were of small importance.

. . .

Voyage into the South Sea

The 15. day of November, in the yeere of our Lord 1577. M. Francis, Drake, with a fleete of five ships and barkes, and to the number of 164. men, gentlemen and sailers, departed from Plimmouth, giving out his pretended voyage for Alexandria: but the wind falling contrary, hee was forced the next morning to put into Falmouth haven in Cornewall, where such and so terrible a tempest tooke us, as few men have seene the like and was in deed so vehement, that all our ships were like to have gone to wracke: but it pleased God to preserve us from that extremitie, and to afflict us onely for that present with these two particulars: The mast of our Admirall which was the Pellican, was cut over boord for the safegard of the ship, and the Marigold was driven ashore, and somewhat bruised: for the repairing of which damages wee returned againe to Plimmouth, and having recovered those harmes, and brought the ships againe to good state, we set forth the second time from Plimmouth, and set saile the 13. day of December following.

The 25. day of the same moneth we fell with the Cape Cantin, upon the coast of Barbarie, and coasting along, the 27. day we found an Island called Mogador, lying one mile distant from the maine, betweene which

49. *Princess Elizabeth Leaves England*, Adam Willaerts.

Island and the maine, we found a very good and safe harbour for our ships to ride in, as also very good entrance, and voyde of any danger.

.   .   .

The 8. of Februarie following, wee fell with the fruitfull Island of Barateve, having in the meane time suffered many dangers by windes and shoalds. The people of this Island are comely in body and stature, and of a civill behaviour, just in dealing, and courteous to strangers, whereof we had the experience sundry wayes, they being most glad of our presence, and very ready to releeve our wants in those things which their Countrey did yeelde. The men goe naked, saving their heads and priviies, every man having something or other hanging at their eares. Their women are covered from the middle downe to the foote, wearing a great number of bracelets upon their armes, for some had 8. upon each armo, being made some of bone, some of horne, and some of brasse, the lightest whereof by our estimation waied two ounces apeece.

With this people linnen-cloth is good marchandize, and of good request, whereof they make rols for their heads, and girdles to weare about them.

Their Island is both rich and fruitfull: rich in golde, silver, copper, and sulphur, wherein they seeme skilfull and expert, not onely to trie the same, but in working it also artificially into any forme and fashion that pleaseth them.

Their fruits be divers and plentiful, as nutmegs, ginger, long pepper, lemmons, cucumbers, cocos, figu, sagu, with divers other sorts: and among all the rest, wee had one fruite, in bignesse, forme, and huske, like a Bay berry, hard of substance, and pleasant of taste, which being sodden, becommeth soft, and is a most good and wholsome victuall, whereof we tooke reasonable store, as we did also of the other fruits and spices: so that to confesse a trueth, since the time that we first set out of our owne Countrey of England, we happened upon no place (Ternate onely excepted) wherein we found more comforts and better meanes of refreshing.

At our departure from Barateve, we set our course for Java major, where arriving, we found great courtesie, and honourable entertainment. This Island is governed by 5. Kings, whom they call Rajah: as Rajah Donaw, and Rajah Mang Bange, and Rajah Cabuccapollo, which live as having one spirite, and one minde.

Of these five we had foure a shipboord at once, and two or three often. They are wonderfully delighted in coloured clothes, as red and greene: their upper parts of their bodies are naked, save their heads, whereupon they weare a Turkish roll, as do the Maluccians: from the middle downward they weare a pintado of silke, trailing upon the ground, in colour as they best like.

The Maluccians hate that their women should bee seene of strangers: but these offer them of high courtesie, yea the kings themselves.

The people are of goodly stature, and warlike, well provided of swords and targets, with daggers, all being of their owne worke, and most artificially done, both in tempering their mettall, as also in the forme, whereof we bought reasonable store.

They have an house in every village for their common assembly: every day they meete twise, men, women, and children, bringing with them such victuals as they thinke good, some fruites, some rice boiled, some hennes roasted, some sagu, having a table made 3. foote from the ground, whereon they set their meate, that every person sitting at the table may eate, one rejoycing in the company of another.

They boile their rice in an earthen pot, made in forme of a sugar loafe, being ful of holes, as our pots which we water our gardens withall, and it is open at the great ende, wherein they put their rice drie, without any moisture. In the meane time they have ready another great earthen pot, set fast in a fornace, boiling full of water, whereinto they put their pot with rice, by such measure, that they swelling become soft at the first, and by their swelling stopping the holes of the pot, admit no more water to enter, but the more they are boiled, the harder and more firme substance they become, so that in the end they are a firme & good bread, of the which with oyle, butter, sugar, and other spices, they make divers sorts of meates very pleasant of taste, and nourishing to nature.

The French pocks is here very common to all, and they helpe themselves, sitting naked from ten to two in the Sunne, whereby the venemous humour is drawen out. Not long before our departure, they tolde us, that not farre off there were such great Ships as ours, wishing us to beware: upon this our Captaine would stay no longer.

From Java Major we sailed for the cape of Good Hope, which was the first land we fell withall: neither did we touch with it, or any other land, untill we came to Sierra Leona, upon the coast of Guinea: notwithstanding we ranne hard aboord the Cape, finding the report of the Portugals to be most false, who affirme, that it is the most dangerous Cape of the world, never without intolerable stormes and present danger to travailers, which come neere the same.

This Cape is a most stately thing, and the fairest Cape we saw in the whole circumference of the earth, and we passed by it the 18. of June.

From thence we continued our course to Sierra Leona, on the coast of Guinea, where we arrived the 22. of July, and found necessarie provisions, great store of Elephants, Oisters upon trees of one kind, spawning and increasing infinitely, the Oister suffering no budde to grow. We departed thence the 24. day.

We arrived in England the third of November 1580. being the third yeere of our departure.

The names of the Kings or Princes of Java at the time of our English mens being there.

Raja Donaw.	Raja Tymbanton.
Raja Rabacapala.	Raja Mawgbange.
Raja Bacabatra.	Raja Patimara.

Certaine wordes of the naturall language of Java, learned and observed by our men there.

Sabuck, silke.	*Larnike,* drinke.
Sagu, bread of the Countrey.	*Paree,* ryce in the huske.
Braas, sodden ryce.	*Bebeck,* a ducke.
Calapa, Cocos.	*Anjange,* a deere.
Cricke, a dagger.	*Popran,* oyntment.
Catcha, a looking glasse	*Coar,* the head.
Arbo, an oxe.	*Endam,* raine.
Vados, a goate.	*Jonge,* a shippe.
Cabo, golde.	*Chay,* the sea.
Gardange, a plantane.	*Sapelo,* ten in number.
Hiam, a henne.	*Dopolo,* twentie.
Sevit, linnen cloth.	*Treda,* no.
Doduck, blew cloth.	*Lau,* understand you.
Totopps, one of their caps.	*Bayer,* goe.
Gula, blacke sugar.	*Adadizano,* I will fetch it.
Tadon, a woman	*Suda,* ynough.

(from *A Selection of the Principal Voyages, Traffiques and Discoveries of the English Nation*)

287

GALILEO

ASTRONOMICAL MESSAGE

*Which contains and explains recent observations made with
the aid of a new spyglass concerning the surface of the moon,
the Milky Way, nebulous stars, and innumerable fixed stars,
as well as four planets never before seen and now named The
Medicean Stars.*

Great indeed are the things which in this brief treatise I propose for
observation and consideration by all students of nature. I say great, because of the excellence of the subject itself, the entirely unexpected and
novel character of these things, and finally because of the instrument by
means of which they have been revealed to our senses.

Surely it is a great thing to increase the numerous host of fixed stars
previously visible to the unaided vision, adding countless more which
have never before been seen, exposing these plainly to the eye in numbers
ten times exceeding the old and familiar stars.

It is a very beautiful thing, and most gratifying to the sight, to behold
the body of the moon, distant from us almost sixty earthly radii, as if it
were no farther away than two such measures—so that its diameter appears almost thirty times larger, its surface nearly nine hundred times,
and its volume twenty-seven thousand times as large as when viewed
with the naked eye. In this way one may learn with all the certainty of
sense evidence that the moon is not robed in a smooth and polished surface but is in fact rough and uneven, covered everywhere, just like the
earth's surface, with huge prominences, deep valleys, and chasms.

Again, it seems to me a matter of no small importance to have ended
the dispute about the Milky Way by making its nature manifest to the
very senses as well as to the intellect. Similarly it will be a pleasant and
elegant thing to demonstrate that the nature of those stars which astronomers have previously called "nebulous" is far different from what has
been believed hitherto. But what surpasses all wonders by far, and what
particularly moves us to seek the attention of all astronomers and philosophers, is the discovery of four wandering stars not known or observed
by any man before us. Like Venus and Mercury, which have their own
periods about the sun, these have theirs about a certain star that is conspicuous among those already known, which they sometimes precede
and sometimes follow, without ever departing from it beyond certain

50. *Fra' Luca Paciolo,* Jacopo de' Barbari.

limits. All these facts were discovered and observed by me not many days ago with the aid of a spyglass which I devised, after first being illuminated by divine grace. Perhaps other things, still more remarkable, will in time be discovered by me or by other observers with the aid of such an instrument. . . .

.   .   .

It would be superfluous to enumerate the number and importance of the advantages of such an instrument at sea as well as on land. But forsaking terrestrial observations, I turned to celestial ones, and first I saw the moon from as near at hand as if it were scarcely two terrestrial radii away. After that I observed often with wondering delight both the planets and the fixed stars, and since I saw these latter to be very crowded, I began to see (and eventually found) a method by which I might measure their distances apart.

.   .

Here we have a fine and elegant argument for quieting the doubts of those who, while accepting with tranquil mind the revolutions of the planets about the sun in the Copernican system, are mightily disturbed to have the moon alone revolve about the earth and accompany it in an annual rotation about the sun. Some have believed that this structure of the universe should be rejected as impossible. But now we have not just one planet rotating about another while both run through a great orbit around the sun; our own eyes show us four stars which wander around Jupiter as does the moon around the earth, while all together trace out a grand revolution about the sun in the space of twelve years.

(from *The Starry Messenger*)

LETTER TO THE
GRAND DUCHESS OF TUSCANY

Some years ago, as Your Serene Highness well knows, I discovered in the heavens many things that had not been seen before our own age. The novelty of these things, as well as some consequences which followed from them in contradiction to the physical notions commonly held among academic philosophers, stirred up against me no small number of professors—as if I had placed these things in the sky with my own hands in order to upset nature and overturn the sciences. They seemed to forget that the increase of known truths stimulates the investigation, establishment, and growth of the arts; not their diminution or destruction.

Showing a greater fondness for their own opinions than for truth, they sought to deny and disprove the new things which, if they had cared to look for themselves, their own senses would have demonstrated to them. To this end they hurled various charges and published numerous writings filled with vain arguments, and they made the grave mistake of sprinkling these with passages taken from places in the Bible which they had failed to understand properly, and which were ill suited to their purposes.

.   .   .

Well, the passage of time has revealed to everyone the truths that I previously set forth; and, together with the truth of the facts, there has come to light the great difference in attitude between those who simply and dispassionately refused to admit the discoveries to be true, and those who combined with their incredulity some reckless passion of their own. Men who were well grounded in astronomical and physical science were persuaded as soon as they received my first message. There were others who denied them or remained in doubt only because of their novel and unexpected character, and because they had not yet had the opportunity to see for themselves. These men have by degrees come to be satisfied. But some, besides allegiance to their original error, possess I know not what fanciful interest in remaining hostile not so much toward the things in question as toward their discoverer. No longer being able to deny them, these men now take refuge in obstinate silence, but being more than ever exasperated by that which has pacified and quieted other men, they divert their thoughts to other fancies and seek new ways to damage me.

I should pay no more attention to them than to those who previously contradicted me—at whom I always laugh, being assured of the eventual outcome—were it not that in their new calumnies and persecutions I perceive that they do not stop at proving themselves more learned than I am (a claim which I scarcely contest), but go so far as to cast against me imputations of crimes which must be, and are, more abhorrent to me than death itself. I cannot remain satisfied merely to know that the injustice of this is recognized by those who are acquainted with these men and with me, as perhaps it is not known to others.

Persisting in their original resolve to destroy me and everything mine by any means they can think of, these men are aware of my views in astronomy and philosophy. They know that as to the arrangement of the parts of the universe, I hold the sun to be situated motionless in the center of the revolution of the celestial orbs while the earth rotates on its axis and revolves about the sun. They know also that I support this position not only by refuting the arguments of Ptolemy and Aristotle, but by producing many counter-arguments; in particular, some which relate to physical effects whose causes can perhaps be assigned in no other way. In addition there are astronomical arguments derived from many things in my new celestial discoveries that plainly confute the Ptolemaic system while admirably agreeing with and confirming the contrary hypothesis. Possibly because they are disturbed by the known truth of other propositions of mine which differ from those commonly held, and therefore mistrusting their defense so long as they confine themselves to the field of philosophy, these men have resolved to fabricate a shield for their fallacies out of the mantle of pretended religion and the authority of the Bible. These they apply, with little judgment, to the refutation of arguments that they do not understand and have not even listened to.

First they have endeavored to spread the opinion that such propositions in general are contrary to the Bible and are consequently damnable and heretical. They know that it is human nature to take up causes whereby a man may oppress his neighbor, no matter how unjustly, rather than those from which a man may receive some just encouragement. Hence they have had no trouble in finding men who would preach the damnability and heresy of the new doctrine from their very pulpits with unwonted confidence, thus doing impious and inconsiderate injury not only to that doctrine and its followers but to all mathematics and mathematicians in general. Next, becoming bolder, and hoping (though vainly) that this seed which first took root in their hypocritical minds would send out branches and ascend to heaven, they began scattering rumors among the people that before long this doctrine would be condemned by the supreme authority. They know, too, that official condemnation would not only suppress the two propositions which I have mentioned, but would render damnable all other astronomical and physical statements and observations that have any necessary relation or connection with these.

In order to facilitate their designs, they seek so far as possible (at least among the common people) to make this opinion seem new and to belong to me alone. They pretend not to know that its author, or rather its restorer and confirmer, was Nicholas Copernicus; and that he was not only a Catholic, but a priest and a canon. He was in fact so esteemed by the church that when the Lateran Council under Leo X took up the correction of the church calendar, Copernicus was called to Rome from the most remote parts of Germany to undertake its reform. At that time the calendar was defective because the true measures of the year and the lunar month were not exactly known. The Bishop of Culm, then superintendent of this matter, assigned Copernicus to seek more light and greater certainty concerning the celestial motions by means of constant study and labor. With Herculean toil he set his admirable mind to this task, and he made such great progress in this science and brought our knowledge of the heavenly motions to such precision that he became celebrated as an astronomer. Since that time not only has the calendar been regulated by his teachings, but tables of all the motions of the planets have been calculated as well.

.   .   .

Now as to the false aspersions which they so unjustly seek to cast upon me, I have thought it necessary to justify myself in the eyes of all men, whose judgment in matters of religion and of reputation I must hold in great esteem. I shall therefore discourse of the particulars which these men produce to make this opinion detested and to have it condemned not merely as false but as heretical. To this end they make a shield of their hypocritical zeal for religion. They go about invoking the Bible, which they would have minister to their deceitful purposes. Contrary to the sense of the Bible and the intention of the holy Fathers, if I am not mistaken, they would extend such authorities until even in purely physical matters—where faith is not involved—they would have us altogether abandon reason and the evidence of our senses in favor of some biblical passage, though under the surface meaning of its words this passage may contain a different sense.

I hope to show that I proceed with much greater piety than they do, when I argue not against condemning this book, but against condemning it in the way they suggest—that is, without understanding it, weighing it, or so much as reading it. For Copernicus never discusses matters of religion or faith, nor does he use arguments that depend in any way upon the authority of sacred writings which he might have interpreted erroneously. He stands always upon physical conclusions pertaining to the celestial motions, and deals with them by astronomical and geometrical demonstrations, founded primarily upon sense-experiences and very exact observations. He did not ignore the Bible, but he knew very well that if his doctrine were proved, then it could not contradict the Scriptures when they were rightly understood. . . .

.   .   .

Therefore I declare (and my sincerity will make itself manifest) not only that I mean to submit myself freely and renounce any errors into which I may fall in this discourse through ignorance of matters pertaining to religion, but that I do not desire in these matters to engage in disputes with anyone, even on points that are disputable. My goal is this alone; that if, among errors that may abound in these considerations of a subject remote from my profession, there is anything that may be serviceable to the holy Church in making a decision concerning the Copernican system, it may be taken and utilized as seems best to the superiors. And if not, let my book be torn and burnt, as I neither intend nor pretend to gain from it any fruit that is not pious and Catholic. And though many of the things I shall reprove have been heard by my own ears, I shall freely grant to those who have spoken them that they never said them, if that is what they wish, and I shall confess myself to have been mistaken. Hence let whatever I reply be addressed not to them, but to whoever may have held such opinions.

The reason produced for condemning the opinion that the earth moves and the sun stands still is that in many places in the Bible one may read that the sun moves and the earth stands still. Since the Bible cannot err, it follows as a necessary consequence that anyone takes an erroneous and heretical position who maintains that the sun is inherently motionless and the earth movable.

With regard to this argument, I think in the first place that it is very pious to say and prudent to affirm that the holy Bible can never speak untruth—whenever its true meaning is understood. But I believe nobody will deny that it is often very abstruse, and may say things which are quite different from what its bare words signify. Hence in expounding the Bible if one were always to confine oneself to the unadorned grammatical meaning, one might fall into error. Not only contradictions and propositions far from true might thus be made to appear in the Bible, but even grave heresies and follies. Thus it would be necessary to assign to God feet, hands, and eyes, as well as corporeal and human affections, such as anger, repentance, hatred, and sometimes even the forgetting of things past and ignorance of those to come. These propositions uttered by the Holy Ghost were set down in that manner by the sacred scribes in order to accommodate them to the capacities of the common people, who are rude and unlearned. For the sake of those who deserve to be separated from the herd, it is necessary that wise expositors should produce the true senses of such passages, together with the special reasons for which they were set down in these words. This doctrine is so wide-

51. Cupola mosaic, after Raphael. Rome, Chigi Chapel, S. Maria del Popolo.

spread and so definite with all theologians that it would be superfluous to adduce evidence for it.

Hence I think that I may reasonably conclude that whenever the Bible has occasion to speak of any physical conclusion (especially those which are very abstruse and hard to understand), the rule has been observed of avoiding confusion in the minds of the common people which would render them contumacious toward the higher mysteries. Now the Bible, merely to condescend to popular capacity, has not hesitated to obscure some very important pronouncements, attributing to God himself some qualities extremely remote from (and even contrary to) His essence. Who, then, would positively declare that this principle has been set aside, and the Bible has confined itself rigorously to the bare and restricted sense of its words, when speaking but casually of the earth, of water, of the sun, or of any other created thing? Especially in view of the fact that these things in no way concern the primary purpose of the sacred writings, which is the service of God and the salvation of souls—matters infinitely beyond the comprehension of the common people.

This being granted, I think that in discussions of physical problems we ought to begin not from the authority of scriptural passages, but from sense-experiences and necessary demonstrations; for the holy Bible and the phenomena of nature proceed alike from the divine Word, the former as the dictate of the Holy Ghost and the latter as the observant executrix of God's commands. It is necessary for the Bible, in order to be accommodated to the understanding of every man, to speak many things which appear to differ from the absolute truth so far as the bare meaning of the words is concerned. But Nature, on the other hand, is inexorable and immutable; she never transgresses the laws imposed upon her, or cares a whit whether her abstruse reasons and methods of operation are understandable to men. For that reason it appears that nothing physical which sense-experience sets before our eyes, or which necessary demonstrations prove to us, ought to be called in question (much less condemned) upon the testimony of biblical passages which may have some different meaning beneath their words. For the Bible is not chained in every expression to conditions as strict as those which govern all physical effects; nor is God any less excellently revealed in Nature's actions than in the sacred statements of the Bible. . . .

WILLIAM SHAKESPEARE

NATURE AND MAN

GLOUCESTER. These late eclipses in the sun and moon portend no good to us. Though the wisdom of nature can reason it thus and thus, yet nature finds itself scourged by the sequent effects. Love cools, friendship falls off, brothers divide. In cities, mutinies; in countries, discord; in palaces, treason; and the bond cracked 'twixt son and father. This villain of mine comes under the prediction, there's son against father. The King falls from bias of nature, there's father against child. We have seen the best of our time. Machinations, hollowness, treachery, and all ruinous disorders follow us disquietly to our graves. Find out this villain, Edmund, it shall lose thee nothing. Do it carefully. And the noble and true-hearted Kent banished! His offense, honesty! 'Tis strange.

[Exit]

EDMUND. This is the excellent foppery of the world, that when we are sick in fortune—often the surfeit of our own behavior—we make guilty of our disasters the sun, the moon, and the stars, as if we were villains by necessity, fools by heavenly compulsion; knaves, thieves, and treachers by spherical predominance; drunkards, liars, and adulterers by an enforced obedience of planetary influence; and all that we are evil in, by a divine thrusting on—an admirable evasion of whoremaster man, to lay his goatish disposition to the charge of a star! My father compounded with my mother under the dragon's tail, and my nativity was under Ursa Major, so that it follows I am rough and lecherous. Tut, I should have been that I am had the maidenliest star in the firmament twinkled on my bastardizing. . . .

(from *King Lear*)

PART IV

A Trinity of Ideas:

New Ordering of
Philosophy and Religion

Three philosophical ideas dominated the Renaissance. Humanism revived interest in Classical writers; Aristotelianism, leaning heavily on logic, emphasized human values; Neoplatonism offered a more personal, more aesthetic approach to God. Religion, undergoing increased secularization, experienced anti-clerical, anti-ritualistic movements that resulted finally in the Reformation.

*Pompanazzi insisted that man has more than immortal long-
ings—he has the very stuff of immortality. Ficino, Castiglione,
and Ronsard, philosopher, diplomat, and poet, each insisted
on man's capacity to realize ideal love and beauty here and
now. But earthly love involves practical considerations, too,
and these Francis Bacon considered with scholarly detach-
ment. Man's proclivity for foolishness was explored by Erasmus, and man's dignity and goodness by Pico. Luther and
Calvin found man cut off from the religious font at which he
had been used to drink, and each preached against corruption within the church, the distortion of its practice and
dogma. Yet visions of perfection were still possible—and
More described a perfect religion even as Shakespeare reflected the perfect civil society as conceived in his own day.*

PIETRO POMPANAZZI

FROM ON IMMORTALITY

*In which it is shown that man is of a twofold ("ancipitis")
nature and a mean between mortal and immortal things.*

Now, I hold that the beginning of our consideration should be made
at this point. Man is clearly not of simple but of multiple, not of certain but of ambiguous (*ancipitis*) nature, and he is to be placed as a
mean between mortal and immortal things. This is plain to see if we
examine his essential operations, as it is from such operations that es-
sences are made known. For in performing the functions of the vegeta-

52. *The Holy Family*, Michelangelo.

tive and of the sensitive soul, which, as is said in *De anima,* Book ii, and in *De generatione animalium,* Book ii, chapter 3, cannot be performed without a bodily and perishable instrument, man assumes mortality. However, in knowing and willing, operations which throughout the whole *De anima* and in *De partibus animalium,* Book i, chapter 1, and in *De generatione animalium,* Book ii, chapter 3, are held to be performed without any bodily instrument, since they prove separability and immateriality, and these in turn prove immortality, man is to be numbered among the immortal things. From these facts the whole conclusion can be drawn, that man is clearly not of a simple nature, since he includes three souls, so to speak—the vegetative, the sensitive, and the intellective—and that he claims a twofold nature for himself, since he exists neither unqualifiedly (*simpliciter*) mortal nor unqualifiedly immortal but embraces both natures.

Therefore the ancients spoke well when they established man between eternal and temporal things for the reason that he is neither purely eternal nor purely temporal, since he partakes of both natures. And to man, who thus exists as a mean between the two, power is given to assume whichever nature he wishes. Hence there are three kinds of men to be found. Some are numbered with the gods, although such are but few. And these are the men who, having subjugated the vegetative and the sensitive, have become almost completely rational. Some from total neglect of the intellect and from occupying themselves with the vegetative and the sensitive alone, have changed, as it were, into beasts. And perhaps this is what the Pythagorean fable means when it says that men's souls pass into different beasts. Some are called normal men; and these are the ones who have lived tolerably according to the moral virtues. They have not, however, devoted themselves entirely to the intellect or held entirely aloof from the bodily powers. Each of these two latter sorts has a wide range, as is plain to see. With this agrees what is said in the Psalm: "Thou hast made him but a little lower than the angels."

.   .   .

By these reasons, I think, other points also can be resolved. For although it is commonly said that, if the soul is mortal, man ought to give himself over completely to bodily pleasures, commit all evils for his own advantage, and that it would be vain to worship God, to honor the divine, to pour forth prayers to God, to make sacrifices, and do other things of this sort, the answer is clear enough from what has been said. For since happiness is naturally desired and misery shunned, and by what has been said happiness consists in virtuous action, but misery in vicious action, since to worship God with the whole mind, to honor the divine, to raise prayers to God, to sacrifice are actions in the highest degree virtuous, we ought hence to strive with all our powers to acquire them. But on the contrary, thefts, robberies, murders, a life of pleasures are vices, which make man turn into a beast and cease to be a man; hence we ought to abstain from them. And note that one who acts conscientiously, expecting no other reward than virtue, seems to act far more virtuously and purely than he who expects some reward beyond virtue. And he who shuns vice on account of the foulness of vice, not because of the fear of due punishment for vice, seems more to be praised than he who avoids vice on account of the fear of punishment, as in the verses:

53. *The School of Athens,* Raphael.

> The good hate sin from love of virtue,
> The evil hate sin from fear of punishment.

Wherefore those who claim that the soul is mortal seem better to save the grounds of virtue than those who claim it to be immortal. For the hope of reward and the fear of punishment seem to suggest a certain servility, which is contrary to the grounds of virtue.

MARSILIO FICINO

COMMENTARY ON PLATO'S SYMPOSIUM

Plato, the father of philosophers, passed away at the age of eighty-one after the food had been cleared away at a banquet on his birthday, November 7. This banquet, which commemorated both his birthday and the anniversary of his death, was renewed every year by all the early Platonists down to the time of Plotinus and Porphyry. But for twelve hundred years after Porphyry these annual feasts were not observed.

At last in our own day, the illustrious Lorenzo de' Medici, wishing to reestablish the Platonic symposium, appointed Francesco Bandini Master of the Feast and so, when Bandini had declared November 7 the date for the celebration, he entertained in regal splendor at the villa, at Careggio, nine guest Platonists: Antonio Agli, Bishop of Fiesole; Ficino, the physician; Cristoforo Landino, the poet; Bernardo Nuzzi, the rhetorician; Tommaso Benci; Giovanni Cavalcanti, our dear friend, whom, because of his virtue of soul and noble appearance, they named Hero of the feast; the two Marsuppini, Cristoforo and Carlo, sons of the poet Carlo Marsuppini; and finally, Bandini wished me to be the ninth, so that with the addition of the name Marsilio Ficino to those already mentioned, the number of the Muses might be rounded out.

When the food had been cleared away, Bernardo Nuzzi took the volume of Plato which is inscribed *Symposium on Love* and read all the speeches of this *Symposium*. When he had finished reading, he asked that each of the guests explain one of the speeches. They all consented, and when the lots had been drawn, the first speech, that of Phaedrus, fell to Giovanni Cavalcanti to explain. The speech of Pausanias fell to the theologian Agli; that of Eryximachus, the physician, to the physician Ficino; that of the poet Aristophanes to the poet Landino; that of Agathon, the young man, to Carlo Marsuppini; to Tommaso Benci was given the discourse of Socrates, and finally the speech of Alcibiades fell to Cristoforo Marsuppini. Everyone approved the lot as it had fallen out; but the bishop and the physician were called away, the one to the care of souls, the other to the care of bodies, and they resigned their parts in the discussion to Giovanni Cavalcanti, to whom the rest then turned and fell silent, ready to listen. The Hero of the feast began the discussion in this way:

By what Rule Love is Praised.
In what its Dignity and Greatness Consist.

. . .

In the beginning, God created the substance of the Angelic Mind, which we also call Essence. This, in the first moment of its creation, was formless and dark, but since it was born from God, it turned toward God, its own source, with a certain innate desire. When turned toward God, it was illumined by the glory of God Himself. In the glow of His

radiance its own passion was set ablaze. When its whole passion was
kindled, it drew close to God, and in cleaving to Him, assumed form.
For God, who is omnipotent, created in the Angelic Mind, as it cleaved
to Him, the forms of all things to be created. In this Mind, therefore,
in some spiritual way was painted, so to speak, everything which we
sense in these bodies [of the material world]. In those forms were conceived the globes of heaven and the elements, the stars, the kinds of
vapors, the forms of stones, metals, plants, and animals. These Prototypes or Forms of everything conceived by the dispensation of God in
the Angelic Mind are, we cannot doubt, the Ideas. That Form or Idea
of the heavens we call the god Uranus, the form of the first planet we
call the god Saturn, of the second Jove, and so on with all the rest of
the planets. Likewise, the Idea of fire we call the god Vulcan, of the air
Jupiter and Juno, of the sea Neptune, and of the earth Pluto. In this way
all the gods are assigned to certain parts of the lower world, the Ideas of
those parts are collected together in the Angelic Mind, but the drawing
near of the Mind to God preceded the completed reception of the Ideas
from God who created them. Before the approach came the kindling of
passion, before that the illumination by the divine light, before that the
first inclination of desire, and before that the substance of the disorderly
Mind. It is that still formless substance which we mean by Chaos; that
first turning toward God we call the birth of Love; the infusion of the
divine light, the nourishing of love; the ensuing conflagration, the incre-
ment of love; the approach to God, the impact of love; and the giving of
the forms, the completion of love. This composite of all the Forms and
Ideas we call in Latin a *mundus,* and in Greek, a *cosmos,* that is, *Orderliness.* The attractiveness of this *Orderliness* is Beauty. To beauty, Love,
as soon as it was born, drew the Mind, and led the Mind formerly unbeautiful to the same Mind made beautiful. And so we may say that
the nature of Love is this, that it attracts to beauty and links the unbeautiful with the beautiful. Who, therefore, will doubt that Love immediately followed Chaos, and preceded the world and all the gods who
were assigned to the various parts of the world? The more so, since the
passion of the Angelic Mind preceded its own acquisition of form, and
in that Mind, once it had taken form, were born the gods and the world.
And so Orpheus was right in naming Love the oldest of the gods, and
also calling him "perfect in himself," as much as to say "self-completing,"
since that first instinct of the Angelic Mind by its own nature seems to
have drawn its own completion from God, and to have shown that com-

pletion to the Mind, which took form from it, and likewise to the gods, who rose from it.

Phaedrus also called Love "most wise," and rightly so, for omniscience, whence all wisdom properly derives, is attributed to the Angelic Mind, because the Mind (when it was turned toward God by Love,) glowed with the light of God Himself. The Angelic Mind was turned toward God in the same way in which the eye is directed toward the light of the sun. For first it looks away, then it sees only the light of the sun, then third, in the light of the sun it perceives the colors and shapes of things. The eye is at first blind, and, like Chaos, formless. When it sees the light, it loves the light and is, in turn, lighted up in looking at it; in receiving the glow, it receives form in the colors and shapes of things.

Now in the same way that the Angelic Mind, just born and formless, was turned by love toward God and received from Him its form, so also the World-Soul turned toward the Mind and toward God, from whom it was born. And, although it was at first formless and a chaos, it was directed by love toward the Angelic Mind, and of forms received from the Mind became a world; and so with the matter of this world, although in the beginning it lay a formless chaos without the ornament of forms, attracted by innate love, it turned toward the Soul and offered itself submissively to it, and by the mediation of this love, it found ornament, from the Soul, of all the forms which are seen in this world; and thus out of a chaos was made a world.

Therefore, there are three worlds, and also three chaoses. Finally, in each case, Love accompanies the chaos, precedes the world, wakens the drowsy, lights the obscure, revives the dead, gives form to the formless, and finishes the incomplete. Certainly no greater praises than these can be spoken of, or even conceived.

.   .   .

On the Two Kinds of Love
and the Double Nature of Venus.

Now we must discuss briefly the two kinds of Love. Pausanias says that for Plato, Cupid was the consort of Venus, and that there are necessarily as many Cupids as there are Venuses. Now, he mentions two Venuses, which are accompanied by two Loves. One Venus he calls the Heavenly, the other the Earthly. The Heavenly one was born of Heaven of no mother; the other was born of Jupiter and Dione. The Platonists call the Supreme God Uranus because just as that sublime body, Heaven, rules over and contains all bodies, so the supreme God surpasses all spirits. But the Platonists call the Angelic Mind many names, for they speak of it now as Saturn, now as Jupiter, and now as Venus, for that Mind has essence, life, and intelligence. They call its essence Saturn, its life Jupiter, and its intelligence Venus. The World-Soul we likewise call Saturn, Jupiter, and Venus. Insofar as it understands the divine, we call it Saturn; insofar as it moves the heavens, we call it Jupiter; and insofar as it begets lower forms, we call it Venus.

The first Venus, which is in the Angelic Mind, is said to have been born of Uranus "of no mother," because for the natural philosophers, *mother* means *matter,* and the Angelic Mind is completely foreign to any relationship with corporeal matter.

The second Venus, which is in the World-Soul, was born of Jupiter and Dione: born of Jupiter, that is, of that faculty of the World-Soul which moves the heavens. She it was who created the power which generates these lower forms. The philosophers attribute a mother as well as a father to this Venus because she is thought to be related to matter, since she is incorporated in the matter of the world. To sum it all up, Venus is two-fold: one is clearly that intelligence which we said was in the Angelic Mind; the other is the power of generation with which the World-Soul is endowed. Each has as consort a similar Love. The first, by innate love is stimulated to know the beauty of God; the second, by its love, to procreate the same beauty in bodies. The former Venus first embraces the Glory of God in herself, and then translates it to the second Venus. This latter Venus translates sparks of that divine glory into earthly matter. It is because of the presence of sparks of this kind that an individual body seems beautiful to us, in proportion to its merits. The human soul perceives the beauty of these bodies through the eyes.

The soul also has two powers. It certainly has the power of comprehension, and it has the power of generation. These two powers in us are the two Venuses which are accompanied by their twin Loves. When the beauty of a human body first meets our eyes, the mind, which is the first Venus in us, worships and adores the human beauty as an image of the divine beauty, and through the first, it is frequently aroused to the second. But the power of generation in us, which is the second Venus, desires to create another form like this. Therefore, there is a Love in each case: in the former, it is the desire of contemplating Beauty; and in the latter, the desire of propagating it; both loves are honorable and praiseworthy, for each is concerned with the divine image.

Of what, therefore, does Pausanias disapprove in love? I shall tell you. If a man is too eager for procreation and gives up contemplation, or is immoderately desirous of copulation with women, or consorts unnaturally with men, or prefers the beauty of the body to that of the soul, insofar he abuses the dignity of love. It is this abuse of love which Pausanias censures. Therefore, a man who properly respects love praises, of course, the beauty of the body; but through it he contemplates the more excellent beauty of the soul, the mind, and God, and admires and loves this more fervently than the other. Moreover, he performs the functions of generation and coition within the bounds prescribed by natural law and civil laws drawn up by men of wisdom. On this subject Pausanias speaks at greater length.

Exhortation to Love. On Simple and Mutual Love.

I urge and beg you all, my friends, to embrace immediately this love, a thing certainly divine, with all your strength and be not deterred by what they say Plato said about a certain lover: "That lover," he said, "is a soul dead in its own body and living in that of another." Likewise, be not dismayed by what Orpheus perchance sang about the wretched and deplorable lot of lovers, for I shall tell you next, if you please, how these grievances are to be understood, and how it is possible to remedy them, so listen carefully.

Plato calls love "something bitter," and correctly so, because whoever loves dies. Orpheus calls it "bitter-sweet" because love is voluntary death. Insofar as it is death, it is bitter, and insofar as it is voluntary, it is sweet. He who loves, dies; for his consciousness, oblivious of himself, is devoted exclusively to the loved one, and a man who is not conscious *of* himself is certainly not conscious *in* himself. Therefore, a soul that is so affected does not function in itself, because the primary function of the soul is consciousness. The soul which does not function in itself does not exist in itself, for function and existence are equivalent. There can be no existence without function, and function cannot survive existence itself; a thing cannot function when it does not exist, and whenever it does exist it functions. Therefore, the soul of a lover does not exist within the man himself, because it does not function in him. If it does not exist in him, it also does not live in him, and he who does not live is dead. Therefore, everyone who loves is dead in himself. But at least he lives in the other person, does he not? Certainly.

There are these two kinds of love: one simple, the other reciprocal. Simple love occurs when the loved one does not return his lover's affections. In this case the lover is completely dead, for he neither lives in himself, as we have already sufficiently proved, nor does he live in his loved one, since he is rejected by him. Where, then does he live? In air, water, fire, earth, or in some animal carcass? In none of these, for the human soul does not live in any but a human body. Will it perhaps eke out an existence in the body of some other person whom it does not love? No, not there either, for if it does not live in that in which it most fiercely desires to live, how can it live in any other? Therefore, the unrequited lover lives nowhere; he is completely dead. Moreover, he never comes back to life unless indignation revives him.

But when the loved one loves in return, the lover leads his life in him. Here, surely, is a remarkable circumstance that whenever two people are brought together in mutual affection, one lives in the other and the other in him. In this way they mutually exchange identities; each gives himself to the other in such a way that each receives the other in return. How they can give themselves up while oblivious of themselves I can see; but how one receives the other, I do not understand; for a man who does not even have possession of himself will that much less take possession of someone else.

The truth must rather be that each has himself and has the other, too. A has himself, but in B; and B also has himself, but in A. When you love me, you contemplate me, and as I love you, I find myself in your contemplation of me; I recover myself, lost in the first place by own neglect of myself, in you, who preserve me. You do exactly the same in me. And then this, too, is remarkable: that after I have lost myself, if I recover myself through you, I have myself through you, and if I have myself through you, I have you sooner and to a greater degree than I have myself. I am therefore closer to you than I am to myself, since I keep a grasp on myself only through you as a mediary.

It is in this that the power of Cupid differs from the force of Mars; indeed it is in this way that military power and love differ: the general possesses others through himself; the lover takes possession of himself through another, and the farther each of the lovers is from himself, the nearer he is to the other, and though he is dead in himself, he comes to life again in the other. In fact, there is only one death in mutual love, but there are two resurrections, for a lover dies within himself the moment he forgets about himself, but he returns to life immediately in his loved one as soon as the loved one embraces him in loving contemplation. He is resurrected once more when he finally recognizes himself in his beloved and no longer doubts that he is loved.

O, happy death, which is followed by two lives. O, wondrous exchange in which each gives himself up for the other, and has the other, yet does not cease to have himself. O, inestimable gain, when two so become one, that each of the two, instead of one alone, becomes two, and as though doubled, he who had one life before, with a death intervening, has now two. For a man who dies once and is twice resurrected has exchanged one life for two and his single self for two selves.

Certainly there is a most just vengeance in reciprocal love, for a homicide must be punished by death, and who will deny that a man who is loved is a homicide since he robs the loving one of his soul? So, likewise, who will deny that that man himself dies when he loves in return the person who loves him? This is a restitution which is certainly due, when each returns to the other the soul he has taken. Each gives up his own to his lover, but by loving in return restores the other through his own. Therefore, anyone who is loved ought in very justice to love in return, and he who does not love his lover must bear the charge of homicide, nay, rather the triple charge of thief, homicide, and desecrator. Money is possessed by the body, the body by the soul, and therefore the man who takes captive a soul, by which both body and money are possessed, thus seizes all three at once: soul, body, and money. Hence it happens that, like a thief, homicide, and desecrator, he is punishable by triple death, and, as though naturally wicked and immoral, he may be killed by anyone with impunity, unless he obeys that law of his own accord, that is, by loving his lover. When his lover dies, he will likewise die, and when his lover returns to life a second time, he will also. In the argument just given, it is conclusively proved that the beloved ought to love his lover in return, not only ought, but must; as is shown.

Likeness generates love. Similarity is a certain sameness of nature in several things. If I am like you, you are necessarily like me; therefore, the same similarity which compels me to love you, forces you to love me. Moreover, a lover withdraws from himself and gives himself to his loved one. The loved one cherishes him like a possession, for one's own possessions are very dear to him.

Moreover, a lover imprints a likeness of the loved one upon his soul, and so the soul of the lover becomes a mirror in which is reflected the image of the loved one. Thereupon, when the loved one recognizes himself in the lover, he is forced to love him.

Astrologers think that the interchange of love is truly reciprocal between those at whose birth there was an exchange of the lights, that is, of the sun and moon (if, for example, at my birth, the sun were in Aries and the Moon in Liber, and at yours the sun were in Liber and the Moon in Aries); or for whom the same sign or a similar one, or the same planet or a similar one was in the ascendant; or on whom friendly planets shone on the same angle of orient; or for whom Venus was in the same mansion and in the same angle. The Platonists add the suggestion that it is those whose lives the same daemon [or certainly a similar one] directs. The natural and moral philosophers would have it that a likeness of complexion, upbringing, education, habit, and attitude is the cause of mutual affection. Finally, where several causes occur together, the passion between the two people is most reciprocal; but where all do, there rise up passions like those of Damon and Pythias, or Orestes and Pylades.

. . .

Beauty is the Splendor of the Divine Countenance.

As soon as the Angelic Mind and the World-Soul were born from Him, the Divine Power over everything beneficently infused into them as His offspring that light in which lay the power of creating everything. In these two, because they were nearest, he depicted the pattern of the whole world much more exactly than it is in the material world. Whence this picture of the world which we see shines whole and more clearly in the Angelic Mind and in the World-Soul. For in these two are the Forms of each planet, the sun, the moon, the rest of the stars, the elements, stones, plants, and each of the animals. Representations of this sort the Platonists call Prototypes, or Ideas in the Angelic Mind, Concepts or mental images in the World-Soul, and Forms or physical images in the material world. They are bright in the material world, brighter in the soul, and brightest in the Angelic

Mind. Therefore the single face of God shines successively in these three mirrors, placed according to their rank: the Angelic Mind, the World-Soul, and the Body of the World. In the first, because it is the nearest to God, the light is most bright; in the second, more remote, it is somewhat darker, and in the last, the farthest away, compared with the others, it is very dark.

Hence the holy Angelic Mind, because it is unimpeded by any attendance upon the body, reflects upon itself where it sees the face of God engraved within its own breast, and seeing there, is struck with awe, and clings most avidly to it forever. The charm of that divine countenance we call beauty; the passion of the Angelic Mind seeking inwardly the face of God, we call love. O, that it might touch us also: but our soul, born into a condition in which it is encased by an earthly body, is inclined to the function of generation. Weighed down by this preoccupation, it neglects the treasure-house concealed within itself, and so, involved in an earthly body, it is servant to the needs of the body for a very long time. To this labor it accommodates sense indeed continuously, and reason also more often than it should. Hence it happens that though it does not notice the glow of that divine countenance shining forever within it until the body has at length become mature and the soul purged, it may with reflection contemplate the countenance of God revealed to our eyes in the handiwork of God. Through just this kind of contemplation we advance to beholding Him who shines forth from within His handiwork. In this kind of reflection, then, it is finally raised to the recognition of God who shines within itself. But since the countenance of the parent is pleasing to the children, it necessarily follows that the countenance of God the Father is most pleasing to souls. The glory and glow of His countenance, to indulge in tiresome repetition, whether in the Angelic Mind, in the Soul, or in the material world, is to be called universal Beauty, and the desire for it is to be called universal Love.

We do not doubt that this beauty is everywhere incorporeal, for it is obviously incorporeal in the Angelic Mind and in the Soul. That it is also incorporeal in bodies we have both shown above and now most clearly understand from this: that the eye sees nothing but the light of the sun, for the shapes and colors of bodies are never seen unless illuminated with light, nor do they come to the eyes with their own matter itself. Yet it seems necessary for them to be in the eyes in order to be seen by them. Therefore, one light of the sun, painted with the colors and shapes of everything illuminated by it, presents itself to the eyes. The eyes, with the help of a certain light of their own, perceive the light thus affected; they see both the perceived light itself, and everything which is in it. Wherefore, this whole order of the visible world is presented [to view], not in the way in which it is infused in the matter of bodies, but in the way in which it is infused in the light streaming into the eyes. In this light, since it is separate from matter, that order is completely independent of body.

This is also evident from the fact that the light itself cannot be body, since it completely fills the whole world in a moment, from its rising to its setting. It penetrates the body of water and air everywhere, without opposition, and though spread over filthy things, it is nowhere soiled.

But these qualities do not in any way correspond with the nature of the bodies, since body does not move in a moment, but in time, nor do two things penetrate each other without opposition from one, the other, or both, but two bodies mixed together stain each other with mutual contagion. We see this in the mixture of water and wine, and of fire and earth. Since, therefore, the light of the sun is incorporeal, whatever it assumes, it does so in the manner of its own nature; therefore, it assumes the colors and shapes of bodies in an incorporeal way, and in the same way it is itself seen, when taken in by the eyes. Hence it happens that this whole earthly beauty, which is the third face of God, presents itself incorporeally to the eyes, through the incorporeal light of the sun.

·   ·   ·

How Many Things are Required of a Thing to be Beautiful and that Beauty is a Spiritual Gift.

What, then, is the beauty of the body? Activity, vivacity, and a certain grace shining in the body because of the infusion of its own idea. This kind of glow does not descend into matter until the matter has been carefully prepared. The preparation of the living body consists in these three things: Arrangement, Proportion, and Adornment. Arrangement means the intervals of its parts, Proportion means their quantity, and Adornment means its shape and color.

In the first place, it is fitting that all the parts of the body should have a natural place: that the ears be in their proper place, the eyes in theirs, the nostrils in theirs, etc., and that the eyes should be at equal distances on either side of the nose, and likewise that both ears be equally distant from the eyes.

Nor is this balance pertaining to the plan of the intervals enough unless there is added a Proportion of parts, to give to each part, keeping the proper proportions of the whole body, its mean size, so that three noses placed end to end will equal the length of one face, and the semi-circles of both ears joined together will equal the circle of the open mouth; the joining of the eyebrows will also give the same result; the length of the nose will match the length of the lips, and so also will that of the ears; the two circles of the eyes will equal one opening of the mouth; eight heads will compass the height of the body: the same distance will also be measured by the spread of the arms, to the side, and likewise of the legs and feet.

Besides these, we consider Adornment necessary, so that the skillful drawing of lines, wrinkles, and the sparkle of the eyes may decorate that Arrangement and Proportion of the parts.

Now, though these three may be in matter, they cannot themselves be any part of the body. The arrangement of the parts is certainly not one of the parts, for the arrangement is found in all the parts, but no one part is found in all of them. There is added the fact that arrangement is nothing else than the appropriate spacing of parts. But what shall we say spacing is but the distance between the parts? Distance, finally, is either nothing, perfectly empty space, or the mere drawing lines, but who will say that lines, which lack breadth and depth, the qualities necessary to body, are bodies?

In the same way, Proportion is not quantity, but the limit of quantity; these limits are surfaces, lines, and points, which, since they lack mass and depth, are not considered bodies. Adornments also, we place in a pleasing harmony of lights and shades and lines, not in matter. From all this it is clear that beauty is so foreign to matter that it never imparts itself to matter unless the matter has been treated with the three incorporeal preparations which we have discussed.

But the basis of these is a temperate combination of the four elements, such that the body is most like heaven, whose substance is temperate, and does not interfere by any excess of humors, with the soul's work of incarnation. For thus the heavenly glow will easily light up in a body much like heaven, and that perfect Form of man which the soul possesses will turn out more accurately in the quiet and compliant matter.

Moreover, in exactly the same way, sounds are prepared to receive their beauty. The Arrangement of sounds is from the low to the octave, and thence descending again. Their Proportion is a progression restricted to thirds, fourths, fifths, and sixths, tones and half-tones; their Adornment is the rich quality of a good tone.

By these three elements, as it were, then, the bodies constructed out of many parts, such as plants, animals, combinations of several sounds, etc., are prepared to receive beauty. But simpler bodies, like the four elements, stones, metals, and single voices are sufficiently well-adapted for the same purpose by a certain inner balance, a richness and clarity of their own natures. Moreover, the soul is the most effectively accommodated to this purpose by its own nature for this reason: that it is both spirit and a mirror, so to speak, next to God, in which, as we have said above, the image of the divine countenance is reflected. Therefore, just as nothing need be added to gold to make it appear beautiful, but if any earthly stains touch it, they must be removed, so the soul needs nothing added to it in order to be beautiful, but anxious care and solicitude for the body must be removed from it, and the disturbance of desire and fear must be dispelled from it; then immediately the natural beauty of the soul will shine out. But lest our speech digress further, let us conclude briefly from what we have said above, that beauty is a certain vital and spiritual charm first infused in the Angelic Mind by the illuminating light of God, thence in the souls of men, the shapes of bodies, and sounds; through reason, sight, and hearing, it moves our souls and delights them; in delighting them, it carries them away, and in so doing, inflames them with burning love.

. . .

Love is the Median between Beauty and its Opposite and is both God and Man.

The lodestone confers upon iron a certain quality of its own by which the iron, made like the stone, is drawn to it. This attraction, inasmuch as it rises in the stone and attracts toward the stone, is said to be certainly the stone's attraction, but inasmuch as it is in the iron, it is equally the iron's and the stone's, for the magnetism is not in the pure matter of the iron of course, but in the iron conditioned by the magnetism of the stone. Therefore it includes the property of each.

So fire, to express it more clearly, by its own quality, that is, heat, kindles the flax. The flax, lifted up by the quality of the heat, flies out into the higher region of the fire. This flying out, inasmuch as it is produced from fire and inclines to fire, we call clearly fiery; inasmuch as it is in the flax (not when it is untouched, but only when it has been ignited), we say is of the nature of both, as much of flax as of fire, equally flaxen and fiery.

The appearance of a man, which because of an interior goodness graciously given him by God, is beautiful to see, frequently shoots a ray of his splendor, through the eyes of those looking at him, into their souls. Drawn by this spark like a fish on a hook, the souls hasten toward the one who is attracting them. This attraction, which is love, since it derives from the beautiful, good, and happy, and is attracted to the same things, we do not hesitate to call Goodness, Beauty, Blessedness, and a God, concurring in the judgment of Agathon and the rest of the previous speakers. But since it is in a soul which is already aroused through the presence of that beautiful ray, we are forced to call it a certain mean passion between beauty and the absence of beauty. Since the soul so long as it has received no image of a beautiful thing does not yet love that thing, which is still unknown, as it were; so also one who possesses the whole beauty is not vexed by the prickings of love. For who desires what he has?

Finally, therefore, a soul burns with glowing love when, having found some pleasing image of a beautiful thing, it is aroused by that foretaste to desire full possession of the beauty. When, therefore, the soul of the lover indeed possesses the beautiful thing in part, but also partly does not possess it, it is, rightly, partly beautiful, and partly not.

And so from this mixed nature of love, we assert that it is a certain mean passion between beauty and absence of beauty, sharing in both. For this reason Diotima, to come now to her, called Love a daemon, because just as daemons are the mediaries between heaven and earth, so Love holds the mean position between beauty and lack of beauty. This middle region of love between the beautiful and the unbeautiful nature [has been explained earlier.]

.   .   .

How the Soul is Raised from Bodily Beauty
to the Beauty of God.

Now, dear fellow-guests, imagine Diotima addressing Socrates thus: No body is beautiful in all parts, O Socrates. For it is either beautiful in one part and ugly in another, or beautiful today and ugly tomorrow, or is judged beautiful by one person and ugly by another. Therefore the beauty of the body, polluted by the contagion of ugliness, cannot be pure, true, and prime beauty; of course, no one suspects beauty of being ugly anywhere, any more than he suspects wisdom of being foolish. But we one time think the appearance of a body is handsome and another time think it ugly, and, various people may think differently about it at the same moment. Therefore the prime and true beauty is not in bodies. Consider also the fact that many bodies are called by the same name, Beauty. Therefore, there must be in many bodies one common nature of beauty through which they are alike called beautiful. But consider that this one nature, as it is in another, that is, matter, must also be dependent on another, for certainly what is not able to support itself is much less able to depend from itself. It will not depend from matter, will it? Never. For nothing ugly and imperfect is able to beautify and perfect itself. But that which is one ought to spring from one; therefore, the one beauty of many bodies depends from some one incorporeal maker. The one artificer of everything is God, who continually renders all worldly matter beautiful through the Angelic Mind and the Souls. Therefore, we ought to expect to find that true concept of beauty in God and in his assistants, rather than in an earthly body. To this, I think, you will easily ascend again, dear Socrates, by these steps. If nature had given you the eyes of a lynx, dear Socrates, so that you might penetrate with your sight to the inside of anything which came in your way, that outwardly most handsome body of your Alcibiades would seem most ugly. How much of him do you love, my friend? His surface appearance only; nay, rather his color wins you; nay, a certain reflection of lights, and a most insignificant shadow. Or else vain imagination deceives you; you love what you dream rather than what you see.

Now, lest I seem to oppose you in earnest, let us say that Alcibiades certainly is handsome. But in what part handsome? In all his parts except his pug-nose, and his eyebrows, which are higher than they ought to be.

Nevertheless, these are beautiful in Phaedrus; but in him the thickness of his legs is not pleasing. These are charming in Charmides, unless perhaps his thin neck might displease you. So, if you observe men individually, you will praise none of them in every detail. Whatever is right anywhere you will gather together and you will make up a whole figure in your mind from the observation of all [the details], so that the absolute beauty of the human species, which is found here and there in many bodies, will be gathered together in your soul in the conception of one image. You value little the beauty of each man, dear Socrates, if you compare it with your Idea. You possess that (Idea), not thanks to the bodies, but thanks to your own soul. So love that image which your soul created and that soul itself, its creator, rather than that crippled and scattered exterior.

But what do I bid you love in the soul?—the beauty of the soul. The beauty of bodies is a visible light, the beauty of the soul is an invisible light; the light of the soul is truth. This alone is what your friend Plato seems to ask of God in his prayers. "Grant," he says, "O God, that my soul may be beautiful and that those things which pertain to my body may not impair the beauty of my soul, and that I may think only the wise man rich." In this Plato declares that the beauty of the soul consists in truth and wisdom; and that this is given men by God. One and the same Truth given to us all by God, acquires the names of various virtues according to its various powers. According as it shows divine things, it is called Wisdom, which Plato asked of God above all else. According as it shows natural things, it is called Knowledge; as human things, Prudence; as it makes men equal, Justice; as it makes them unconquered, Courage; and as tranquil, Temperance.

Hence, two kinds of virtues are delineated: moral virtues, so to speak, and intellectual virtues, prior to them. The intellectual virtues are: Wisdom, Knowledge, and Prudence; the moral virtues: Justice, Courage, and Temperance. The moral virtues, because of their functions and public applications, are better known. The intellectual virtues, because of their recondite truth, are more esoteric. But he who is brought up with noble breeding, because he is purer than others, is easily raised to the intellectual virtues. Therefore I bid you consider the beauty of the soul, which consists in moral virtues, to be the first beauty, so that you may understand that there is one principle of all moral virtues, through which men are called alike, noble. That is, there is one truth of the pure life, which, through exercise of Justice, Courage, and Temperance, leads us to true happiness. Therefore, esteem as highest this one truth of moral virtue and the beautiful light of the soul. Know also that you will rise immediately above moral virtue to the clear truth of wisdom, knowledge, and prudence, if you will consider these to be conceded to the soul brought up in the best virtues, and that in them is the best rule of a moral life; but however varied are the doctrines of wisdom, knowledge, and prudence you see, nevertheless, remember that there is one single light of truth in them all, through which all alike are called beautiful. I charge you to love this supremely as the supreme beauty of the soul. But this one truth in the numerous doctrines, first of all, cannot be the supreme truth, since it is in another (being distributed in many doctrines). Whatever lies in another certainly depends upon another. But one truth is never born from a multitude of doctrines, for what is one ought to rise from one. Therefore there must be one wisdom above the soul of man, which is not divided among many diverse doctrines, but is one Wisdom from whose single truth the multiform truth of man springs.

O Socrates, remember that that single light of the single truth is the beauty of the Angelic Mind, which you must worship above the beauty of the soul. This, as we have shown in the foregoing discussion, excels the beauty of bodies, because it is neither limited to space nor divided according to the parts of matter, nor is it corrupted. It excels the beauty of the soul because it is fundamentally eternal and is not disturbed by the passage of time, but since the light of the Angelic Mind shines in the series of innumerable ideas, and it is fitting that there be a unity above all the multitude of everything, a unity which is the origin of all number; this light necessarily flows from one single principle of everything, which we call the One Itself.

So the simple light of the One Itself in everything is infinite beauty, because it is neither soiled by the stains of matter, like the beauty of the body, nor, like the form of the soul is it changed by the passage of time, nor, like the beauty of the Angelic Mind, is it spent in vast number; and every quality separate from extraneous additions is called infinite by the natural philosophers. If there is heat in itself, not limited by cold and moisture and not weighted down with the weight of matter, the heat is called infinite, because its force is free and is not limited by any additional restrictions. Similarly, the light from every body is free and infinite, for it shines without measure or limit, because it shines of its own nature and is limited very little by the body. So the light and beauty of God, which is pure, freed from all other things, is called, without the slightest question, infinite beauty. But infinite beauty demands a vast love also. Wherefore, I ask you, Socrates, to esteem other things with a definite limit and restriction; but you must worship God truly with infinite love, and let there be no limit to divine love.

BALDASSARE CASTIGLIONE

BEAUTY AND LOVE

"I say, then, that according to the definition of the ancient sages love is naught but a certain desire to enjoy beauty; and as desire longs only for things that are perceived, perception must needs always precede desire, which by its nature wishes good things, but in itself is blind and does not perceive them. Therefore nature has so ordained that to every faculty of perception there is joined a certain faculty of appetite; and since in our soul there are three modes of perceiving, that is, by sense, by reason, and by intellect: from sense springs appetite, which we have in common with the brutes; from reason springs choice, which is peculiar to man; from the intellect, by which man is able to commune with the angels, springs will. Thus, just as sense perceives only things that are perceptible by the senses, appetite desires the same only; and just as intellect is directed solely to the contemplation of things intellectual, the will feeds only upon spiritual benefits. Being by nature rational and placed as a mean between these two extremes, man can at pleasure (by descending to sense or mounting to intellect) turn his desires now in the one direction and now in the other. In these two ways, therefore, it is possible to desire beauty, which universal name applies to all things (whether natural or artificial) that are framed in good proportion and due measure according to their nature.

"But speaking of the beauty we have in mind, which is only that which is seen in the bodies and especially in the faces of men, and which excites this ardent desire that we call love,—we will say that it is an effluence of divine goodness, and that although it is diffused like the sun's light upon all created things, yet when it finds a face well proportioned and framed with a certain pleasant harmony of various colours embellished by lights and shadows and by an orderly distance and limit of outlines, it infuses itself therein and appears most beautiful, and adorns and illumines that object whereon it shines with grace and wonderful splendour, like a sunbeam falling upon a beautiful vase of polished gold set with precious gems. Thus it agreeably attracts the eyes of men, and entering thereby, it impresses itself upon the soul, and stirs and delights her with a new sweetness throughout, and by kindling her it excites in her a desire for its own self.

"Then, being seized with desire to enjoy this beauty as something good, if the soul allows herself to be guided by the judgment of sense, she runs into very grievous errors, and judges that the body wherein the beauty is seen is the chief cause thereof; and hence, in order to enjoy that beauty, she deems it necessary to join herself as closely to that body as she can; which is false: and accordingly, whoever thinks to enjoy the beauty by possessing the body deceives himself, and is moved, not by true perception through reasonable choice, but by false opinion through sensual appetite: wherefore the pleasure also that results therefrom is necessarily false and vicious.

"Hence all those lovers who satisfy their unchaste desires with the women whom they love, run into one of two errors: for as soon as they have attained the end desired, they either not only feel satiety and tedium, but hate the beloved object as if appetite repented its error and perceived the deceit practised upon it by the false judgment of sense, which made it believe evil to be good; or else they remain in the same desire and longing, like those who have not truly attained the end they sought. And although, by reason of the blind opinion wherewith they are intoxicated, they think they feel pleasure at the moment, as the sick sometimes dream of drinking at some clear spring, nevertheless they are not contented or appeased. And since the possession of a wished-for joy always brings quiet and satisfaction to the mind of the possessor, if that joy were the true and worthy object of their desire, they would remain quiet and satisfied in possessing it; which they do not. Nay, deceived by that likewise, they soon return to unbridled desire, and with the same distress they felt at first, they find themselves furiously and very ardently athirst for that which they vainly hope to possess perfectly.

"Such lovers as these, therefore, love most unhappily; for either they never attain their desires (which is great unhappiness), or if they do attain thereto, they find they have attained their woe, and finish their miseries with other miseries still greater; because even in the beginning and midst of their love naught else is ever felt but anguish, torments, sorrows, sufferings, toils. So that to be pale, melancholy, in continual tears and sighs, to be sad, to be ever silent or lamenting, to long for death, in short, to be most unhappy, are the conditions that are said to befit lovers.

"The cause, then, of this havoc in the minds of men is chiefly sense, which is very potent in youth, because the vigour of flesh and blood at that period gives to it as much strength as it takes away from reason, and hence easily leads the soul to follow appetite. For, finding herself plunged into an earthly prison and deprived of spiritual contemplation by being set the task of governing the body, the soul cannot of herself clearly comprehend the truth; wherefore, in order to have perception of things, she must needs go begging first notions from the senses, and so she believes them and bows before them and allows herself to be guided by them, especially when they have so much vigour that they almost force her; and as they are fallacious, they fill her with errors and false opinions.

"Hence it nearly always happens that young men are wrapped in this love which is sensual and wholly rebellious to reason, and thus they become unworthy to enjoy the graces and benefits which love bestows upon its true subjects; nor do they feel any pleasures in love beyond those which the unreasoning animals feel, but anguish far more grievous.

"This premise being admitted then,—and it is most true,—I say that the contrary happens to those who are of maturer age. For if such as these (when the soul is already less weighed down by bodily heaviness and when the natural heat begins to become tepid) are inflamed by beauty and turn thereto a desire guided by rational choice,—they are not deceived, and possess beauty perfectly. Therefore their possession of it always brings them good; because beauty is good, and hence true love of beauty is most good and holy, and always works for good in the mind of those who restrain the perversity of sense with the bridle of reason; which the old can do much more easily than the young.

"Hence it is not beyond reason to say further that the old can love without blame and more happily than the young; taking this word old, however, not in the sense of decrepit, nor when the bodily organs have already become so weak that the soul cannot perform its functions through them, but when our knowledge is at its true prime.

"I will not refrain from saying also this: which is, that I think that although sensual love is evil at every age, yet in the young it deserves excuse, and is perhaps in a measure permitted. For although it gives them anguish, dangers, toils, and those woes that have been told, still there are many who, to win the favour of the ladies of their love, do worthy acts, which (although not directed to a good end) are intrinsically good; and thus from that mass of bitterness they extract a little sweet, and through the adversities which they endure they at last perceive their error. Hence, just as I deem those youths divine who control their appetites and love in reason, so I excuse those who allow themselves to be overcome by sensual love, to which they are so strongly inclined by human frailty: provided they show therein gentleness, courtesy and worth, and the other noble qualities of which these gentlemen have told; and provided that when they are no longer of youthful age, they abandon it altogether, shunning this sensual desire as it were the lowest round of the ladder by which true love can be attained. But if, even after they are old, they preserve the fire of appetite in their chill heart and subject stout reason to frail sense, it is not possible to say how much they are to be blamed. For like fools they deserve to be numbered with perpetual infamy among the unreasoning animals, since the thoughts and ways of sensual love are too unbecoming to mature age."

. . .

"My lords, I would not have any of us, like profane and sacrilegious men, incur God's wrath by speaking ill of beauty, which is a sacred thing. Therefore, to the end that my lord Morello and messer Federico may be warned, and not lose their sight, like Stesichorus (which is a very fitting punishment for one who scorns beauty), I say that beauty springs from God, and is like a circle of which goodness is the centre. And hence, as there can be no circle without a centre, there can be no beauty without goodness. Thus a wicked soul rarely inhabits a beautiful body, and for that reason outward beauty is a true sign of inward goodness. And this grace is impressed upon bodies, more or less, as an index of the soul, whereby she is known outwardly, as in the case of trees, in which the beauty of the blossom gives token of the excellence of the fruit. The same is true in the case of human bodies, as we see that

323

the Physiognomists often recognize in the face the character and sometimes the thoughts of men; and what is more, in beasts also we discern from the aspect the quality of the mind, which is expressed as much as possible in the body. Think how clearly we read anger, ferocity and pride in the face of the lion, the horse, the eagle; a pure and simple innocence in, lambs and doves; cunning malice in foxes and wolves, and so of nearly all other animals.

"The ugly are therefore for the most part wicked too, and the beautiful are good: and we may say that beauty is the pleasant, gay, acceptable and desirable face of good, and that ugliness is the dark, disagreeable, unpleasant and sad face of evil. And if you will consider all things, you will find that those which are good and useful always have a charm of beauty also.

"Look at the state of this great fabric of the world, which was made by God for the health and preservation of every created thing. The round firmament, adorned with so many heavenly lights, and the earth in the centre, surrounded by the elements and sustained by its own weight; the sun, which in its revolving illumines the whole, and in winter approaches the lowest sign, then little by little mounts to the other side; the moon, which derives her light from it, according as it approaches her or withdraws from her; and the five other stars, which separately travel the same course. These things have such influence upon one another through the linking of an order thus precisely framed, that if they were changed for an instant, they could not hold together, and would wreck the world; they have also such beauty and grace that human wit cannot imagine anything more beautiful.

"Think now of the shape of man, which may be called a little world; wherein we see every part of the body precisely composed with skill, and not by chance; and then the whole form together so beautiful that we could hardly decide whether more utility or more grace is given to the human features and the rest of the body by all the members, such as the eyes, nose, mouth, ears, arms, breast, and other parts withal. The same can be said of all the animals. Look at the feathers of birds, the leaves and branches of trees, which are given them by nature to preserve their being, and yet have also very great loveliness."

.　　.　　.

"Therefore the lover who considers beauty in the body only, loses this blessing and felicity as soon as his beloved lady by her absence leaves his eyes without their splendour, and his soul consequently widowed of its blessing. Because, her beauty being far away, that amorous influence does not warm his heart as it did in her presence; wherefore his pores become arid and dry, and still the memory of her beauty stirs a little those forces of his soul, so that they seek to scatter abroad the spirits; and these, finding the ways shut, have no exit, and yet seek to issue forth; and thus hemmed in by those goads, they sting the soul and give it keenest suffering, as in the case of children when the teeth begin to come through the tender gums. And from this proceed the tears, the sighs, the anguish and the torments of lovers, because the soul is ever in affliction and travail, and becomes almost raging until her dear beauty appears to it again; and then it suddenly is calmed and breathes, and all intent upon that beauty it feeds on sweetest food, nor would ever part from so delightful a spectacle.

"Hence, to escape the torment of this absence and to enjoy beauty without suffering, there is need that the Courtier should, with the aid of reason, wholly turn his desire from the body to the beauty alone, and contemplate it in itself simple and pure, as far as he can, and fashion it in his imagination apart from all matter; and thus make it lovely and dear to his soul, and enjoy it there, and have it with him day and night, in every time and place, without fear of ever losing it; bearing always in mind that the body is something very different from beauty, and not only does not enhance it, but diminishes its perfection.

"In this wise will our unyouthful Courtier be beyond all the bitterness and calamities that the young nearly always feel: such as jealousies, suspicions, disdainings, angers, despairings, and certain furies full of madness whereby they are often led into such error that some of them not only beat the women whom they love, but deprive themselves of life. He will do no injury to the husband, father, brothers or kinsfolk of his beloved lady; he will put no infamy upon her; he will never be forced to bridle his eyes and tongue with such difficulty in order not to disclose his desires to others, or to endure suffering at partings or absences;—because he will always carry his precious treasure with him shut up in his heart, and also by force of his imagination he will inwardly fashion her beauty much more beautiful than in fact it is.

"But besides these blessings the lover will find another much greater still, if he will employ this love as a step to mount to one much higher; which he will succeed in doing if he continually considers within him-

325

54. *Sacred and Profane Love,* Titian.

self how narrow a restraint it is to be always occupied in contemplating the beauty of one body only; and therefore, in order to escape such close bounds as these, in his thought he will little by little add so many ornaments, that by heaping all beauties together he will form an universal concept, and will reduce the multitude of these beauties to the unity of that single beauty which is spread over human nature at large. In this way he will no longer contemplate the particular beauty of one woman, but that universal beauty which adorns all bodies; and thus, bewildered by this greater light, he will not heed the lesser, and glowing with a purer flame, he will esteem lightly that which at first he so greatly prized.

"This stage of love, although it be very noble and such as few attain, still cannot be called perfect; for since the imagination is merely a corporeal faculty and has no perception except through those means that are furnished it by the senses, it is not wholly purged of material darkness; and hence, although it considers this universal beauty in the abstract and intrinsically, yet it does not discern that beauty very clearly or without some ambiguity, because of the likeness which phantoms bear to substance. Thus those who attain this love are like tender birds beginning to put on feathers, which, although with their frail wings they lift themselves a little in flight, yet dare not go far from their nest or trust themselves to the winds and open sky.

"Therefore when our Courtier shall have reached this goal, although he may be called a very happy lover by comparison with those who are plunged in the misery of sensual love, still I would have him not rest content, but press boldly on following along the lofty path after the guide who leads him to the goal of true felicity. And thus, instead of going outside himself in thought (as all must needs do who choose to contemplate bodily beauty only), let him have recourse to himself, in order to contemplate that beauty which is seen by the eyes of the mind, which begin to be sharp and clear when those of the body lose the flower of their loveliness. Then the soul,—freed from vice, purged by studies of true philosophy, versed in spiritual life, and practised in matters of the intellect, devoted to the contemplation of her own substance,—as if awakened from deepest sleep, opens those eyes which all possess but few use, and sees in herself a ray of that light which is the true image of the angelic beauty communicated to her, and of which she then communicates a faint shadow to the body. Grown blind to things earthly, the soul thus becomes very keen-sighted to things heavenly; and sometimes, when the motive forces of the body are absorbed by earnest contemplation or fettered by sleep, being unhampered by them, she is conscious of a certain far-off perfume of true angelic beauty, and ravished by the splendour of that light, she begins to kindle and pursues it so eagerly that she almost becomes phrensied with desire to unite herself to that beauty, thinking that she has found God's footstep, in the contemplation of which she seeks to rest as in her beatific end. And thus, glowing in this most happy flame, she rises to her noblest part, which is the intellect; and here, no longer darkened by the gloomy night of things earthly, she sees the divine beauty; but still she does not yet quite enjoy it perfectly, because she contemplates it in her own particular intellect only, which cannot be capable of the vast universal beauty.

(from *The Book of the Courtier*)

PIERRE DE RONSARD

SONNET

Avant qu' Amour du Chaos ocieux

Ere Love from barren Chaos drew the skies,
 Piercing its womb that hid the light of day,
 Beneath primaeval earth's and water's sway
The shapeless Heavens lay whelmed, in dark disguise.

Even so my sluggish soul, too dull to rise,
  Within this body's gross and heavy clay
  Without or form or feature shapeless lay
Until Love's arrow pierced it from your eyes.

Love brought me life and power and truth and light,
  Made pure my inmost heart through his control,
  And shaped my being to a perfect whole.

He warms my veins, he lights my thoughts, his flight
  Snatches me upward, till in Heaven's height
  I find the ordered pathway of my soul.

FRANCIS BACON

OF LOVE

The stage is more beholding to Love then the life of man. For as to
the stage, Love is ever matter of comedies, and now and then of tragedies: but in life it doth much mischiefe; sometimes like a Syren, sometimes like a Fury. You may observe that amongst all the great and
worthy persons (whereof the memory remaineth, either ancient or
recent) there is not one that hath beene transported to the mad degree
of Love: which shewes that great spirits and great businesse doe keepe
out this weake passion. You must except neverthelesse Marcus Antonius,
the halfe partner of the empire of Rome; and Appius Claudius, the
decemvir and law-giver; whereof the former was indeed a voluptuous
man, and inordinate; but the latter was an austere and wise man: and
therefore it seemes (though rarely) that Love can finde entrance not
only into an open heart, but also into a heart well fortified, if watch
be not well kept. It is a poore saying of Epicurus: *Satis magnum alter
alteri theatrum sumus:* as if man, made for the contemplation of heaven
and all noble objects, should doe nothing but kneele before a little
idoll, and make himselfe subject, though not of the mouth (as beasts
are), yet of the eye; which was given him for higher purposes. It is a
strange thing to note the excesse of this passion, and how it braves the
nature and value of things, by this, that the speaking in a perpetuall

hyperbole is comely in nothing but in Love. Neither is it meerely in the phrase; for whereas it hath beene well said that the arch-flatterer, with whom all the petty flatterers have intelligence, is a man's selfe; certainly the lover is more. For there was never proud man thought so absurdly well of himselfe as the lover doth of the person loved; and therefore, it was well said; *That it is impossible to love and to be wise.* Neither doth this weaknesse appeare to others onely, and not to the party loved; but to the loved, most of all, except the love be reciproque. For it is a true rule, that love is ever rewarded either with the reciproque or with an inward and secret contempt. By how much the more men ought to beware of this passion, which loseth not only other things, but it selfe. As for the other losses, the poet's relation doth well figure them; that he that preferred Helena, quitted the gifts of Juno, and Pallas. For whosoever esteemeth too much of amorous affection quitteth both riches and wisedome. This passion hath his flouds in the very times of weaknesse; which are great prosperitie and great adversitie; though this latter hath beene less observed: both which times kindle Love and make it more fervent, and therefore shew it to be the childe of folly. They doe best, who if they cannot but admit Love, yet make it keepe quarter: and sever it wholly from their serious affaires and actions of life: for if it checke once with businesse, it troubleth men's fortunes, and maketh men that they can no wayes be true to their owne ends. I know not how, but martiall men are given to love: I thinke it is but as they are given to wine; for perils commonly aske to be paid in pleasures. There is in man's nature a secret inclination and motion towards love of others; which, if it be not spent upon some one or a few, doth naturally spread it selfe towards many, and maketh men become humane and charitable; as it is seene sometimes in Friars. Nuptiall Love maketh mankinde; friendly Love perfecteth it; but wanton Love corrupteth & imbaseth it.

DESIDERIUS ERASMUS

FROM THE PRAISE OF FOLLY

My Dear More:
While I was on my way to England from Italy I needed an occupa-

tion for my mind during the long hours on horseback. My fellow-travellers were strangers to the Muses, and their conversation soon grew wearisome; therefore I rode by myself, my thoughts full of the theological and classical studies that engage us both, and of the sympathetic and cultivated friends I had left behind when I last quit your country. Of these friends, you, my dear More, were oftenest in my mind; for I delight in the thought of you when we are apart almost as much as I do in your company when we are together, and I must solemnly declare to you that nothing in life gives me greater pleasure than that.

So it came about that, resolved to do something, and circumstances making serious work impossible, a panegyric on folly occurred to me as a pastime. 'What, in the name of goodness, can have put such a thought in your head?' you will ask. Well, what first made me think of it was your surname, as much like the Greek word *moria* for 'folly' as you by common consent are unlike its meaning. I promised myself that you would appreciate this diversion, since I know you are given to humour, the more so if it is inclined to be learned, and not without some underlying wisdom, as I flatter myself this is; in fact I believe you regard the whole of human life with something of the satirical humour of a Democritus. The peculiar acuteness of your mind raises you above the level of ordinary men, but you are so extremely agreeable and kind that you can be, and like to be, what Tiberius called 'a man for all occasions' in any company.

.   .   .

If there is anyone still not satisfied with my excuses, he had better comfort himself with the thought that there is no harm in being abused by a fool, still less by Folly herself, in whose person, and therefore in whose character, I speak throughout.

Need I say all this to you, my learned friend? Are you not the most skilful advocate to whom a weak case can possibly be entrusted? I take leave of you, my dear More, bidding you defend your Moria to the last.

From the country:

June 12th, 1508

Ladies and Gentlemen:

Bad as my reputation is among mortals, and well I know that it is not good even among the most foolish, I stand before you as the sole possessor of the divine power to cheer the hearts of gods and men. You would have believed me the more readily if you could have seen how the faces of this crowded assembly lit up when I rose to address you. You would hardly have known yourselves if you had seen what I saw. Your brows smoothed out, and you greeted me with such good-humoured laughter that I seemed all at once to be surrounded by so many Homeric deities warmed with a mixture of nectar and nepenthe. A moment before I had seen rows of sour individuals looking as worried as though they had just emerged from the oracle's cave at Trophonis.

The effect of my appearance on your faces was like the dawning rays of the glorious sun over the face of the earth or the earliest spring breezes after a hard winter giving new colour and new youth to the whole face of nature. How many practised orators with all their calculated and laborious effects could have done as much as I by simply showing my countenance?

. . .

I snap my fingers at the wise who tell me it is ill-mannered and impudent to praise oneself. That may be; but if so, they must own it becomes me all the better. What could be more fitting than that Folly should *blow her own trumpet?* Is there anyone better qualified? No, I always say if you want a thing well done, do it yourself.

I declare there is less effrontery in what I am doing than in the mock-modesty of the common run of magnates who hire a hack to write them up, and spread abroad mercenary lies to ingratiate them with the public. If you call me impudent, what word will you find for the honourable hypocrite chuckling at his portrait and striking attitudes as his venal publicist lauds him to the skies as the sum of all the virtues? Go and tell him that puffing cannot make a frog into a bull, and that it is lost labour *whitewashing an Ethiope!* If need be, I can fall back on the old proverb that a man who has no kind neighbours must needs praise himself.

I pause for a moment to comment on the ingratitude—or is it only forgetfulness?—of mankind towards me. All are devotees of mine, and many are the favours they have received at my hands; yet not one in all literary history has thought of writing the panegyric on Folly that I had the right to expect.

. . .

You know what I am, and will not mind if I speak plainly. I ask you: is it the head, is it the face, or the hands, the ears, the breast, or any other mentionable part of the body that generates gods or men? No; it is a part so absurd that I cannot name it without raising a laugh. This is the sacred fountain of all life; and do not talk to me about Pythagoras and his fourfold natural cause. Without folly there would be no union for the procreation of children. Who would put his neck into the noose of wedlock if he first, like a wise man, weighed all the disadvantages? What woman would let a man come near her if she knew or considered in time the dangers of childbirth or the drudgery of bringing up a child? If, then, you owe your being to a lawful union, you have to thank my servant *Anoia* for it: unless you are a first-born, you owe your existence to *Lethe*. Even Aphrodite could, I think, be made to confess that without my help her power would be vain, whatever Lucretius may say as to Venus being lady of all. I hope I have convinced you that from a silly and often drunken sport of mine come even the highest-browed philosophers, monks, reverend clerics, kings and our holy father the Pope, not to mention all the throng of poet-made gods, so many that, according to Lucian, Olympus for all its breadth can barely hold them.

To make good my claim to divinity I must prove not only that I am the giver of life, but that I make life worth living. That ought not to be difficult. Would life without pleasure be worthy of the name? I am glad to hear you applaud; I thought none of you would be so wise— I mean foolish—no, let us call it wise—as to differ from me. We know that even the Stoics do not really despise pleasure; they only decry it in public in the hope of having it all the more to themselves. Can they tell us of any age in life that is not repulsive, tedious and unhappy if it has no seasoning of pleasure, that is to say, of folly? One would have thought the authority of Sophocles enough to establish it: did he not leave the noblest eulogy of us—peace be to his bones—*to avoid thinking is the secret of a happy life?*

Let us consider man's ages one by one. Who will gainsay that the first is by far the happiest and prettiest? What makes us want to fondle and protect babies, and even an enemy spare them, unless it is silliness acting the go-between? Provident Nature endows the new-born with childish graces with which to repay those who look after them and win favours from all about them. And then youth; how everyone loves it, watches over it, provides for it, and tries in all manner of ways to give it a helping hand! Can you explain the charm of young people except by saying it comes from me, who save them from much thinking, and so from much worry? No sooner do they gain some manly wisdom from experience and discipline than they begin to lose their looks, their vivacity, their attraction and their vigour. The further a man departs from me, the less life he has in him until at last *grievous old age* comes on, hateful alike to him and to all who see him. No one could bear his last age unless I stood by him when he came near to the grave, and just as the mythical gods were said to save their favourites from perishing by some miraculous transformation, so I save the old, as far as in me lies, by turning them into children again. It is not without reason that people commonly speak of *second childhood.*

.   .   .

The male was given a little extra reason, because he was born to control; and in order to obtain the soundest advice on how to act for the best, he naturally consulted me. I instantly gave him a piece of my mind truly worthy of me; and that was that he should get a woman to help him. Now, woman is a foolish creature with pleasing ways, and her foolishness is beneficial in the home as an antidote to the austerity of the masculine character. When Plato hesitated between classing woman among rational beings and relegating her to the brute creation, he was only seeking to emphasize the silliness of womankind. Such is her nature that if she tries to seem wise, she only looks the more foolish; the world says she is unsexing herself, like a crowing hen. We know that those who try unsuccessfully to cloak their deformities make themselves doubly ridiculous. Just as an ape in a scarlet robe is still an ape, a woman is always a fool, and conceal it she cannot.

For my part, I shall not suppose that women will be so silly as to mind my calling them silly, being myself a woman and the personification of silliness. On reflection they will see that I have made them in many respects better-off than men. For one thing, they have physical attraction and rightly prize it above all else, for it gives them power to lord it over the lords of creation. For another, I have given them a measure of perpetual youth; for, whereas the disease of wisdom makes men past their prime ugly, wrinkled and bearded, women, being immune from that infection, keep their smooth skins and shrill voices all the days of their lives. What do they want more than anything else? Men's admiration. Hence all this washing and bathing, all these trinkets, cosmetics and scents, this everlasting dressing-up, titivating, dyeing and painting of themselves. It is folly that makes women so much nicer than men. What, if not that, is the secret of their power? If you doubted that it was man's leaning towards folly that made him so fond of woman, you need only call to mind his absurd behaviour and the rubbish he talks when he is making love to her.

·   ·   ·

I hear someone say, 'Stop! This is dangerous'; and rightly; for one of the audience who tried to unmask the actors in a play so as to show up their real faces would be spoiling the entertainment, and would undoubtedly be bundled out neck and crop into the street. We are creating a new species, one minute a man and the next a woman, young and old at the same time, both a prince and a peasant, either a god or an insect. Such a heresy would indeed spoil our earthly comedy. We must not open the eyes of the audience to any such thing; for what is life but a play in which everyone acts a part until the curtain comes down? I do not mean that one actor may not come on in several different roles, first as a king in ermine and later as a beggar in rags, but every player must have at any given moment a single, recognisable character, otherwise our play would not run for long.

Imagine some wise man (fallen, perhaps, from the skies) proclaiming to all and sundry that the lords of the earth are less than men because they are swayed by their appetites; mean slaves, therefore, to mean masters. Suppose he were to tell a son grieving for his father's death to cheer up because our life is a kind of death, and therefore his father is more truly alive than ever before, or to remind someone boasting of his noble ancestry that virtue is the only true nobility. Would not such a busybody be taken for a halfwit? Sense out of season is as senseless as wisdom carried too far is unwise: a man who will not accommodate himself to circumstances, and in Rome do as Rome does, is not playing the game of life fairly. *Conform or quit,* in the Greek phrase: the sensible man does not question conventions. If he will not embrace the prevailing errors, at least he turns a blind eye to them.

·   ·   ·

It is worthy of remark by the way that the nearer a science approximates to folly, the greater is the demand for it. Theologians go hungry, astronomers go bare, chemists are laughed at, logicians are ignored, but still, as in Homer's day, *a leech is worth many another man.* In medicine the more ignorant, rash, and unthinking the practitioner, the more highly he is esteemed, particularly in the most exalted circles. It is well known nowadays that medicine, like oratory, is a branch of the art of flattery. A degree less popular than the doctors are the lawyers. I shall not assume to pronounce on their profession; but you know how much amusement their asinine doctrines give the philosophers, with whom, for once, I find myself agreeing. All the same, the most momentous affairs, as well as the most trifling, are constantly being submitted to the judgment of these pettifoggers. Consequently the lawyer piles up a fortune while the theologian, having digested the whole body of divinity, sits gnawing a crust, perpetually battling with fleas and lice. The most profitable arts, I say, are those that have most to do with folly, least to do with learning; in other words, those that suit man's natural bent. We prove over and over again that nature gives us all the guidance we need, so long as we do not seek to transcend the limits of earthly things. Yes; nature unadorned excels your work of art.

Now look at the animal world, and see how much the happiest are the creatures that live least artificially and most naturally. Could any be happier or more marvellous than the bees? Yet, so far are the bees from being intelligent, that they lack some of our five senses; but can our architecture be compared to theirs, or could a philosopher have imagined such a well-ordered community? The horse, on the other hand, is akin to man in temperament, and keeping human company, partakes of human misfortune. Many a steed has cracked his wind straining to escape defeat on the race-course; many a one, too, seeking glory on the field of battle has bitten the dust in company with his rider. Need I dwell on the tragedy of equine servitude, the bits, whips, spurs, halters, tethers, riders, horses have brought on themselves in trying, as Horace tells us, to revenge themselves with manly courage on the original enemies of their race? How much more joyful are the birds, living for the present, and solely as nature bids them! But, once let man's wiles ensnare them and shut them in cages, they may learn to copy human speech, but their natural beauty of plumage will decline in a marvellous manner. So much lovelier is Nature's handiwork than anything the art of man can compass.

·   ·   ·

Poets, I confess, are less beholden to me. Still, they are generally considered to be of my flock; for they are a motley tribe whose aim is to tickle fools' ears with useless information and silly fables. So conceited are they that they count on immortality for themselves and confidently promise it to others. My attendants Self-Love and Flattery are very much hand-in-glove with the poets, nor does any kind of man worship me more sincerely than they.

The orators are of my faction, hard as it may be to disentangle them from the philosophers in particular instances. Several things go to prove it, this in particular, that among their rubbishy writings there are so many voluminous treatises on humour. The author of the anonymous work addressed to Herennius considers facetiousness useful in speechmaking. Quintilian, chief among rhetoricians, has a chapter on laughter more long-winded than the 'Iliad'. These authorities recommend the insinuation of a joke where a difficult objection cannot be fairly met by argument—but perhaps you will say that making people laugh on purpose is not folly.

Much like them are the authors and editors in quest of undying fame, specially dear to me being those who spoil good paper with worthless scribbles. Those few who write for a small learned public are pitiable to my mind rather than amusing, for they lead a life of torment. They must puzzle out every obscure classical text, even Persius and Laelius, and spend a lifetime adding glosses and emendations. Their days are wasted in detecting spuria, restoring readings, expounding, copying, correcting, never to their own satisfaction. The prize, if they get it, is no more than praise from one or two critics. Think of the price they pay—loss of the greatest of all blessings—sleep, with waste of money and sweat, and all manner of vexation. Think what the scholar endures in the way of ill-health, wasting away, eyestrain or even blindness, poverty, jealousy, abstinence from pleasure, premature old age, untimely death. What is the reward that these wiseacres think compensates them for all that? The approval of one or two other blind old bookworms!

How far better to be a writer of my sort, never needing to study or think but putting down whatever comes readiest to his pen. He has but to jot down his day-dreams, and rush them post-haste to the printer. The work costs no more than a few sheets of paper! Well the fellow knows that the more trivial his writing, the better he will please the only public that pays, the vast world of ignorant fools. Is he troubled by the thought that two or three good judges might chance to read and despise him? What are their pence to him, with his eye on the great golden multitude?

.　　.　　.

Dear me! I am forgetting myself and *talking out of character*. If I have been prolix and a little saucy, remember that you have been listening to a fool and a female. Bear in mind, too, the Greek proverb, '*A foolish man may stumble on a truth*'—though perhaps one may not apply it to a woman.

I can feel that you expect a peroration; but that is carrying folly too far, to expect me to remember what I have been driving at in all this farrago of verbiage. Let me leave you with the old saying: '*I hate a drinker with a long memory*'; and a new one of my own: '*I hate an audience with any memory*.'

'So farewell, friends, our play is done.'

Long life and good drinking to you, my illustrious votaries!

Pico della Mirandola

from ORATION ON THE DIGNITY OF MAN

I have read in the records of the Arabians, reverend Fathers, that Abdala the Saracen, when questioned as to what on this stage of the world, as it were, could be seen most worthy of wonder, replied: "There is nothing to be seen more wonderful than man." In agreement with this opinion is the saying of Hermes Trismegistus: "A great miracle, Asclepius, is man." But when I weighed the reason for these maxims, the many grounds for the excellence of human nature reported by many failed to satisfy me—that man is the intermediary between creatures, the intimate of the gods, the king of the lower beings, by the acuteness of his senses, by the discernment of his reason, and by the light of his intelligence the interpreter of nature, the interval

337

between fixed eternity and fleeting time, and (as the Persians say) the bond, nay, rather, the marriage song of the world, on David's testimony but little lower than the angels. Admittedly great though these reasons be, they are not the principal grounds, that is, those which may rightfully claim for themselves the privilege of the highest admiration. For why should we not admire more the angels themselves and the blessed choirs of heaven? At last it seems to me I have come to understand why man is the most fortunate of creatures and consequently worthy of all admiration and what precisely is that rank which is his lot in the universal chain of Being—a rank to be envied not only by brutes but even by the stars and by minds beyond this world. It is a matter past faith and a wondrous one. Why should it not be? For it is on this very account that man is rightly called and judged a great miracle and a wonderful creature indeed.

But hear, Fathers, exactly what this rank is and, as friendly auditors, conformably to your kindness, do me this favor. God the Father, the supreme Architect, had already built this cosmic home we behold, the most sacred temple of His godhead, by the laws of His mysterious wisdom. The region above the heavens He had adorned with Intelligences, the heavenly spheres He had quickened with eternal souls, and the excrementary and filthy parts of the lower world He had filled with a multitude of animals of every kind. But, when the work was finished, the Craftsman kept wishing that there were someone to ponder the plan of so great a work, to love its beauty, and to wonder at its vastness. Therefore, when everything was done (as Moses and Timaeus bear witness), He finally took thought concerning the creation of man. But there was not among His archetypes that from which He could fashion a new offspring, nor was there in His treasure-houses anything which He might bestow on His new son as an inheritance, nor was there in the seats of all the world a place where the latter might sit to contemplate the universe. All was now complete; all things had been assigned to the highest, the middle, and the lowest orders. But in its final creation it was not the part of the Father's power to fail as though exhausted. It was not the part of His wisdom to waver in a needful matter through poverty of counsel. It was not the part of His kindly love that he who was to praise God's divine generosity in regard to others should be compelled to condemn it in regard to himself.

At last the best of artisans ordained that that creature to whom He had been able to give nothing proper to himself should have joint possession of whatever had been peculiar to each of the different kinds of being. He therefore took man as a creature of indeterminate nature and, assigning him a place in the middle of the world, addressed him thus: "Neither a fixed abode nor a form that is thine alone nor any function peculiar to thyself have we given thee, Adam, to the end that according to thy longing and according to thy judgment thou mayest have and possess what abode, what form, and what functions thou thyself shalt desire. The nature of all other beings is limited and constrained within the bounds of laws prescribed by Us. Thou, constrained by no limits, in accordance with thine own free will, in whose hand We have placed thee, shalt ordain for thyself the limits of thy nature. We have set thee at the world's center that thou mayest from thence more easily observe whatever is in the world. We have made thee neither of heaven nor of earth, neither mortal nor immortal, so that with freedom of choice and with honor, as though the maker and molder of thyself, thou mayest fashion thyself in whatever shape thou shalt prefer. Thou shalt have the power to degenerate into the lower forms of life, which are brutish. Thou shalt have the power, out of thy soul's judgment, to be reborn into the higher forms, which are divine."

O supreme generosity of God the Father, O highest and most marvelous felicity of man! To him it is granted to have whatever he chooses, to be whatever he wills. Beasts as soon as they are born (so says Lucilius) bring with them from their mother's womb all they will ever possess. Spiritual beings, either from the beginning or soon thereafter, become what they are to be for ever and ever. On man when he came into life the Father conferred the seeds of all kinds and the germs of every way of life. Whatever seeds each man cultivates will grow to maturity and bear in him their own fruit. If they be vegetative, he will be like a plant. If sensitive, he will become brutish. If rational, he will grow into a heavenly being. If intellectual, he will be an angel and the son of God. And if, happy in the lot of no created thing, he withdraws into the center of his own unity, his spirit, made one with God, in the solitary darkness of God, who is set above all things, shall surpass them all. Who would not admire this our chameleon? Or who could more greatly admire aught else whatever? It is man who Asclepius of Athens, arguing from his mutability of character and from his self-transforming nature, on just grounds says was symbolized by Proteus in the mysteries.

·   ·   ·

I come now to the things I have elicited from the ancient mysteries of the Hebrews and have cited for the confirmation of the inviolable Catholic faith. Lest perchance they should be deemed fabrications, trifles, or the tales of jugglers by those to whom they are unfamiliar, I wish all to understand what they are and of what sort, whence they come, by what and by how illustrious authors supported, and how mysterious, how divine, and how necessary they are to the men of our faith for defending our religion against the grievous misrepresentations of the Hebrews. Not only the famous doctors of the Hebrews, but also from among men of our opinion Esdras, Hilary, and Origen write that Moses on the mount received from God not only the Law, which he left to posterity written down in five books, but also a true and more occult explanation of the Law. It was, moreover, commanded him of God by all means to proclaim the Law to the people but not to commit the interpretation of the Law to writing or to make it a matter of common knowledge. He himself should reveal it only to Iesu Nave, who in his turn should unveil it to the other high priests to come after him, under a strict obligation of silence. It was enough through guileless story to recognize now the power of God, now his wrath against the wicked, his mercy to the righteous, his justice to all; and through divine and beneficial precepts to be brought to a good and happy way of life and the worship of true religion. But to make public the occult mysteries, the secrets of the supreme Godhead hidden beneath the shell of the Law and under a clumsy show of words—what else were this than to give a holy thing to dogs and to cast pearls before swine? Therefore to keep hidden from the people the things to be shared by the initiate, among whom alone, Paul says, he spoke wisdom, was not the part of human deliberation but of divine command. This custom the ancient philosophers most reverently observed, for Pythagoras wrote nothing except a few trifles, which he intrusted on his deathbed to his daughter Dama. The Sphinxes carved on the temples of the Egyptians reminded them that mystic doctrines should be kept inviolable from the common herd by means of the knots of riddles. Plato, writing certain things to Dion concerning the highest substances, said: "It must be stated in riddles, lest the letter should fall by chance into the hands of others and what I am writing to you should be apprehended by others." Aristotle used to say that his books of *Metaphysics,* in which he treated of things divine, were both published and not published. What further? Origen asserts that Jesus

Christ, the Teacher of life, made many revelations to his disciples, which they were unwilling to write down lest they should become commonplaces to the rabble. This is in the highest degree confirmed by Dionysius the Areopagite, who says that the occult mysteries were conveyed by the founders of our religion ἐκ νοῦ εἰς νοῦν διὰ μέσον λόγου, from mind to mind, without writing, through the medium of speech.

In exactly the same way, when the true interpretation of the Law according to the command of God, divinely handed down to Moses, was revealed, it was called the Cabala, a word which is the same among the Hebrews as "reception" among ourselves; for this reason, of course, that one man from another, by a sort of hereditary right, received that doctrine not through written records but through a regular succession of revelations. But after the Hebrews were restored by Cyrus from the Babylonian captivity, and after the temple had been established anew under Zorobabel, they brought their attention to the restoration of the Law. Esdras, then the head of the church, after the book of Moses had been amended, when he plainly recognized that, because of the exiles, the massacres, the flights, and the captivity of the children of Israel, the custom instituted by their forefathers of transmitting the doctrine from mouth to mouth could not be preserved, and that it would come to pass that the mysteries of the heavenly teachings divinely bestowed on them would be lost, since the memory of them could not long endure without the aid of written records, decided that those of the elders then surviving should be called together and that each one should impart to the gathering whatever he possessed by personal recollection concerning the mysteries of the Law and that scribes should be employed to collect them into seventy volumes (about the number of elders in the Sanhedrin). That you may not have to rely on me alone in this matter, Fathers, hear Esdras himself speak thus: "And it came to pass, when the forty days were fulfilled, that the Most High spake unto me, saying, The first that thou hast written publish openly, and let the worthy and the unworthy read it: but keep the seventy last books, that thou mayst deliver them to such as be wise among thy people: for in them is the spring of understanding, the fountain of wisdom, and the stream of knowledge. And I did so." And these are the words of Esdras to the letter. These are the books of cabalistic lore. In these books principally resides, as Esdras with a clear voice justly declared, the spring of understanding, that is, the ineffable theology of the supersubstantial deity; the fountain of wisdom, that is, the exact metaphysic of the intellectual and angelic forms; and the stream of knowledge, that is, the most steadfast philosophy of natural things. Pope Sixtus the Fourth who last preceded the pope under whom we are now fortunate to be living, Innocent the Eighth, took the greatest pains and interest in seeing that these books should be translated into the Latin tongue for a public service to our faith, and, when he died, three of them had been done into Latin. Among the Hebrews of the present day these books are cherished with such devotion that it is permitted no man to touch them unless he be forty years of age.

When I had purchased these books at no small cost to myself, when I had read them through with the greatest diligence and with unwearying toil, I saw in them (as God is my witness) not so much the Mosaic as the Christian religion. There is the mystery of the Trinity, there the Incarnation of the Word, there the divinity of the Messiah; there I have read about original sin, its expiation through Christ, the heavenly Jerusalem, the fall of the devils, the orders of the angels, purgatory, and the punishments of hell, the same things we read daily in Paul and Dionysius, in Jerome and Augustine. But in those parts which concern philosophy you really seem to hear Pythagoras and Plato, whose principles are so closely related to the Christian faith that our Augustine gives immeasurable thanks to God that the books of the Platonists have come into his hands. Taken altogether, there is absolutely no controversy between ourselves and the Hebrews on any matter, with regard to which they cannot be refuted and gainsaid out of the cabalistic books, so that there will not be even a corner left in which they may hide themselves. I have as a most weighty witness of this fact that very learned man Antonius Chronicus who, when I was with him at a banquet, with his own ears heard Dactylus, a Hebrew trained in this lore, with all his heart agree entirely to the Christian idea of the Trinity.

Martin Luther

from THE NINETY-FIVE THESES

The pope does excellently when he grants remission to the souls in purgatory on account of intercessions made on their behalf, and not by the power of the keys (which he cannot exercise for them).

There is no divine authority for preaching that the soul flies out of purgatory immediately the money clinks in the bottom of the chest.

It is certainly possible that when the money clinks in the bottom of the chest avarice and greed increase; but when the church offers intercession, all depends on the will of God.

Who knows whether all souls in purgatory wish to be redeemed in view of what is said of St. Severinus and St. Paschal?

No one is sure of the reality of his own contrition, much less of receiving plenary forgiveness.

One who *bona fide* buys indulgences is as rare as a *bona fide* penitent man, i.e., very rare indeed.

All those who believe themselves certain of their own salvation by means of letters of indulgence, will be eternally damned, together with their teachers.

We should be most carefully on our guard against those who say that the papal indulgences are an inestimable divine gift, and that a man is reconciled to God by them.

For the grace conveyed by these indulgences relates simply to the penalties of the sacramental "satisfactions" decreed merely by man.

It is not in accordance with Christian doctrine to preach and teach that those who buy off souls, or purchase confessional licenses, have no need to repent of their own sins.

Any Christian whatsoever, who is truly repentant, enjoys plenary remission from penalty and guilt, and this is given him without letters of indulgence.

Any true Christian whatsoever, living or dead, participates in all the benefits of Christ and the Church; and this participation is granted to him by God without letters of indulgence.

Yet the pope's remission and dispensation are in no way to be despised, for, as already said, they proclaim the divine remission.

55. *The Sale of Indulgences,* woodcut after Holbein.

It is very difficult, even for the most learned theologians, to extol to the people the great bounty contained in the indulgences, while, at the same time, praising contrition as a virtue.

A truly contrite sinner seeks out, and loves to pay, the penalties of his sins; whereas the very multitude of indulgences dulls men's consciences, and tends to make them hate the penalties.

Papal indulgences should only be preached with caution, lest people gain a wrong understanding, and think that they are preferable to other good works: those of love.

Christians should be taught that the pope does not at all intend that the purchase of indulgences should be understood as at all comparable with works of mercy.

Christians should be taught that one who gives to the poor, or lends to the needy, does a better action than if he purchases indulgences;

Because, by works of love, love grows and a man becomes a better man; whereas, by indulgences, he does not become a better man, but only escapes certain penalties.

Christians should be taught that he who sees a needy person, but passes him by although he gives money for indulgences, gains no benefit from the pope's pardon, but only incurs the wrath of God.

344

Christians should be taught that, unless they have more than they need, they are bound to retain what is necessary for the upkeep of their home, and should in no way squander it on indulgences.

Christians should be taught that they purchase indulgences voluntarily, and are not under obligation to do so.

Christians should be taught that, in granting indulgences, the pope has more need, and more desire, for devout prayer on his own behalf than for ready money.

Christians should be taught that the pope's indulgences are useful only if one does not rely on them, but most harmful if one loses the fear of God through them.

Christians should be taught that, if the pope knew the exactions of the indulgence-preachers, he would rather the church of St. Peter were reduced to ashes than be built with the skin, flesh, and bones of his sheep.

THE LORD'S SUPPER

The first thing for me to do is to deny that there are seven sacraments, and, for the present, to propound three: baptism, penance, and the Lord's Supper. All these have been taken for us into a miserable servitude by the Roman curia and the church has been robbed of all her liberty. If, however, I were to use the language of Scripture, I should say that there was only one sacrament, but three sacramental signs of which I shall speak in detail in the proper place.

In regard to the sacrament of the Lord's Supper, which is the most important of all, I shall discuss in what way my ideas have progressed while meditating on the administration of this sacrament. For, at the time, when I published my tractate on the Eucharist, I held to the common usage, quite undisturbed by what was right or wrong according to the pope. But now that I have been cited and attacked, and even forcibly thrust into the arena, I shall give free expression to my ideas, no matter whether the Papists all join together to mock or reproach me.

In the first place, John 6 is to be totally set on one side, on the ground that it does not utter a syllable about the sacrament. The sacrament was not yet instituted; and, a more important point, the chapter is plainly and obviously speaking about faith, as is shown by the warp and woof of the words and thoughts. For Jesus said: "My words are spirit and they are life," showing that He was speaking of spiritual eating, by doing which any partaker would live; whereas the Jews understood Him to mean eating His flesh, and so raised the dispute. No sort of eating gives life except eating in faith. This is the true eating, the spiritual. Accordingly, Augustine says: "Why do you make your teeth and stomach ready? Believe, and thou hast eaten." In itself, sacramental eating does not give life, for many eat unworthily. Therefore Jesus cannot be understood to have spoken of the sacrament in this passage.

. . . But it is one thing to use the Scriptures wrongly, and another to understand them properly. Otherwise, if Jesus had intended it to be a commandment to eat of the sacraments when He said: "Unless you eat my flesh and drink my blood, you will not have life," He would have condemned all infants, all the sick, all those kept back by any cause and prevented from partaking of the sacraments, no matter how firm their faith. Hence Augustine, in the second book of *Contra Julianum,* proves from Innocent that even infants, who do not yet partake of the sacrament, eat the flesh and drink the blood of Christ; i.e., they communicate through the faith of the church. Let us then regard this proposition as proved, and that John 6 is not relevant here. . . .

Thus there remain two records which deal, and that very clearly, with this subject, viz.: the gospel passages on the Lord's Supper, and St. Paul in I Corinthians II. Let us consider them. For, as Matthew, Mark, and Luke all agree, Christ gave all His disciples both kinds. And that Paul gave both kinds is so certain that no one has had the effrontery to say anything to the contrary. A further fact is that, according to Matthew, Christ did not say of the bread: "All of you eat of this"; but he does say of the cup: "All of you drink of this"; and in Mark He does not say: "All of you ate," but "All of you drank from it." Each writer attaches the mark of universality to the cup, but not to the bread. It is as if the Spirit foresaw the coming division forbidding the communion of the cup to some, though Christ would have had it common to all. You may be sure the Romanists would let us feel their anger smartly if they found the word "all" applied to the bread and not to the cup. They would leave us no loophole; they would cry aloud, brand us as heretics, and damn us as schismatics. But now, when Scripture is on our side and against them, they refuse in their perversity to be bound by logic, even in those things which be of God; they change, change again, and tangle everything together.

Now, suppose I were to approach my lords the Romanists, and ask them whether the whole sacrament, under both kinds, at the Lord's Supper is to be given only to the priests, or also to the laity. If, as they wish, only to the priests, then logically neither kind is to be given to the laity on any excuse; for it is not to be lightly given to anyone to whom Christ did not give it when He first instituted the rite. Otherwise, if we allow an alteration in one institution of Christ's, all His ordinances are immediately brought to nought, and any one whatever is in a position to say that he is not bound by anything Christ ordained or instituted; for a single exception, especially in the Scriptures, dis-. proves any universal law. But, if the cup was given to the laity also, the logical consequence is that no one can deny both kinds to the laity. If, nevertheless, the administration is denied to those who desire it, that is done impiously and against Christ's act, example, and institution.

This argument seems unassailable, and I confess that it has convinced me. I have neither heard of, nor discovered, anything opposed to it. Christ's word and example stand here as firmly as possible. When He says, "All ye drink of it," He is not giving a permission, but issuing a command. Everyone ought to drink of it, and that commandment ought not to be understood as addressed only to the priests. Hence, it is undoubtedly impious to deny it to the laity who ask for it; yes, even if an angel from heaven were to do so. To support the Romanists' view that it was entrusted to the free judgment of the church to administer which kind she preferred, they bring forward no reasons, and no proofs from Scripture. The question is more easily passed over than proved; but their contention avails nothing against an opponent who faces them with the words or the works of Christ. Such a person must be refuted with the Word of Christ, the very thing we Romanists lack.

If, however, in the Lord's Supper, either kind could be denied to the laity, so also might a part of the rites of baptism and penitence be withheld from them, equally, at the free dispensation of the church; because in each instance they have equal grounds and authority for so doing. Therefore, just as the rites of baptism and absolution are administered to the laity in their complete form, so also should the complete sacrament of the Supper, if asked for. I am greatly astonished that the Romanists insist that, under pain of mortal sin, the priests must never receive only one kind at mass. The reason given by them all, with one voice, is that the two kinds constitute a full and complete sacrament, and should not be sundered. I would like them to tell me why the two kinds are separated for the laity, whereas the undivided sacrament must be administered only to themselves. Do they not acknowledge, by their own practice, either that both kinds should be given to the laity, or that the true and genuine sacrament is not in fact given them under the one form? Or is it that, in the case of the priests, the sacrament in one kind is not complete, but is complete in the case of the laity? Why do they appeal at this point to the free choice of the church and the power of the pope? Yet no such appeal abolishes either the Word of God or the testimony of the truth.

Further, if the church has authority to withhold the wine from the laity, she can also withhold the bread; and, on the same basis, she could withhold the whole sacrament of the altar from the laity, and deprive the laity altogether of what Christ instituted. But, I deny that she has such authority. If, on the other hand, she is commanded to administer either the bread alone, or both kinds (according to the desire of the communicant), it is not in her choice to withhold the wine. No attack on this position can succeed. Either the church has authority over both kinds, and the same authority applies to each separately; or else it is not valid over both together, and neither is it valid over each separately. I am hoping to hear what answer the toadies of Rome will give to that.

The most important proof, and, to me, a fully cogent one, is that Christ said: "This is my blood, shed for you and for many for the remission of sins." Here you may see very plainly that the blood was given to all, and that it was shed for the sins of all. No one will dare to say that it was not shed for the laity, for it is clear who was addressed, when Jesus was speaking of the cup. Did He not address all? He used the words "for you." Good, let us grant these words referred to the priests. Even so, the words Jesus added, viz., "and for many," cannot also apply to them only. Besides all this, He said: "All ye drink of it." I could easily make a little word-play here, and jest with Christ's words, as does that trifler whom I have already mentioned. But those who rely on Scripture to refute us, must be overcome by Scripture.

(from *The Pagan Servitude of the Church*)

348

JOHN CALVIN

ARTICLES OF FAITH

Article I. Of Baptism.

We must believe, with sure and firm faith, that to all, even infants, Baptism is necessary for salvation, and that by means of it the grace of the Holy Spirit is given.

Proof.—Because otherwise there would be no efficacy in the baptism given by women, which is founded expressly on the belief that baptism is one of the essentials of salvation, though the Council of Carthage declared, without any exception, that women must not presume to baptize. Nay, what is stronger, Doctors still debate, as a difficult question, whether an infant, at the point of death, (*in periculo mortis,*) if water is not at hand, ought to be plunged into a well rather than commended to God, to wait the event; whereas, if baptism is not essential to salvation, the act would be a murder deserving of death. There are also other questions, as to whether, in the absence of ordinary water, an infant ought to be baptized with lotion, or with artificial or distilled waters, rather than left as it is till water be procured; also, whether, in a case of necessity, it be not true baptism to spit in the face! All these questions would not only be superfluous, but foolish also, did we not hold this principle.

Antidote to Article I.

That in baptism remission of sins, as well as the grace of the Holy Spirit, is offered and exhibited to us, all the pious confess. They also acknowledge that infants have need of it, not as a necessary help to salvation, but as a seal divinely appointed to seal upon them the gift of adoption. For Paul teaches that the children of believers are born holy. And, indeed, baptism would not be at all suitable to them if their salvation were not already included in this promise,—"I will be a God unto thee, and to thy seed after thee." For they do not become the sons of God through baptism; but because, in virtue of the promise, they are heirs of adoption, therefore the Church admits them to baptism. And as of old, when the children of the Israelites died before the eighth day,

they suffered not by wanting the sacrament of circumcision, so now, provided there is no contumacy or negligence on the part of the parents,
the simple promise by which the children of believers are from the womb
adopted into the fellowship of the Church suffices for their salvation.
For injury is done to Christ if we imagine that the grace of God is impaired by his advent. But God once gave the name of *sons* to all who
should be born of Israel. Nor do we read that John was baptized, though
he was the minister of baptism to others. We ought, therefore, to hold
that, as in Abraham, the father of the faithful, the righteousness of faith
preceded circumcision, so in the children of the faithful, in the present
day, the gift of adoption is prior to baptism. According to the words of
the promise, "I will be a God to thy seed." Baptism, however, is a confirmation of this gift, and a help to our faith.

Article III. Of Penitence.

*It is not less certain that to adults, and those having the use
of reason, after the commission of mortal sin, penitence is
necessary; which penitence consists in contrition, and in sacramental confession, to be made audibly to a priest, and likewise in satisfaction.*

Proof.—It is to be noted that the Lutherans do not speak doctrinally
of penitence, when they say that it is a turning unto God, which springs
from hatred and displeasure at sin and love of righteousness; also, that
man ought to renounce his own will that he may be governed by God.
Also, that he ought to be humbled by perceiving the wrath of God and
the terrors of death. For contrition is sufficient for mortal sins, in this
sense, that to each single sin a single act of contrition is commensurate.
In regard to confession, it is to be observed that the matter is of divine,
but the form is of positive law; on this point not only the Lutherans err,
but also the Canonists, who hold that the law of confession is merely
positive. But the matter is proved to be of divine obligation by this,
that James says, "Confess one to another." This is the raw material; for,
were it not brought into form *ab extra,* it would follow that priests
ought to confess to laics, since "one another" means reciprocally; or
that laics would not be capable of confessing, because then they could
not hear the confession of others, but the form was superadded by Pope
Innocent, viz., that the confession should be made to one's own priest.

This is the magisterial distinction adopted by all Schools. But the necessity of giving satisfaction to God is thus proved—without it there would be no place for what is said of works of supererogation, and, moreover, what the School holds with regard to remission of the fault, and retention of the penance, would be false. And so the Lutherans would make out their point, that there is nothing we can do which we owe not to God; also that we are reconciled to God freely through the satisfaction of Christ. But we ought never to concede this to them, because, as will be seen farther on, it drags too long a tail after it, and, in fact, would leave no room for purgatory.

Antidote to Article III.

The Spirit of God calls us to repentance every where, in the law, the prophets, and the gospel; at the same time, he also defines what he understands by the term, when he orders us to be renewed in our hearts, to be circumcised to the Lord, to be washed, and to cease from wicked pursuits, to loose the bond of iniquity bound within us, to rend our hearts and not our garments, to put off the old man, to renounce our own desires, and be renewed in the image of God; besides enumerating, as the fruits of repentance, acts of charity, and the exercises of a pious and holy life. Of confession to be made in the ear of a priest there is no where any mention. Of satisfaction still less. Nay, it is even certain, that before Innocent the Third, no necessity of confession was imposed on the Christian people; for his decree, made at the Lateran Council, is extant. Therefore, for about twelve hundred years the Christian Church had no knowledge of the dogma, that to repentance auricular confession was essentially requisite. And the words of Chrysostom are clear: "I do not say that you must confess to your fellow servant; let it be to the Lord." Again, "It is not necessary to confess before witnesses. Let a searching out of sins be made in thought: let the decision be without a witness: let God alone see thee confessing." Again, "I call thee not into the view of men. Show thy wounds to God, the best physician, that he may cure them." I do not, indeed, deny, that the practice of confessing is very ancient. But I say that it was free, as Sozomen relates in his Ecclesiastical History, where he also attests that it was abolished at Constantinople, because a certain matron, under the pretext of confessing, had been caught with a deacon. But that a few only confessed is apparent from his mentioning that only one presbyter was allotted to the office in each bishopric. Whence it may easily be inferred, that the practice had arisen from the solemnity used in public repentance. But public repentance does not refer to God in the forum of conscience, but looks to the judgment of the Church, that the sinner may, by some sign, declare before man what his mind is before God. In regard to satisfaction, the Scripture claims, out and out, for Christ this honour, that he is an expiator for sin, that the chastisement of our peace was upon him, that through his name only is obtained forgiveness of sins. In regard to ourselves, it is completed gratuitously and without works, since Paul declares it to be our high privilege, that sins are not imputed to us. At the same time, we disapprove not of the satisfaction which the Church exacts of sinners in token of repentance.

REFORMING THE CHURCH

.   .   .

We maintain, then, that at the commencement, when God raised up Luther and others, who held forth a torch to light us into the way of salvation, and who, by their ministry, founded and reared our churches, those heads of doctrine in which the truth of our religion, those in which the pure and legitimate worship of God, and those in which the salvation of men are comprehended, were in a great measure obsolete. We maintain that the use of the sacraments was in many ways vitiated and polluted. And we maintain that the government of the Church was converted into a species of foul and insufferable tyranny. But, perhaps these averments have not force enough to move certain individuals until they are better explained. This, therefore, I will do, not as the subject demands, but as far as my ability will permit. Here, however, I have no intention to review and discuss all our controversies; that would require a long discourse, and this is not the place for it. I wish only to show how just and necessary the causes were which forced us to the changes for which we are blamed. To accomplish this, I must take up together the three following points.

First, I must briefly enumerate the evils which compelled us to seek for remedies.

Secondly, I must show that the particular remedies which our Reformers employed were apt and salutary.

Thirdly, I must make it plain that we were not at liberty any longer to delay putting forth our hand, in as much as the matter demanded instant amendment.

The first point, as I merely advert to it for the purpose of clearing my way to the other two, I will endeavour to dispose of in a few words, but in wiping off the heavy charge of sacrilegious audacity and sedition, founded on the allegation, that we have improperly, and with intemperate haste, usurped an office which did not belong to us, I will dwell at greater length.

If it be inquired, then, by what things chiefly the Christian religion has a standing existence amongst us, and maintains its truth, it will be found that the following two not only occupy the principal place, but comprehend under them all the other parts, and consequently the whole substance of Christianity, viz., a knowledge, *first,* of the mode in which God is duly worshipped; and, *secondly,* of the source from which salvation is to be obtained. When these are kept out of view, though we may glory in the name of Christians, our profession is empty and vain. After these come the Sacraments and the Government of the Church, which, as they were instituted for the preservation of these branches of doctrine, ought not to be employed for any other purpose; and, indeed, the only means of ascertaining whether they are administered purely and in due form, or otherwise, is to bring them to this test. If any one is desirous of a clearer and more familiar illustration, I would say, that rule in the Church, the pastoral office, and all other matters of order, resemble the body, whereas the doctrine which regulates the due worship of God, and points out the ground on which the consciences of men must rest their hope of salvation, is the soul which animates the body, renders it lively and active, and, in short, makes it not to be a dead and useless carcase.

As to what I have yet said, there is no controversy among the pious, or among men of right and sane mind.

Let us now see what is meant by the due worship of God. Its chief foundation is to acknowledge Him to be, as He is, the only source of all virtue, justice, holiness, wisdom, truth, power, goodness, mercy, life, and salvation; in accordance with this, to ascribe and render to Him the glory of all that is good, to seek all things in Him alone, and in every want have recourse to Him alone. Hence arises prayer, hence praise and thanksgiving—these being attestations to the glory which we attribute to Him. This is that genuine sanctification of His name which

353

He requires of us above all things. To this is united adoration, by which we manifest for Him the reverence due to his greatness and excellency, and to this ceremonies are subservient, as helps or instruments, in order that, in the performance of divine worship, the body may be exercised at the same time with the soul. Next after these comes self-abasement, when, renouncing the world and the flesh, we are transformed in the renewing of our mind, and living no longer to ourselves, submit to be ruled and actuated by Him. By this self-abasement we are trained to obedience and devotedness to his will, so that his fear reigns in our hearts, and regulates all the actions of our lives. That in these things consists the true and sincere worship which alone God approves, and in which alone He delights, is both taught by the Holy Spirit throughout the Scriptures, and is also, antecedent to discussion, the obvious dictate of piety. Nor from the beginning was there any other method of worshipping God, the only difference being, that this spiritual truth, which with us is naked and simple, was under the former dispensation wrapt up in figures. And this is the meaning of our Saviour's words, "The hour cometh, and now is, when the true worshippers shall worship the Father in spirit and in truth." For by these words he meant not to declare that God was not worshipped by the fathers in this spiritual manner, but only to point out a distinction in the external form, viz., That while they had the Spirit shadowed forth by many figures, we have it in simplicity. But it has always been an acknowledged point, that God, who is a Spirit, must be worshipped in spirit and in truth.

Moreover, the rule which distinguishes between pure and vitiated worship is of universal application, in order that we may not adopt any device which seems fit to ourselves, but look to the injunctions of Him who alone is entitled to prescribe. Therefore, if we would have Him to approve our worship, this rule, which he everywhere enforces with the utmost strictness, must be carefully observed. For there is a twofold reason why the Lord, in condemning and prohibiting all fictitious worship, requires us to give obedience only to his own voice. First, it tends greatly to establish His authority that we do not follow our own pleasure, but depend entirely on his sovereignty; and, secondly, such is our folly, that when we are left at liberty, all we are able to do is to go astray. And then when once we have turned aside from the right path, there is no end to our wanderings, until we get buried under a multitude of superstitions. Justly, therefore, does the Lord, in order to assert his full right of dominion, strictly enjoin what he wishes us to do, and at once reject all human devices which are at variance with his command. Justly, too, does he, in express terms, define our limits, that we may not, by fabricating perverse modes of worship, provoke His anger against us.

I know how difficult it is to persuade the world that God disapproves of all modes of worship not expressly sanctioned by His Word. The opposite persuasion which cleaves to them, being seated, as it were, in their very bones and marrow, is, that whatever they do has in itself a sufficient sanction, provided it exhibits some kind of zeal for the honour of God. But since God not only regards as fruitless, but also plainly abominates, whatever we undertake from zeal to His worship, if at variance with His command, what do we gain by a contrary course? The words of God are clear and distinct, "Obedience is better than sacrifice." "In vain do they worship me, teaching for doctrines the commandments of men." Every addition to His word, especially in this matter, is a lie. Mere "will worship" . . . is vanity. This is the decision, and when once the judge has decided, it is no longer time to debate.

Will your Imperial Majesty now be pleased to recognise, and will you, Most Illustrious Princes, lend me your attention, while I show how utterly at variance with this view are all the observances, in which, throughout the Christian world in the present day, divine worship is made to consist? In word, indeed, they concede to God the glory of all that is good, but, in reality, they rob him of the half, or more than the half, by partitioning his perfections among the saints. Let our adversaries use what evasions they may, and defame us for exaggerating what they pretend to be trivial errors, I will simply state the fact as every man perceives it. Divine offices are distributed among the saints as if they had been appointed colleagues to the Supreme God, and, in a multitude of instances, they are made to do his work, while He is kept out of view. The thing I complain of is just what every body confesses by a vulgar proverb. For what is meant by saying, "the Lord cannot be known for apostles," unless it be that, by the height to which apostles are raised, the dignity of Christ is sunk, or at least obscured? The consequence of this perversity is, that mankind, forsaking the fountain of living waters, have learned, as Jeremiah tells us, to hew them out "cisterns, broken cisterns, that can hold no water." For where is it that they seek for salvation and every other good? Is it in God alone? The whole tenor of their lives openly proclaims the contrary. They say, indeed, that they seek salvation and every other good in Him; but it is mere pretence, seeing they seek them elsewhere.

355

Of this fact, we have clear proof in the corruptions by which prayer was first vitiated, and afterwards in a great measure perverted and extinguished. We have observed, that prayer affords a test whether or not suppliants render due glory to God. In like manner, will it enable us to discover whether, after robbing Him of his glory, they transfer it to the creatures. In genuine prayer, something more is required than mere entreaty. The suppliant must feel assured that God is the only being to whom he ought to flee, both because He only can succour him in necessity; and also, because He has engaged to do it. But no man can have this conviction unless he pays regard both to the command by which God calls us to himself, and to the promise of listening to our prayers which is annexed to the command. The command was not thus regarded when the generality of mankind invoked angels and dead men promiscuously with God, and the wiser part, if they did not invoke them instead of God, at least regarded them as mediators, at whose intercession God granted their requests. Where, then, was the promise which is founded entirely on the intercession of Christ? Passing by Christ, the only Mediator, each betook himself to the patron who had struck his fancy, or if at any time a place was given to Christ, it was one in which he remained unnoticed, like some ordinary individual in a crowd. Then, although nothing is more repugnant to the nature of genuine prayer than doubt and distrust, so much did these prevail, that they were almost regarded as necessary, in order to pray aright. And why was this? Just because the world understood not the force of the expressions in which God invites us to pray to him, engages to do whatsoever we ask in reliance on his command and promise, and sets forth Christ as the Advocate in whose name our prayers are heard. Besides, let the public prayers which are in common use in Churches be examined. It will be found that they are stained with numberless impurities. From them, therefore, we have it in our power to judge how much this part of divine worship was vitiated. Nor was there less corruption in the expressions of thanksgiving. To this fact, testimony is borne by the public hymns, in which the saints are lauded for every blessing, just as if they were the colleagues of God.

Then what shall I say of adoration? Do not men pay to images and statues the very same reverence which they pay to God? It is an error to suppose that there is any difference between this madness and that of the heathen. For God forbids us not only to worship images, but to regard them as the residence of his divinity, and worship it as residing in them. The very same pretexts which the patrons of this abomination employ in the present day, were formerly employed by the heathen to cloak their impiety. Besides, it is undeniable that saints, nay, their very bones, garments, shoes, and images, are adored even in the place of God. But some subtle disputant will object, that there are divers species of adoration,—that the honour of *dulia*, as they term it, is given to saints, their images, and their bones; and that *latria* is reserved for God as due to him only, unless we are to except *hyperdulia*, a species which, as the infatuation increased, was invented to set the blessed Virgin above the rest. As if these subtle distinctions were either known or present to the minds of those who prostrate themselves before images. Meanwhile, the world is full of idolatry not less gross, and if I may so speak, not less capable of being felt, than was the ancient idolatry of the Egyptians, which all the Prophets everywhere so strongly reprobate.

I am merely glancing at each of these corruptions, because I will afterwards more clearly expose their demerits.

I come now to ceremonies, which, while they ought to be grave attestations of divine worship, are rather a mere mockery of God. A new Judaism, as a substitute for that which God had distinctly abrogated, has again been reared up by means of numerous puerile extravagancies, collected from different quarters; and with these have been mixed up certain impious rites, partly borrowed from the heathen, and more adapted to some theatrical show than to the dignity of our religion. The first evil here is, that an immense number of ceremonies, which God had by his authority abrogated, once for all, have been again revived. The next evil is, that while ceremonies ought to be living exercises of piety, men are vainly occupied with numbers of them that are both frivolous and useless. But by far the most deadly evil of all is, that after men have thus mocked God with ceremonies of one kind or other, they think they have fulfilled their duty as admirably as if these ceremonies included in them the whole essence of piety and divine worship.

With regard to self-abasement, on which depends regeneration to newness of life, the whole doctrine was entirely obliterated from the minds of men, or, at least, half buried, so that it was known to few, and to them but slenderly. But the spiritual sacrifice which the Lord in an especial manner recommends, is to mortify the old, and be transformed into a new man. It may be, perhaps, that preachers stammer out something about these words, but that they have no idea of the things meant by them is apparent even from this,—that they strenuously oppose us in our attempt to restore this branch of divine worship. If at any time they discourse on repentance, they only glance, as if in contempt, at the points of principal moment, and dwell entirely on certain external exercises of the body, which, as Paul assures us, are not of the highest utility. What makes this perverseness the more intolerable is, that the generality, under a pernicious error, pursue the shadow for the substance, and, overlooking true repentance, devote their whole attention to abstinences, vigils, and other things, which Paul terms "beggarly elements" of the world.

Having observed that the Word of God is the test which discriminates between his true worship and that which is false and vitiated, we thence readily infer that the whole form of divine worship in general use in the present day is nothing but mere corruption. For men pay no regard to what God has commanded, or to what he approves, in order that they may serve him in a becoming manner, but assume to themselves a licence of devising modes of worship, and afterwards obtruding them upon him as a substitute for obedience. If in what I say I seem to exaggerate, let an examination be made of all the acts by which the generality suppose that they worship God. I dare scarcely except a tenth part as not the random offspring of their own brain. What more would we? God rejects, condemns, abominates all fictitious worship, and employs his Word as a bridle to keep us in unqualified obedience. When shaking off this yoke, we wander after our own fictions, and offer to him a worship, the work of human rashness, how much soever it may delight ourselves, in his sight it is vain trifling, nay, vileness and pollution. The advocates of human traditions paint them in fair and gaudy colours; and Paul certainly admits that they carry with them a show of wisdom; but as God values obedience more than all sacrifices, it ought to be sufficient for the rejection of any mode of worship, that it is not sanctioned by the command of God.

PRESERVING THE PURITY
OF THE CHRISTIAN RELIGION

My dear Brother,

I feel extremely sorry on your account, and, as in duty bound, pity your situation, in not being able to come forth out of that Egypt in which so many Idols and so much monstrous Idolatry are daily presented to your eyes. While pious ears shudder at the very mention of these things, how much more grievously must they offend the eye whose perceptions are at once more vivid and more keen? You are forced, as you mention, to behold foul forms of impiety in monks and priestlings, a thousand kinds of superstition in the common people, numerous mockeries of True Religion. In all quarters around you these teem and resound. As I count those happy who can spare their eyes such spectacles, so your condition, as you describe it, I regard as truly miserable.

First of all, The Mass, that head of all abominations, forces itself upon your view, and takes the lead among all those species of iniquity. In it every imaginable kind of gross profanity is perpetrated. Were such spectacles exhibited in derision, you might perhaps be able to laugh at them; but now, when they are performed in earnest, with the greatest contumely to God, I doubt not, from your well-known piety, that, instead of exciting mirth, they arouse your indignation, or rather call forth your tears.

.   .   .

When the Lord, by his Law, forbade Idols to be reverenced or worshipped, he, under that head, comprehended the whole of the external worship which the ungodly are wont to bestow upon their Idols. Such is the natural force of the terms which he employed—the one, meaning to bow down; the other, to bestow honour: and it is evident that the species of adoration struck at, is that by which Images of wood or stone are worshipped by bodily gestures. The Lord, therefore, by his interdict, does not simply prohibit his people from standing in stupid amazement like the Gentiles before wood or stone, but forbids any imitation of their profane stolidity in any form, by prostrating themselves before Images for the purpose of paying honour to them, or giving any other indication of religious reverence, such as we are accustomed to give by uncovering the head or bending the knee. Accordingly, when he describes his pure worshippers, the mark by which he distinguishes them is this—"I have preserved to myself seven thousand men." What! is it those whose hearts are not infatuated by the vanity and lies of Baal? Not only so, but those also "whose knees have never been bent to Baal, and whose lips have never kissed his hand." In another place he employs the same symbol, when declaring that his majesty must be acknowledged by "all things in heaven and on earth, and under the earth."

359

He thus describes the mode of acknowledgement: "Every knee shall bow to me, and every tongue shall swear by my name." Here it is obviously implied that an Image receives the worship due to God when reverence for it is expressed by any bodily gesture.

To establish the guilt of those who express such reverence, it is of no consequence under what pretence, or with what sincerity they do it. Whoever bestows any kind of veneration on an Idol, be the persuasion of his own mind what it may, acknowledges it to be God, and he who gives the name of divinity to an Idol withholds it from God. Accordingly, the three companions of Daniel have taught us what estimate to form of this dissimulation. To them it seemed easier to allow their bodies to be cruelly consumed by the flames of a fiery furnace than to please the king's eye, by bending their thighs for a little before his statue! Let us either deride their infatuation in inflaming the anger of a mighty king against them, to the danger of their lives, and for a thing of no moment, or let us learn by their example, that to perform any act of idolatry, in order to gain the favour of man, is more to be shunned than death in its most fearful form. Wherefore, when they had only two alternatives between which to choose—either to shake off the fear of God and obey an impious edict, or to despise men when brought into competition with God, they wished it to be notified to the king that they would not worship his gods nor bow down to the statue which he had set up. The equal constancy of Daniel, in a very similar case, is mentioned by the writer, whoever he was, who added the appendix to his prophecy. He says that Daniel chose rather to be torn to pieces by the claws of lions, than bend the knee in worship of the dragon which others worshipped as God. But as this history is not received by all, I refrain from quoting it as an authority.

Moreover, lest any one might suppose that he had done all that was required of him by merely withholding his head or his knee from the worship of Idols, the Lord has added numerous precepts concerning the holy keeping of his ceremonies, and utterly shunning the ways of the Gentiles. In the Prophet, he by a single expression declared how completely clear he would have his people to be from all communion with impiety, when he prohibited the Jews who had been transported to Babylon from even touching what was unclean. This clause, as Paul interprets summarily, implies that they were not to pollute themselves by any observance or ceremony unbecoming the sanctity of their religion. For, giving injunctions to the Church of Corinth on that subject, he was contented to borrow a summary of his whole sentiments on the subject from this one passage.

It is a fact, believe me, not to be idly or giddily overlooked, that those only duly preserve the holy Religion of God who profane it by no defilements of unhallowed superstitions, and that those violate, pollute, and lacerate it, who mix it up with impure and impious rites. Believers who duly meditate on this consideration, will carefully give heed not to involve themselves in such sacrilege. In this way, Abraham, Isaac, and the other Patriarchs, though they sojourned in countries which teemed with the abominations of Idols—although they mourned over the infatuations of their hosts, which as they could not cure, they bore with, took anxious care, however, to keep themselves within the pure and untainted worship of God. And though they did not publicly proclaim their dissent from the superstitions practised around them, they gave no indication of a pretended compliance.

Of this simplicity a distinguished specimen appears in Daniel. Although he was living in Babylon amid the pollutions of Idolatry, yet being as far from holding communion with it as if he had been placed at an immense distance away from it, he contracted no stain. Seeing, however, that there would be no place for true piety in presence of the people, he withdrew from their sight, and shutting the doors of his chamber, worshipped his God apart with becoming purity. Thus, notwithstanding the public error of the city and nation, he deviated not from the right faith. To the same effect is the injunction laid upon the Jews in the law, that they should not covet gold or silver from the graven Images of the nations and bring it into their houses, but should regard it as an impure unclean thing which was an abomination in the sight of the Lord. He taught them to detest and abominate everything which had once borne the name of Idol, that thus they might the more zealously shun the impure superstitions of the Gentiles.

But if it was the will of God, that under the Old Testament his Religion, though still obscure and only shadowed forth by figures, should be observed with so much external purity of profession, how much more necessary must this be in the Christian Church to which he himself, by the appearance of his only begotten Son, has unlocked the mysteries of his wisdom, as it were completely encircling it with the light of His Truth? This may be easily confirmed by the doctrine of the Apostles. The argument which Paul uses against fornication, holding equally true with regard to this matter, may without absurdity be accommodated

56. *The Last Supper*, Andrea del Castagno.

to it. "Know ye not," he says, "that your bodies are the members of Christ? Shall I then take the members of Christ and make them the members of a harlot? Far from it!" In the same way, may we too argue; seeing our members are the members of Christ, shall we defile them by the worship of Idols, or by impure Superstitions? What were this but either to subject the glory of Christ to ignominy, or dissever our body from the body of Christ to commit fornication with Idols? The precept with which he concludes has a general application to all kinds of modification: "Let us remember that our body is the temple of the Holy Spirit; that we are not our own, but have been bought with a great price, and ought therefore to bear and glorify God in our body." Will the glory of God be displayed in our body after it has been rolled in the mire of Sacrilege? Will the sacred sanctity of the temple of God be preserved if it be polluted by alien and profane rites?

If on any subject Paul is an urgent exhorter to duty, his urgency is more particularly displayed when he admonishes Christians not to exhibit anything unworthy of their profession before the eyes of men by using vicious ceremonies. Referring to two great evils, the dishonour of God and the offence of men, the natural consequence of all simulate compliance with Idolatry, or of other imitations of it on whatever ground undertaken, he at great length warns us against committing either. In regard to the profanation of the Divine Name and honour, his words are, "Dearly beloved, flee the worship of Idols." (That under the term *worship* he comprehended all external rites which are used by the ungodly, is manifest from the subsequent context,) "I speak as to wise men; judge ye what I say. The cup of blessing which we bless, is it not the Communion of the blood of Christ? And the bread which we break, is it not the Communion of the body of Christ? Therefore we many are one bread, and one body; for we all partake of one bread." "You see Israel according to the flesh. Are not those who eat the Sacrifices partakers of the altar? What then? Do I say that what is sacrificed to idols is any thing? or that an idol is any thing? But that which the Gentiles sacrifice they sacrifice to demons and not to God. Now I would not have you to be partakers of demons. You cannot drink the cup of the Lord and the cup of demons: you cannot partake of the table of the Lord and the table of demons."

. . .

To interdict the Eating of Flesh under the name of Religion, and bind the consciences of believers by such an interdict, was plainly tyrannical, and as the Apostle expresses it, "devilish." And seeing the Lord had left it optional to eat flesh daily, or abstain for a lifetime from eating it, nothing forbids you to abstain on particular days. For why may not that be occasionally lawful which is at all times free? Thus you may without sin obey an iniquitous command, provided your intention be to make a concession to the ignorance of the weak, and not also to enthral your mind by those fetters of tradition. To prohibit them from Marrying who are not constitutionally permitted to decline marriage, is tyranny of the same description: and you have not the same liberty to submit to it, unless the gift of abstinence have been specially bestowed upon you.

. . .

Then, any one who throws his pence into the coffer where Pardons are set out for sale, or purchases anything for himself out of that prolific and abundant treasury of Indulgences and Dispensations, enrols his name as a sharer in those nefarious traffickings, and declares his consent to them as clearly as if he wore their badge! I cannot admit the excuse which is commonly made, that just as wild beasts are calmed by throwing offal to them, so the rage of Priestlings is to be softened by throwing them a few coins, or occasionally bestowing upon them a large sum of money, seeing that where lucre is in question, they gape over their prey and are more ravenous than a hungry lion; always, like the false prophets and false priests of old, sounding the tocsin of war against every man who will not put something into their mouths! This excuse, I say, I cannot accept. For what do those Bulls, the favour of which you make a pretence of desiring, imply? Do they not with loud voice proclaim that in return for the money you leave, you carry off Indulgences full of anathema, and deserving of the utmost execration? Have not those who understand this, (and everybody understands it!) and who see you offer money, (did you not wish to be seen you would not do it!) an abundantly clear testimony that you are desirous to have a share in Indulgences? If you thoroughly examine what is concealed under them, you will nowhere find Christ and his cross more systematically insulted.

.　　.　　.

Now, dearest brother, let my discourse have reference to yourself. Although you are already aware what course remains for you, since you see the direction in which you are led by the Word of God, to which all your deliberations ought to be conformed and confined, still, that I may not be wanting to you in your great straits, I will proceed, with all possible brevity, to lay down The Rule of Duty, as requested in your letter. Only be you, on your part, prepared and eager to listen to the voice of the Lord, and to execute his commandments with intrepid and unwavering constancy; and, finally, remember that in truth it is not so much a counsel given you by man, as an oracle pronounced by man's lips, but received from the sacred lips of Almighty God.

I. First, then, consider it a thing altogether interdicted to allow any man to see you communicating in the Sacrilege of the Mass, or uncovering your head before an Image, or observing any form of Superstition belonging to the class of those by which, as shewn above, the glory of God is obscured, his religion profaned, and his truth corrupted. None of these things can you do without giving the wicked a confession most insulting to God, and dragging weak brethren to fatal ruin by your example. But while you conduct yourself thus, (if, indeed, it is not your intention to proceed to a more open confession,) you must at the same time take good heed, as far as in you lies, that those miserable and blind idolators (to whom, when their superstition is removed, God and Religion appear to be utterly abolished) are not led to imagine, when they see you holding their Idols in ridicule or contempt, that you are a derider and contemner of God also. This you will in some measure accomplish if you seldom appear at their sacred meetings, and regulate your whole life so as to give it something of a religious character. Come then, most excellent sir, let such zeal for piety, goodness, continence, charity, chastity, and inoffensiveness appear, as may completely clear you in the eyes of all men from any suspicion of impiety, so that, while the weak and superstitious are offended at your not being like themselves, they may be forced, whether they will or no, to acknowledge that you are a servant of God.

II. In the second place, unless you are preparing to give any one an exposition of your faith, indulge their bigotry so far as not to push yourself forward at the time when they are performing their Rites, causelessly to make a display of contempt, which you are aware that they (such is their ignorance!) will regard as sheer impiety against God. For what gain can accrue to yourself or others from being suspected to be an atheist, utterly devoid of all religious feeling? But, while I advise you not voluntarily, or of set purpose, to give ground for such suspicion, still, if by circumstances you are accidentally brought into a dubious position, any suspicion is better far than to let them see you acting the idolater! If in your general conduct you exhibit the sanctity of a Christian man, your integrity will afford you sufficient protection against the shafts of slander.

Then you must be particularly careful in regulating your household, over which you should consider that you have been set, not merely that each may yield you obedience and service, but be religiously brought up in the fear of the Lord, and imbued with the best discipline. For if it is truly said by Aristotle, that "Every man's house is the image of a little kingdom, in which the head of the family, as chief, makes laws by which he may train those under him to all justice and innocence," not even in human judgment is he excusable who, careless as to the regulation of his family, provided it is sedulous and dutiful towards himself, allows it to be flagitious in regard to God and man. You ought even to rise higher in your thoughts, and consider, that those persons of whom the Lord has made you master are committed to your trust, He having placed them under you that you may teach and accustom them, first of all, to obey and serve him; and next, under him, obey and serve yourself.

Not, therefore, without cause did the Apostle, when speaking of those who cast off all anxiety as to the administration of their household, inflict on them the heavy censure that they have "denied the faith, and are worse than infidels." For what else is it than to refuse and desert the post assigned by God, and to renounce His vocation? But then most servants are of a very bad disposition, and the old proverb almost always holds true—"As many servants in the house, so many enemies!" This, indeed, is vulgarly thought and alleged, but it is not so. We get them not as enemies, but make them so by our own fault, while we bring them up like brute beasts, without doctrine, without the knowledge of God, without pious training, forgetting that they are our fellow-servants, and have been committed to our charge by a heavenly Master. Will the Scripture never bestow praise on a Christian man, without adding that he and his whole house believed, and shall we boast of faith in Christ, while fostering the denial of him within the walls of our house, in the persons of our servants? Wherefore, if the first requisite in a good householder is to manage his household rightly, and in order—and the household of a Christian man can then only be considered duly arranged, when it exhibits the appearance of a little Bethel—it must be your careful endeavour not to leave yours ignorant or devoid of piety.

There is no ground for being deterred by such vulgar scruples as these —Shall I make a servant the disposer of my life? Shall I put a drawn sword into his hand to kill me? Grant, first, that the members of your household are of such disposition and natural temper as promise no good, still, having obtained them, dare to imbue them with the doctrine of God, and to sow within them the seed of his word. God himself will provide the rest, and give a success which will never allow you to repent of having obeyed His commands. And certainly, if you are not willing to impose upon yourself, you must see how much more annoyance you must have, to how much greater danger you must be exposed, within the recesses of your house, among persons whom you consider as sentinels placed over you, whose snares you are always fearing, and the fear of whom meets you at every corner, so that you scarcely dare to breathe without looking round to see whether they observe you. Surely this were worse than once for all to try their fidelity, though it should be at your peril!

The Lord has many ways of avenging contempt of his Word. In contracting Marriage (seeing that the Lord has hitherto left your liberty in this respect entire) consider in what fetters you entangle yourself, if you take a wife differing from you in religion! And yet, why should I bid you consider those labyrinths, which no one can well comprehend but he who has actually had experience of them? I wish you may rather fear and beware, than be willing to make the trial. I know the flattering thought. She now opposes in such a manner that I am confident she will gradually give in! Do not vainly promise this of yourself, but of the Lord, seeing a good wife is His special gift. And how can you expect a good wife from Him whom you will not hear while strictly prohibiting you from being "yoked with unbelievers?"

You have the advice which you asked of me, or rather you have it from the Lord, through my hand—an advice indeed perilous, and little flattering to your faith, but faithful and salutary to your soul; I add, altogether necessary to you, if you do not wish to shake off the yoke of the Lord from your neck, and abjure His Religion!

Your part now is to render to the Lord the confession of praise which he demands of you, to exhort yourself to be instant and urgent, to arouse and collect your courage. For the servant of God to give way, especially at such an important crisis of Religion, were most foolish and unworthy. That you may ever and anon call to mind and daily yield submission to what I have declared above, I now in your presence call God and his holy Angels to witness, that the controversy now agitated is no less than this—How are we to avoid denying Christ before men, so as not to be denied by Him, when seated for judgment on his Supreme Tribunal?

That you may not think any special burden is laid upon you, which every one is not called to bear, I can easily meet any such erroneous impression. I do not ask you openly to profess your piety; all I ask is, that you do not abjure it for the profession of impiety! For what else have I aimed at in the whole of this Discussion, or what do I wish to obtain now, but just that you may not pollute the holy Religion of God by horrible sacrilege—that you may not profane your body, which he has dedicated as a temple to himself, by foul abominations—that you may not inscribe your name on execrable blasphemies? Do we account all these things to be of so little moment, that we are not prepared to shun them at some peril to our life, or, if need be, at the shedding of our blood? Nay, surely we estimate this brief miserable life too highly, if we think it worthy to be ransomed by such impiety; and we have too much fear of death, if we think it in any respect more grievous than to purchase pardon from man by becoming sacrilegious, apostate, perfidious, treacherous before God—if we would rather hear Christ pronounce us unworthy of being counted his disciples, than be counted by men worthy to die—if, in short, from fear of death we resign the hope of eternal life!

O the empty vanity of our boasting, whether we found it on our faith in Christ, or on any other title! Can we allow the Poet, who thought death "terrible destruction," to exclaim in the person of another uttering his own sentiment, "Is it so very miserable a thing to die?" And shall we, who have been taught by the Word of God that it is nothing else than an entrance, by momentary pain, into immortal life and blessed rest, reply, that it is indeed a miserable thing to die? O seven times wretched we, whom Paul declares to be "of all men the most miserable," if we have confidence in the present life only!

Perhaps you will say, It is easy for men sitting in the lap of ease thus to talk of flames, just as it is easy to philosophize on war while in the shade; but were the reality before you, your feelings would be different! Though I hope better things from the goodness of Him by whose power we can do all things, and doubt not that in whatever contest he may permit me to be engaged, he will maintain me in the same resolution to my last breath, still I am unwilling that you should turn your eyes upon myself.

The things which I set before you are not those which I have meditated with myself in my shady nook, but those which the invincible martyrs of God realized amid gibbets, and flames, and ravenous beasts! Had not their courage been thus whetted, they would in an instant have perfidiously abjured the eternal truth, which they intrepidly sealed with their blood. They did not set us an example of constancy in asserting the truth that we should now desert it, when handed down to us so signed and sealed; but they taught us the art by which, trusting to the Divine protection, we stand invincible by all the powers of death, hell, the world, and Satan! Farewell.

(from *Tracts and Treatises on the Reformation of the Church*)

Sir Thomas More

OF THE RELIGIONS IN UTOPIA

There be divers kindes of religion not only in sondrie partes of the ilande, but also in divers places of every citie. Some worship for God, the sonne; some, the mone; some, some other of the planettes. There be that give worship to a man that was ones of excellente vertue or of famous glory, not only as God, but also as the chiefest and hyghest God.

But the moste and the wysest parte (rejectynge al these) beleve that there is a certayne godlie powre unknowen, everlastinge, incomprehensible, inexplicable, farre above the capacitie and retche of mans witte, dispersed throughoute all the worlde, not in bignes, but in vertue and power. Him they call the father of al. To him alone they attribute the beginninges, the encreasinges, the procedinges, the chaunges and the endes of al thinges. Neither they geve any divine honours to any other then to him. Yea al the other also, though they be in divers opinions, yet in this pointe they agree all togethers with the wisest sorte, in beleving that there is one chiefe and principall God, the maker and ruler of the whole worlde: whome they all commonlye in their countrey language call Mythra. But in this they disagree, that among some he is counted one, and amonge some another. For every one of them, whatsoever that is whiche he taketh for the chief God, thinketh it to be the very same nature, to whose only divine mighte and majestie, the summe and soveraintie of al thinges by the consent of al people is attributed and geven.

Howbeit they all begyn by litle and litle to forsake and fall from this varietie of superstitions, and to agre togethers in that religion whiche semethe by reason to passe and excell the residewe. And it is not to be doubted, but all the other would long agoo have bene abolished, but that whatsoever unprosperous thynge happened to anie of them, as he was mynded to chaunge his religion, the fearefulnesse of people did take it, not as a thinge comminge by chaunce, but as sente from GOD out of heaven. As thoughe the God whose honoure he was forsakynge would revenge that wicked purpose against him. But after they hearde us speake of the name of Christe, of his doctrine, lawes, myracles, and of thee no lesse wonderful constancie of so manye martyrs, whose bloude wyllinglye shedde broughte a great numbre of nations throughoute all partes of the worlde into their sect; you will not beleve with howe gladde mindes, they agreed unto the same: whether it were by the secrete inspiration of GOD, or elles for that they thought it nieghest unto that opinion, which among them is counted the chiefest. Howbeit I thinke this was no smale helpe and furtheraunce in the matter, that they harde us say, that Christ instituted among his, al thinges commen; and that the same communitie doth yet remaine amongest the rightest Christian companies.

Verely howsoever it came to passe, manye of them consented togethers in our religion, and were wasshed in the holy water of baptisme. But because among us foure (for no mo of us was left alive, two of our companye beyng dead) there was no priest; which I am right sorie for; they beynge entered and instructed in al other pointes of our religion, lacke onely those sacramentes, whiche here none but priestes do minister. Howbeit they understand and perceive them and be very desierous of the same. Yea, they reason and dispute the matter earnestly among themselves, whether without the sending of a Christian bishop, one chosen out of their own people may receave the ordre of priesthod. And truely they were minded to chuese one. But at my departure from them they had chosen none.

They also which do not agree to Christes religion, feare no man from it, not speake against any man that hath received it. Saving that one of our company in my presence was sharpely punished. He as soone as he was baptised began against our willes, with more earneste affection then wisedome, to reason of Christes religion; and began to waxe so hote in his matter, that he did not onlye preferre our religion before al other, but also did utterly despise and condempne all other, calling them prophane, and the folowers of them wicked and develish and the children of everlastinge dampnation. When he had thus longe reasoned the matter, they laide holde on him, accused him and condempned him into exile, not as a despiser of religion, but as a sedicious person and a raiser up of dissention amonge the people.

For this is one of the auncientest lawes amonge them; that no man shall be blamed for resoninge in the maintenaunce of his owne religion. For kyng Utopus, even at the firste beginning, hearing that the inhabitauntes of the land wer, before his comming thether, at continuall dissention and strife amonge themselves for their religions; perceyving also that this common dissention (whiles every severall secte tooke severall partes in fighting for their countrey) was the only occasion of his conquest over them al, as sone as he had gotten the victory; firste of all he made a decree, that it should be lawfull for everie man to favoure and folow what religion he would, and that he mighte do the best he could to bring other to his opinion, so that he did it peaceablie, gentelie, quietly and soberlie, without hastie and contentious rebuking and invebing against other. If he could not by faire and gentle speche induce them unto his opinion yet he should use no kinde of violence, and refraine from displeasaunte and seditious woordes. To him that would vehemently and ferventlye in this cause strive and contende was decreed banishment or bondage. This lawe did kynge Utopus make not only for the maintenaunce of peace, which he saw through continuall contention and mortal hatred utterly extinguished; but also because he thought this decrie should make for the furtheraunce of religion. Wherof he durst define and determine nothing unadvisedlie, as douting whether God desiering manifolde and diverse sortes of honour, would inspire sondry men with sondrie kindes of religion. And this suerly he thought a very unmete and folish thing, and a point of arrogant presumption, to compell all other by violence and threateninges to agre to the same that thou belevest to be trew.

Furthermore thoughe there be one religion whiche alone is trew, and al other vaine and superstitious, yet did he wel foresee (so that the matter were handeled with reason, and sober modestie) that the trueth of the own powre would at the last issue out and come to lyghte. But if contention and debate in that behalfe should continuallye be used, as the woorste men be mooste obstinate and stubbourne, and in their evyll opinion mooste constante; he perceaved that then the beste and holyest religion woulde be troden underfote and destroyed by most vaine supersticions, even as good corne is by thornes and weedes overgrowen and chooked.

Therfore all this matter he lefte undiscussed, and gave to everye man free libertie and choise to beleve what he woulde. Savinge that he earnestelye and straitelye charged them, that no man should conceave so vile and base an opinion of the dignitie of mans nature, as to think that the soules do die and perishe with the bodye; or that the world runneth at al aventures governed by no divine providence. And therfore thei beleve that after this life vices be extreamelye punished and vertues bountifully rewarded. Hym that is of a contrary opinion they counte not in the numbre of men, as one that hathe avaled the heighe nature of hys soule to the vielnes of brute beastes bodies, muche lesse in the numbre of their citiziens, whose lawes and ordenaunces, if it were not for feare, he wold nothing at al esteme. For you maye be suer that he will studie either with craft prively to mocke, or els violently to breake the commen lawes of his countrey, in whom remaineth no further feare then of the lawes, nor no further hope then of the bodye. Wherfore he that is thus minded is deprived of all honours, excluded from all offices and reject from all common administrations in the weale publique. And thus he is of all sortes despised, as of an unprofitable and of a base and vile nature. Howbeit they put him to no punishment, because they be persuaded that it is in no mans power to beleve what he list. No nor they constraine hym not with threatninges to dissemble his minde and shew countenaunce contrarie to his thought. For deceit and falshod and all maners of lies, as nexte unto fraude, they do mervelouslic deteste and abhorre. But they suffer him not to dispute in his opinion, and that onelye amonge the commen people. For els aparte amonge the priestes and men of gravitie they do not onelye suffer, but also exhorte him to dispute and argue, hoping that at the last, that madness will geve place to reason.

(from *Utopia*)

WILLIAM SHAKESPEARE

DEGREE, PRIORITY, AND PLACE

The specialty of rule hath been neglected.
And look how many Grecian tents do stand
Hollow upon this plain, so many hollow factions.
When that the general is not like the hive
To whom the foragers shall all repair,
What honey is expected? Degree being vizarded,
The unworthiest shows as fairly in the mask.
The heavens themselves, the planets and this center,
Observe degree, priority, and place,
Insisture, course, proportion, season, form,
Office, and custom, in all line of order.
And therefore is the glorious planet Sol
In noble eminence enthroned and sphered
Amidst the other, whose medicinable eye
Corrects the ill aspécts of planets evil,
And posts like the commandment of a king,
Sans check to good and bad. But when the planets
In evil mixture to disorder wander,
What plagues and what portents, what mutiny,
What raging of the sea, shaking of earth,
Commotion in the winds, frights, changes, horrors,

57. Tympanum. Vezelay, Church of St. Madeleine.

Divert and crack, rend and deracinate,
The unity and married calm of states
Quite from their fixure! Oh, when degree is shaked,
Which is the ladder to all high designs,
The enterprise is sick! How could communities,
Degrees in schools and brotherhoods in cities,
Peaceful commerce from dividable shores,
The primogenitive and due of birth,
Prerogative of age, crowns, scepters, laurels,
But by degree, stand in authentic place?
Take but degree away, untune that string,
And hark, what discord follows! Each thing meets
In mere oppugnancy. The bounded waters
Should lift their bosoms higher than the shores,
And make a sop of all this solid globe.
Strength should be lord of imbecility,
And the rude son should strike his father dead.
Force should be right, or rather, right and wrong,

58. *The Last Judgment*, Michelangelo. Rome, the Sistine Chapel of The Vatican.

Between whose endless jar justice resides,
Should lose their names, and so should justice too.
Then everything includes itself in power,
Power into will, will into appetite,
And appetite, a universal wolf,
So doubly seconded with will and power,
Must make perforce a universal prey,
And last eat up himself. Great Agamemnon,
This chaos, when degree is suffocate,
Follows the choking.
And this neglection of degree it is
That by a pace goes backward, with a purpose
It hath to climb. The general's disdained
By him one step below, he by the next,
That next by him beneath. So every step,
Exampled by the first pace that is sick
Of his superior, grows to an envious fever
Of pale and bloodless emulation.
And 'tis this fever that keeps Troy on foot,
Not her own sinews. To end a tale of length,
Troy in our weakness stands, not in her strength.

(from *Troilus and Cressida*)